4867'

WHITEFACE MT. - 9 miles

MONTREAL
96 miles

PROLOGUE

There are few ways in which universal understanding is achieved among the peoples of the world. The disciplines of art, music, drama, literature and athletics are international in nature, and transcend cultural, economic and governmental differences between nations. The Olympic games represent an idealism initiated by the ancient Greeks in 776 B.C.

The modern Olympic games perpetuate the ideology of competition in stadiums, rather than on battlefields.

It is with this thought in mind that we dedicate this book; to encourage and promote the youth of our country to participate in a meaningful activity, supported by our free enterprise system.

UNITED STATES OLYMPIC COMMITTEE
ICE SKATING INSTITUTE OF AMERICA

The Meaning of the Olympic Symbol

The five rings or circles which form the Olympic Symbol originally represented the five major continents, namely Europe, Asia, Africa, Australia, and America (both North and South). However, the true concept is that the rings are linked together to denote the sporting friendship of the peoples of the earth, whatever their creed or color. The colors are chosen because at least one of them (blue, yellow, black, green, and red) appears in the flag of every nation of the world.

The Olympic Creed

"The most important thing in the Olympic Games is not to win but to take part, just as the most important thing in life is not the triumph but the struggle. The essential thing is not to have conquered but to have fought well." — **Baron Pierre de Coubertin, founder of the Modern Olympic Games.**

XIII
Olympic Winter Games
Lake Placid • 1980

Dr. Eugene H. Baker, *Editor in Chief*
Donna Baker, *Editorial Director*

The Ice Skating Institute of America

Staff, Contributors, and Consultants

Editor in Chief **Eugene H. Baker**
Editorial Director **Donna Baker**
Consulting Editor **William Frazer**

Design and Art Director **Z. Basil Thomas**
Art Production **John Cather**
Production Consultant **Richard Kashner**
Editorial Consultant **C. Robert Paul, Jr.**
Research Adviser **Einar Jonland, Thomas Hall**
Research Assistants **Lisa Baker, Ruth Jahnke, Lori Jessen**
Cover Illustrations **Richard Mlodick**

Created and Marketed By **T. A. Chacharon and Associates LTD.**

Photograph Contributors

United States Olympic Committee
United States Ski Team
United States Bob Sled Association
United States Amateur Hockey Association
United States International Speed Skating Association
United States Figure Skating Association
Ice Skating Institute of America

Wide World Photos
George Christian Ortloff
Ann J. Bates
Irving Jaffee
United States Ski Hall of Fame
William Markland
Lake Placid Organizing Committee
United States Hockey Hall of Fame
Donald Clark
Arthur Goodfellow
Carol Heiss
Dick Button
Recreational Ice Skating Magazine
Flags © Rand McNally & Co.

All Archive Photographs
of Lake Placid, courtesy of
Macromedia Inc. © 1976

Manufacturers/Suppliers

Wisconsin Cuneo Press Inc./*Printing*
John F. Cuneo Company/*Binding/Packaging*
Hobart McIntosh Paper Company/*Paper Converter*
Kolor Kraft Inc./*Film Separations*
J&L Lithographers/*Typesetting/Film Reproductions*
Master Graphic Services/*Film Separations*

ISBN Hardbound edition 0-9602988-1-7
ISBN Paperback edition 0-9602988-2-7
Library of Congress
Catalog Card Number 79-89008

Table of Contents

Gold Medal Advisory Board

UNITED STATES OLYMPIC COMMITTEE OFFICERS

Back Row: L to R: Joel Ferrell, Jr., Third V.P.; John B. Kelly, Jr., First V.P.; William E. Simon, Treas.; E. Newbold Black, IV, Second V.P.
Front Row: L to R: Tenley Albright, M.D., Secretary; Robert J. Kane, Pres.

Introduction

BY ROBERT J. KANE, PRESIDENT
UNITED STATES OLYMPIC COMMITTEE

Over the years there have been many fine testimonials to the Olympic Games. Two of my favorites are these:

"The aims of the Olympic movement are to promote the development of those fine physical and moral qualities which are the basis of amateur sport and to bring together the athletes of the world in a great quadrennial festival of sports, thereby creating international respect and goodwill and thus helping to construct a better and more peaceful world." This was contributed by Baron Pierre de Coubertin, founder of the modern Olympic Games, following an International Athletics Congress in Paris in 1894.

When asked to comment on the place of the Olympic Games in today's society, Avery Brundage, president of the International Olympic Committee, 1952-1972, and an outstanding amateur sportsman for more than sixty years, said, "In an imperfect world, if participation in sport is to be stopped every time the laws of humanity are violated, there will never be any international contests. Is it not better to try to expand the sportsmanship of the athletic field into other areas?"

As we prepare for the XIII Olympic Winter Games in Lake Placid, February 13-24, 1980, Americans may well be proud of the achievements of our athletes in the Olympic Winter Games because we are not, in truth, a nation of winter sports. In recent years the United States of America has been among the strongest in both figure skating and speed skating and we are looking forward to new successes at Lake Placid.

Although the Olympic Winter Games were inaugurated only in 1924, we can be proud that the XIII Olympic Winter Games marks the third time that our nation has hosted the games; no other country has hosted so many of them. Previously the games were held at Lake Placid in 1932 and again in 1960 at Squaw Valley, California, now the site of a U.S. Olympic Committee training center.

Reminiscing. The U.S. athletes at Lake Placid forty-eight years ago, for the only time in history, earned more medals than those from the Scandinavian countries who have enjoyed great success in these games. And in 1960 the United States won its only ice hockey championship.

IX

FINLAND

NETHERLANDS

THE MODERN OLYMPIC MOVEMENT

The governing body for the Olympic Games is the International Olympic Committee (IOC), which is responsible for insuring the regular celebration of the games, maintaining their high ideals, selecting the host cities for the games and establishing the broad-scale eligibility rules for athletes.

The first International Olympic Committee in 1894 consisted of fourteen men, including W. M. Sloane, a Princeton professor of history who was personally selected by de Coubertin. Members are self-recruited, and today there are about ninety from more than sixty countries. Members of the IOC are regarded as ambassadors to their countries from the international body. Upon taking their oath as members, these men swear not to accept instructions from governments or from any other organizations that shall in any way bind them or interfere with their independence to vote.

Incidentally, the president of the IOC is selected by the individual members for an eight-year term of office. He may be elected for successive terms of four years.

The U.S. Olympic Committee, parenthetically, consists of representatives from 134 nations, territories or geographic areas recognized by the IOC for the purposes of identifying, selecting and training athletes and entering them in the Olympic Games. There may be only one such organization in each nation thus recognized by the IOC.

The IOC since 1920 has transferred to the international sports federations, world governing bodies for each of the sports on the program for the Olympic Games, the responsibility for conducting the actual competitions, including drawing up the schedules and appointing the referees, judges and other officials. For the Olympic Winter Games the recognized sports are biathlon, bobsledding, figure skating, ice hockey, skiing (Alpine and Nordic), luge and speed skating.

A fundamental principle of the IOC decrees that no recognized country shall discriminate among its citizens on grounds of race, religion or politics. Furthermore, every person or organization that plays any part whatsoever in the Olympic movement shall be bound by this principle and all of the other regulations of the Olympic charter, and shall accept the supreme authority of the IOC.

Olympiana

The Olympic Motto. The words *Citius, Altius, Fortius,* which appear under the five interlocked circles, were conceived in 1895 by the famous Father Didon, headmaster of Arceuil College (near Paris), while delivering a speech glorifying the athletic achievements of his pupils. Literally translated

UNITED KINGDOM

YUGOSLAVIA

from the Latin the words mean "faster, higher, braver." But the universally accepted modern version is "swifter, higher, stronger," indicative of the athletes' endeavor to run faster, jump higher and throw more strongly.

The Olympic Creed. "The most important thing in the Olympic Games is not to win but to take part, just as the most important thing in life is not the triumph but the struggle. The essential thing is not to have conquered but to have fought well." The creed was enunciated by de Coubertin at the Organizing Congress in 1894.

The Olympic Flag. In the center of the flag, on a plain white background with no border, are five interlocked rings—blue, yellow, black, green and red, arranged in that order from left to right. The Olympic flag was first flown in public at Alexandria, Greece, in 1914 and made its first appearance at the games of the VII Olympiad at Antwerp, Belgium, in 1920.

The Olympic flag symbolizes the union of the five continents and the meeting of athletes from all over the world at the Olympic Games in a spirit of fair and equal competition and good friendship.

The Spirit of Fair and Equal Competition. The Olympic Games must be regarded as contests between individuals and not between countries or political ideologies.

The Olympic Oath. On behalf of all the athletes participating in the Olympic Games, an athlete of the host country during the opening ceremony takes the following oath: "In the name of all competitors I promise we shall take part in these games, respecting and abiding by the rules which govern them, in the true spirit of sportsmanship, for the glory of sport and the honor of our teams."

The Olympic Order

In 1975 the International Olympic Committee created the Olympic Order, involving the award of gold, silver and bronze medals. The award is to honor "any person who has illustrated the Olympic ideals through his/her action, has achieved remarkable merit in the sporting world, or has rendered outstanding services to the Olympic cause, either through his own personal achievement or his/her contribution to the development of sports."

Among the distinguished Americans in the Olympic movement to be honored are the following:

Gold—Avery Brundage, IOC president (1952-1972), former president of the U.S. Olympic Committee (USOC) and a member of the 1912 U.S. Olympic track and field team in the decathlon and pentathlon.

Silver—Miguel de Capriles, two-time Olympic medalist in fencing, past president of the International Federation for Fencing, long-time member of

KOREA, NORTH

KOREA, SOUTH

the U.S. Olympic Committee in several capacities and currently U.S. delegate to the Pan American Sports Organization.

Dan Ferris (deceased 1977), long-time secretary-treasurer of the Amateur Athletic Union of the United States and member of the ruling council of the International Federation for Track and Field.

Jesse Owens, winner of four gold medals in track and field at the Olympic Games in Berlin (1936). Owens is perhaps the best-known Olympic champion in the world.

Bronze—Al Oerter, only man in the history of the Olympic Games to win a gold medal in four successive Olympic Games (1956, 1960, 1964 and 1968) for the discus throw. He was presented with his Olympic Order award at the annual meeting of the USOC House of Delegates in April 1979 at Colorado Springs. Currently the Olympic Order is the only award bestowed by the IOC.

Eligibility for the Olympic Games

Since 1896 there have been many changes and frequent updating in the Athletes' Eligibility Code for participation in the Olympic Games, recognizing changes in society. Since the participation of Socialist countries in the games (1952) the IOC no longer uses the words *amateur* and *amateurism* in defining "eligibility." In fact, the IOC rule on eligibility is very simply stated:

"To be eligible for participation in the Olympic Games, a competitor must—

"—observe and abide by the Rules of the IOC and, in addition, the rules of his or her International Federation, as approved by the IOC, even if the federation's rules are more strict than those of the IOC;

"—not have received any financial rewards or material benefits in connection with his or her sports participation, except as permitted in the By-Laws to this Rule."

The bylaw to the rule delineates the types of remuneration that an athlete may receive, and permits him or her to be a physical education teacher or a coach of youngsters being introduced to sports.

Under this bylaw, also, an athlete may not endorse a commercial product except when the remuneration is contracted for with his or her national federation, such as we now see in skiing, track and field, and swimming.

Age Limit. There is no age limit stipulated by the IOC for competitors in the Olympic Games. The international federations, however, may adopt "lower" age limits as are currently prescribed by the ruling organizations for boxing and gymnastics.

SWITZERLAND

SPAIN

Citizenship. In general, only nationals of a country entered by their national Olympic committee may take part in the Olympic Games and represent their country. If an athlete has represented one country in the Olympic Games—or in world championships, area games, or international competition—he or she may not represent another country in the games unless he has become a naturalized citizen of the second country and has secured permission of the first country's national sports federation.

Doping. Under Rule 27, doping is forbidden. The IOC in 1968 prepared a list of prohibited drugs in an effort to preserve the health of the athletes, as well as to militate against any unfair advantages accruing from the use of such substances.

All Olympic athletes are liable to medical control and examination to be carried out at the site of the games, under the rules and procedures drawn up by the IOC Medical Commission. Any Olympic competitor who refuses to submit to such control or examination, or who is found guilty of doping, shall be excluded.

Competitors in sports restricted to women must comply with the prescribed test for femininity. Currently the test consists of a simple buccal smear of the upper roof of the mouth and is in no way denigrating to the athlete. Since femininity control was introduced at the 1968 Olympic Winter Games in Grenoble, France, no competitor has "failed" the test.

Entries. The maximum number of entries from each national Olympic committee in each event is fixed by the IOC in consultation with the appropriate international federation.

By and large, for individual events in such sports as track and field and swimming, a maximum of three competitors is permitted. For skiing four are permitted. Entries must be filed before the opening of the games and no substitutions are permitted in the case of illness or injury.

For team sports, one team from each country is permitted and pre-Olympic qualifying tournaments are conducted. The United States qualified for competition in the Olympic ice hockey tournament by virtue of its finish place in the 1979 World Ice Hockey Tournament.

ROLE OF NATIONAL OLYMPIC COMMITTEES

The national Olympic committee of a country, duly recognized by the IOC, is the only organization that can enter athletes in the Olympic Games. In the United States the national Olympic committee is the U.S. Olympic Committee.

CZECHOSLOVAKIA

FRANCE

There are more than 130 national Olympic committees recognized by the IOC today. One of the qualifications for recognition is that a country have a *minimum* of five national sports bodies affiliated with international bodies. The United States is one of the few countries that have national sports federations affiliated with every international body recognized for competitions on the programs for the Olympic Games and Olympic Winter Games. The USOC is the only national Olympic committee that enters athletes in every sport and for every individual event for which the United States has been qualified.

The national Olympic committees for Rhodesia and South Africa have been denied recognition by the IOC since 1968 because of the national policies of apartheid, prohibiting free competition between all athletes, as well as policies prohibiting general activities within each country without regard to race.

Under IOC regulations, national Olympic committees must be independent and autonomous and in a position to resist all political, religious or commercial pressure.

Furthermore, it is the responsibility of each national Olympic committee to identify the athlete who will bear the nation's flag during the opening ceremony. The USOC invites the athletes to designate the flagbearer, the selection being made at the site of the games immediately preceding the opening ceremony.

THE U.S. OLYMPIC COMMITTEE

When the Olympic Games were revived in 1896, the task of arousing American interest and obtaining the participation of American athletes in Athens was accepted by James E. Sullivan, one of the founders of the Amateur Athletic Union of the United States and a great champion of amateur athletics.

In 1900 A. G. Spalding, a prominent sports publisher and sporting goods manufacturer, was named first president of the committee. Sullivan himself continued as secretary until his death in 1914. Actually, there was no formal committee until an organization meeting was held at the New York Athletic Club on November 28, 1921, when a formal constitution, bylaws and rules of procedures were adopted.

The Governance Structure

The House of Delegates consists of all officers, current and past, representatives of organizations serving as national sports governing bodies, national multisport organizations, certain national organizations selected for membership because they may be on the program for the Olympic or Pan

SWEDEN

AUSTRALIA

American Games one day, and representatives of the fifty-one state and District of Columbia Olympic organizations. The House of Delegates has the authority to elect the USOC officers the year following the Olympic Games (the president may serve only one-four term) and to enact, amend or repeal provisions of the constitution, bylaws and general rules at its annual meeting.

Member organizations may either elect or appoint representatives to the House of Delegates, each to serve until a replacement is named by the appointing member organization.

The Administrative Committee

This committee, presided over by the USOC president, has the responsibility for supervising the conduct of the daily affairs of the USOC. The committee consists of the six officers and seven other voting members selected by those serving on the Executive Board. In addition there are eight nonvoting members.

The Executive Board

The board has general charge of the business affairs and activities of the USOC and is charged with defining policies to be followed in carrying out the purposes and objectives of the USOC. In addition to the current officers (and IOC members to the United States), the organizations holding membership also either elect or appoint representatives to serve until they are replaced. The state and District of Columbia organizations have a single representative, and an amendment adopted in April 1979 provided for the addition of six representatives from the general public. The constitution specifies that at least six members of the board be elected by the athletes themselves, but at least 20 percent of the members of the board must be persons who have been athletes in the Olympic or Pan American Games or other major international competitions within the preceding ten years.

Currently there are seventy-nine members of the Executive Board. The board meets quarterly.

Athletes' Advisory Council

The Athletes' Advisory Council, organized in 1973, consists of athletes from each of the sports on the programs for the Olympic Games, Olympic Winter Games and Pan American Games. This council serves in an advisory capacity to the USOC Executive Board. The current chairman is Edward Williams, a member of the 1968 U.S. Olympic biathlon squad.

Standing and Special Committees

The USOC president, with the approval of the Executive Board, appoints members to a number of standing and special committees under the constitution, including those concerned with budget and audit, development, finance, games preparation, investment, sports medicine, USOC-International Olympic Academy and team services.

Olympic House

Headquarters of the U.S. Olympic Committee are at the Olympic House in Colorado Springs. The headquarters were removed from New York City on July 1, 1978.

In charge of Olympic House is Executive Director Colonel F. Don Miller, U.S.A. (ret.), who serves as chief administrative official. Although he does not have the status of an officer, Colonel Miller is entitled to attend meetings of the House of Delegates, the Administrative Committee and the Executive Board, where he has a voice but no vote. He is also an ex-officio member of all committees.

The executive director is also in charge of all facilities operated by the USOC. He directs staff services, operations at the national training centers and operations at the site of the Olympic Games.

THE NATIONAL TRAINING CENTERS

The USOC Executive Board in December 1976 adopted the national training center concept by authorizing the establishment of several regional training centers to help develop and prepare potential international-class athletes, as well as other athletes, without regard to age or level of ability.

Subsequently the USOC opened two training centers: one at Squaw Valley, California, site of the 1960 Olympic Winter Games, and the other, in late 1977, at Colorado Springs, on the site of the former Ent Air Force Base.

Operated by the USOC, the training centers are available to all athletes nominated by the thirty-two national sports governing bodies for the sports on the programs for the Olympic and Pan American Games. It is the responsibility of the national sports governing bodies to select the athletes and to handle the transportation expenses for all athletes, coaches, trainers and administrative officials. The USOC underwrites all expenses of athletes during their stay at the training centers.

The National Training Center in Action

XVII

THE NATIONAL SPORTS FESTIVAL

One of the most significant undertakings of the USOC was the inauguration of the National Sports Festival in 1978 at Colorado Springs. It was the implementation of a concept that I originally jotted down fifteen years earlier—a summertime mini-Olympics with a dual purpose:

First, we were providing a first-class showcase for the finest amateur athletes in the country for top-level midsummer competition in an Olympic-like atmosphere.

Secondly, we not only were offering sports fans of the United States an opportunity to watch our top amateur athletes in head-to-head competition, but also were giving all America an opportunity to watch a number of Olympic sports that they may previously only have read about.

A basic premise in establishing the National Sports Festival was the desire to introduce all sports on the Olympic program to the youth of America. We firmly believe that our youth who may see these sports either in person or through national telecasts will have their sports appetites whetted to the point of giving some new sports a try. We are further convinced that through this exposure we can enlarge the reservoir of potential Olympians in many of those sports which have not attracted broad-scale participation.

In National Sports Festival I we brought together more than two thousand athletes from all sections of the country to participate in twenty-six different sports on the programs of the Olympic and Pan American Games. The athletes were chosen by various selection methods by our thirty-two national sports governing bodies. For National Sports Festival II we added five more sports and increased the number of athletes to 2600.

National Sports Festival I was underwritten almost 100 percent by the USOC. The impact of the festival on athletes and athletic America was gratifying. As a result, the National Broadcasting Company secured the television rights and Coca Cola U.S.A. became the national sponsor for the festival. Along with a guarantee from the community of Colorado Springs, in its second year the festival was self-sustaining.

On the basis of the success of the first two festivals, we can forecast not only that the festival will become a summer fixture, but also that it should blossom into the premier amateur sports event in the country.

Currently it is planned to hold the festival annually except in Olympic years. This schedule has been adopted so that potential Olympians and elite-class athletes will set their training schedules to include the festival. In an Olympic year our total effort must be concerned with the preparation of all athletes for Olympic competition.

XVIII

The National Sports Festival

XIX

CANADA

GERMANY,
FEDERAL
REPUBLIC

The dedicated effort of the spirited Colorado Springs citizens was instrumental in the selection of this city for the first two festivals. It may be expected, however, that the site of the festival will be moved around the country to expose athletes and sports to other areas in the coming years.

The future success of the United States in the Olympic Games may be directly tied in with the effectiveness of the National Sports Festival. We are convinced that the future was never brighter.

THE SPORTS MEDICINE PROGRAM

Concomitant with the establishment of the national training centers has been the implementation of a broad-scale, coordinated, sophisticated sports medicine program designed to cater to the specific needs of our athletes to improve their skills, techniques, health and knowledge of their own bodies.

Unlike similar sports medicine programs in other countries designed to amass medical data for further studies by doctors, this program is structured for the athlete. Any findings, however, will be made available to doctors, coaches, trainers, other athletes and anyone in the United States interested in the broad field of sports medicine, comprising those sciences concerned with the development of athletes of all ages and at all levels of ability.

The program embraces the following areas:

● Biomechanics, or body engineering, designed to make athletes aware of more efficient use of their muscles and strength to increase skills and techniques.

● Sports physiology, to bring to the attention of athletes a better understanding of their bodies.

● Nutrition, to make the athlete aware of proper eating habits.

● Sports psychology, embracing a study of the importance of the proper mental attitude when faced with competitive situations.

Both training centers have excellently appointed sports medicine complexes designed to handle special testing for the athletes in the areas of body fat, strength and flexibility and weight training, along with laboratories for visual acuity and dental examinations.

It may be expected that in the coming years more and more elite-class athletes will take advantage of both the training opportunities and the special testing and exposure available. Through the sponsorship of the Burger King Corporation we have been able to step up the sports medicine programs at the training centers. Also, through the generosity of a number of national corporations, the USOC has obtained valuable equipment, so important in a

NEW ZEALAND

NORWAY

modern, up-to-date sports medicine complex.

Definitely, the progress of the American athlete in international competitions, including the Olympic Games, is tied to the work now being done in sports medicine. However, sports medicine cannot be expected to furnish all the answers. The ultimate success of our athletes depends on the continued dedicated efforts and serious training regimen of all elite-class athletes.

THE OLYMPIC JOB OPPORTUNITIES PROGRAM

For many years it has been evident that a sound employment program must be developed for the mature athlete to enable him or her to combine a career job with opportunities for daily training.

Howard C. Miller, president of the Canteen Corporation of Chicago, blueprinted such a program for the consideration of the USOC.

Highlights of the Olympic Job Opportunities Program designed by Miller, and accepted by the USOC, embraced the placing of athletes in career jobs for which they qualify, the cooperation of almost a hundred national corporations interested in employing elite-class athletes, a promise to provide the athlete with time off daily (without loss of pay) for daily training and freedom for additional time off to participate in important national and international competitions.

The USOC has been gratified with the response of national corporations offering to consider for career positions mature athletes under the conditions laid down for those companies cooperating with the Olympic Job Opportunities Program.

Here is an ongoing program that will have a constructive impact on athletes. For the first time the USOC is encouraging our top athletes to remain competitive by combining a career job with regular training.

Athletes have been encouraged to submit job résumés to the USOC. After review by the Olympic House staff, the résumé is forwarded to the appropriate national sports governing body for certification of the applicant as a potential Olympian. Only then is the athlete's application forwarded to the Canteen Corporation for further screening prior to arranging for job interviews.

This is an open-ended program. Canteen Corporation continues to solicit participation by national corporations. It is expected that there will be no limitation placed on the number of positions or the number of corporations seeking to employ potential Olympians. There must be unlimited job opportunities for our mature athletes permitting them to remain in athletics.

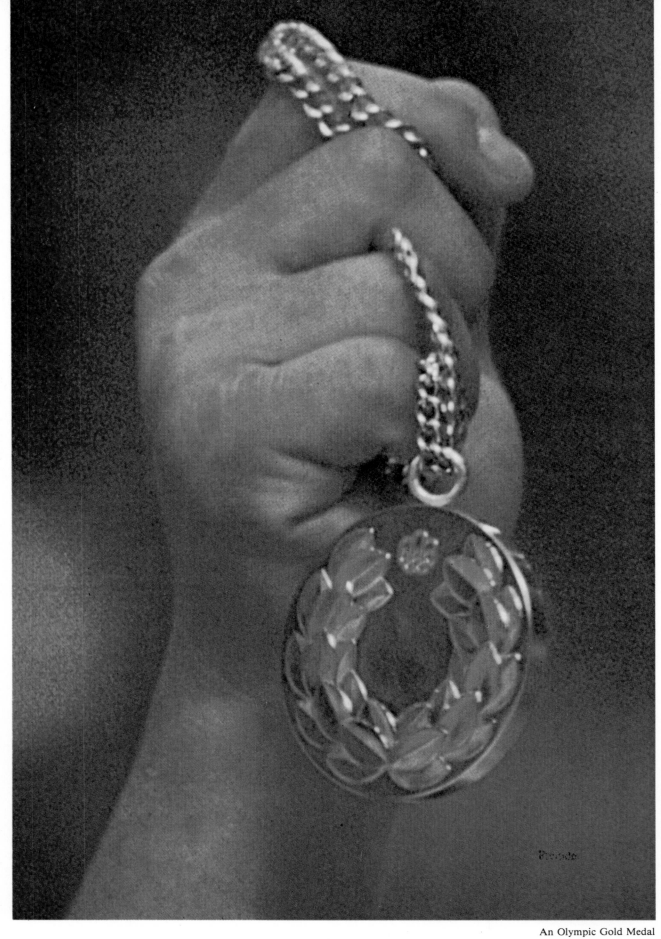

An Olympic Gold Medal

JAPAN

SELECTION OF U.S. OLYMPIC AND PAN AMERICAN TEAMS

AUSTRIA

Long experience has taught the U.S. Olympic Committee that the tryout method is the fairest and most satisfactory method of selecting team members for the Olympic and Pan American Games. It is recognized that some athletes who have been highly regarded (on the basis of previous performances) have failed to qualify in the final selection trials, but these cases are exceptions. In the United States, with a plethora of talented athletes, it is considered a good policy to require that all athletes who have either qualified or been selected to participate in the final selection trials start on an equal basis.

Arbitrary selection of an athlete who did not compete or qualify in the tryouts could arouse charges of politics or racial or religious prejudice on the part of athletes, or friends of athletes, who would have been displaced on the team.

Under a recent USOC change the responsibility of identifying athletes for the final selection trials and conducting the trials belongs to the national sports governing bodies. However, it is also the responsibility of each national sports governing body to present the criteria for selection at the trials for the review of the USOC Games Preparation Committee prior to approval by the USOC Executive Board.

In addition to selecting the dates and sites of the final selection trials, the national sports governing body must detail the process to be used in selecting athletes for the trials, the sequence of events and the selection of team officials (coaches, managers and ancillary personnel, as required).

All final selection trials are open to athletes eligible under the rules of the IOC, the international sports federations and the national sports governing bodies. No gifts or prizes are awarded at the final selection trials unless the trial is an established event (such as a national championship used by the U.S. Figure Skating Association). The established event may use the traditional prizes for the event.

All members qualifying for the Olympic or Pan American teams must pass the USOC medical examination before being accepted on the team.

Expenses are awarded to all athletes selected for the final trials. The USOC also pays full travel and living expenses from the date an athlete is selected until he returns to his home, including the inclusive dates for any special training organized by his particular sport.

The United States is probably the only nation in the worldwide Olympic movement that uses advertised head-to-head competition for the selection of all members of the Olympic and Pan American teams.

ITALY

HUNGARY

THE AMATEUR SPORTS ACT OF 1978

The Amateur Sports Act of 1978 represents the most significant sports federal legislation adopted by the Congress of the United States. When signed by the President of the United States on November 8, 1978, the restructuring of amateur sports in the United States was assured.

Under this act the USOC was identified as the coordinating body for all amateur sports on the programs of the Olympic and Pan American Games. With humility and compassion we have accepted the challenge for the enhancement of amateur sports in the United States.

For the first time in more than fifty years we have the national sports organizations working toward a single objective—amateur sports programs designed for amateur athletes.

The main change in the structure of amateur sports in America has been from a horizontal to a vertical structure. Under the vertical structure, provision has been made for all national sports organizations to become integral and active partners in the governance of the thirty-two national sports governing bodies.

The provisions of the act implemented the USOC constitution, delineating the criteria for the recognition of national sports governing bodies, as well as reinforcing the procedures for the resolution of all disputes between athletes and sports governing bodies and disagreements between two or more sports organizations.

The act further recognizes the role of the athlete in the governance of amateur sports. Specifically, at least 20 percent of the governance structure of the USOC and of all national sports governing bodies must consist of athletes. In the last seven years the USOC has included ''recent athletes'' (those who have been on Olympic teams within the last ten years) on its Executive Board and standing committees.

A bill of rights for athletes, guaranteeing every athlete's freedom of choice in competing in important meets and matches leading to qualification for national and international teams and the Pan American and Olympic Games—under the provisions of the USOC constitution—has been recognized in the act.

Where there may have been some question about the powers of national sports governing bodies to act on their own in the past, autonomy has been decreed under the act. Thus, no longer can there be cross-pollenization

U.S.S.R.

GERMAN
DEMOCRATIC
REPUBLIC

among several national governing bodies. In effect, in the future swimmers will make rules of competition for swimmers, boxers for boxers, and the like. The act put an end to a limited prevailing practice among national governing bodies of forming umbrella organizations.

With enactment of the Amateur Sports Act of 1978, the blueprint was drawn for the future development of amateur sports, pointing to a broad-scale national program for the enhancement of amateur sports for athletes of all ages and at all levels of ability.

EPILOGUE

The USOC is concerned with the enhancement of all amateur sports programs for the youth of America. Of course, emphasis is placed on those sports on the programs for the Olympic and Pan American Games.

Along with the International Olympic Committee, the USOC encourages all amateur sports, especially those sports which one day may be on the programs for either the Olympic or the Pan American Games.

In a recent national poll conducted by the National Broadcasting Company, the work of the USOC was identified as "vitally important" by more than 73 percent of those queried. In addition, parents questioned on preferences for their sons and daughters showed an overwhelming preference (55 percent) for participation in amateur athletics, as opposed to 30 percent opting for professional sports.

The amateur sports programs for the youth of our country have seldom enjoyed the acceptance and popularity found today. This renewed interest in amateur sports will have a profound effect on the stimulation and development of elite-class athletes. In fact, 93.6 percent felt it was important for children to take pride in the achievements of U.S. athletes in the Olympic Games, regardless of the number of medals won.

The biggest challenge facing the United States is the development of a broader base of elite-class athletes. The popularity of these exciting sports in Europe still eclipses that in our country. With the expansion of programs and the development of new facilities, however, it may be expected that within the next decade our success and worldwide respect in winter sports will attain all-time highs.

Sonja Henie
ONE IN A MILLION

Sonja Henie without a doubt was truly the most famous woman skater in the world. She was sometimes described by the name of her first movie in the United States, "One in a Million."

In 1927 Jack Dempsey was in training again. He was getting ready for a return boxing championship match with Gene Tunney. In 1927 Babe Ruth was hitting his 416th home run. In 1927 Bobby Jones was winning his third national golf championship. In 1927 five thousand American marines were sent to Nicaragua to preserve order. And in 1927 Sonja Henie, a pretty little Norwegian girl, had just won her first world's figure-skating championship.

This was the first of ten consecutive world championship titles. She won her first Olympic championship in 1928 at St. Moritz, her second in 1932 at Lake Placid and finally won her third gold medal in 1936 at Garmisch-Partenkirchen. She was the only woman figure skater to win the first-place gold medal in three consecutive Olympiads.

She brought to figure skating a new look. Her routines included numerous jumps and increased speed and, although her moves were graceful, they were demanding. This new look was enthusiastically welcomed by the sports world.

1

Sonja Henie was born during an unusual April blizzard in Oslo in 1912. One of the first things that she remembered about Oslo was "snow on the hill, sleds, the fine, clean cut of ice winds, and the fact that older boys and girls had fun going skating at Frogner Stadium."

She immediately loved outdoor sports and began skiing when she was four years old. The family had a winter home in a mountain village named Geilo, famous for winter sports. Now on skis, she could follow her older brother everywhere.

Because of the early experience on skis, Sonja felt she had a head start in competing with other children on skates. Skiing gave her excellent balance and rhythm in movement. Sonja stated, "What I do know is that Geilo meant skiing, and skiing was like flying, and this flying made me winter-drunk, an affliction I have never got over."

Another activity that influenced Sonja Henie's skating career was her early interest in dancing. At about age four she seemed compelled to put her feeling into motion whenever she heard music. Raiding her mother's closet for "costumes," she made up her own dance recitals by turning on the music and dancing around her house. After a year of this with no signs of her interest in dancing diminishing, her parents gave her ballet lessons. The lessons were very successful. Sonja continued ballet instruction throughout the many years of her skating competitions, feeling that it gave added dimension to her free-skating routines. Dancing turned out to be one of her contributions to figure skating. By introducing a dance choreography to her part of the free-skating program of the 1928 Olympics at St. Moritz, she gave form and flow to the usual sequence of spins and jumps. Most skaters in all countries of the world now use this blend of dancing and skating in their routines.

With such a high interest in dancing, it would seem that there would be no time for anything else. As little sister Sonja saw it, however, older brother Leif had skates, went to the popular Frogner skating rink with his friends and returned glowing from the fun he had had. She was missing out on fun.

Using every persuasion she knew, she finally won from her parents a pair of skates. They were the kind that fitted onto the shoes, but they were ice-going and that is what mattered. Finally able to tag along with Leif, she did

2

just that—sometimes being a bother but more often learning from his earnest advice.

Since she had done well on skis, Sonja was sure ice skating would give her no problems. The first time on the new skates she struck out after big brother toward center ice. Coming to her aid after a jarring fall, Leif said to her, "If you are going to skate, you are going to fall," and taught her to relax when falling. He went on, "Who do you think you are to think you can learn to skate without falling? Ten years from now you'll still be falling, maybe less often."

Comforted because he didn't plan to convince their parents that she was too unbalanced to become a good skater, she relaxed and took his instruction. Thus she learned the rudiments of skating from her brother Leif.

The next thing her family knew, skating was the big thing in Sonja's life. It filled her days. She found in it the same excitement she had found in dancing.

Then a member of a private skating club at Frogner noticed the enthusiastic six-year-old and led her through a few simple figures that Leif had taught her. Impressed with the youngster, the young woman gave Sonja amateur lessons for the next few months. When Sonja turned seven and was presented with a pair of boot skates, the young woman convinced Sonja's father he should allow her to enter the children's competition held at the rink each year. Sonja won the event over children twice her age. Her family was enthusiastic over her victory. Her father had been a champion bicyclist and a skater of note as well. Sonja's career in competition was launched.

The next year, at age eight, she won the next step higher, the junior Class C competition. It was decided that she should skip the junior Classes B and A and the senior C and B and enter the senior A national championship of Norway to be held the following winter.

Planning began in earnest and Sonja took professional lessons from Oscar Holte, the leading instructor in Oslo. Her mother and father kept close watch over her skating. A regular supervised practice schedule was arranged and time spent at Frogner was no longer fun time but serious training. Sonja didn't mind doing anything that meant she could keep on skating. She was

3

thrilled that she was improving. Proper eating habits took on more significance, and the Henie household routines revolved around Sonja's skating. Sonja's parents accepted the travel, the new acquaintances, the tensions and the terrific pace without regret. When Father had to attend business concerns, Mother took over Sonja's supervision completely. Sonja found the whole affair to be a fairy tale of happiness.

In the spring before the national competition she resumed her ballet lessons, and during the summer her mother took her to London for instruction from the woman who guided Pavlova in the Russian ballet for many years, Madame Karsavina. School studies were tutored and remained that way throughout most of Sonja's school career. This is another factor that Sonja Henie felt contributed to her becoming a skating champion. Had her family not had the means to have her tutored, to travel, to have her coached by top instructors, to give her experience skating in places away from home, there would have been no championship career.

The Norwegian national championship competition was held at Frogner Stadium, but the crowd that assembled that day was far larger than the one Sonja had skated for in the children's and junior titles. It was an overwhelming experience to rise when her name was called and skate out onto the ice before all those people. Once she was in her place on the ice, however, she was "at home and alone with [her] fun." It was to be the same throughout her career—tension disappeared when she felt the smooth, hard surface and thought about the motions she loved to do.

She carefully cut the school figures she knew so well. Then, during the free-skating program, she flew over the ice and let go during jumps in a manner she had done only when she was by herself. When she finished, she was the national champion of Norway. She was heady with excitement.

Skating became her whole life after that. It was agreed that she would go abroad for lessons and experience. She was introduced into a world of color and commotion and the glitter of international fame. She looked forward to becoming a real part of it someday.

In the winter of 1924 she was entered in the Olympic Games at Chamonix. She won no honors, coming in last, but the experience prepared her for the four years of training necessary for the next Olympics.

Then, after she had successfully retained the Norwegian championship twice more, in 1925 and 1926, it was announced that the world championship would be held in Oslo in 1927. It was a competition of almost Olympic magnitude. If she retained her Norwegian title again in 1927, she would be the logical representative for her country.

Sonja Henie would be fifteen, fourteen at the time of entry. The authorities at the 1924 Olympics had opposed a child's entry into the games at Chamonix on the grounds that it would "turn the affair into a farce." At that time her father countered with the fact that she was her country's "national champion and therefore entitled to enter any international contest of her choosing."

There was a little tension over her being accepted by the world championship authorities, but the papers were filed anyway. There was no objection from the committee. Sonja was dazzled by the idea of again competing with the stars of the ice-skating world. Her family was determined that she would make a good showing on their own "back ice." There was increased concentration on guidance from skating experts, there were dancing and music lessons and the design of an appropriate costume. Her mother chose a tight-fitting white velvet dress with a bell skirt. There would be no extra folds or ruffles to detract from the skater's movements. It was a revolution compared to costumes that had been worn by skaters in the past.

The world championship was a challenging goal. Ice conditions were excellent at home that fall, so there was no need to go abroad. Sonja worked steadily, getting her school figures absolutely accurate. She exercised for balance, limberness and strength. She worked constantly on the jumps that were to be the specialty of her free-skating program. Sonja loved it all.

With her instructors she planned the most daring free-skating program she could manage. Her training was controlled for her well-being, but she worked as hard as she could during her hours on the ice. Sometimes her muscles felt like lead, and sometimes she felt as though she could fly over all of Norway. She didn't mind any of it when the work was skating and the goal was better skating.

During the winter of 1926-27 the ice-skating elite began to arrive in Oslo and to fill the ice at Frogner Stadium. On the afternoon before the opening

5

of the world championships Sonja Henie stood in the middle of what had been her home territory. She watched representatives from all the countries of Europe and a few from other parts of the world going through their practice routines. They all seemed confident and looked brilliant.

One of the boxes in the grandstands had been draped with flags and surrounded by silk ropes in anticipation of the appearance of the king and queen of Norway. She thought of how much better she would have to be than those brilliant, unerring champions around her, all older and more experienced. She was the youngest skater who had ever entered a world championship. She thought of what the disgrace would be like if she failed. She went home to an endless night.

After the final spin of her free-skating program late the next afternoon, the icy wind blowing across Frogner Stadium awoke her to the fact that her effort was over. A few moments later, thirteen-year-old Sonja Henie was presented to King Haakon and Queen Maude of Norway as the new world champion figure skater.

This victory led the way to St. Moritz and the 1928 Olympic Games. Again it was unnecessary to go abroad to train, as the ice near home was excellent. Besides, Sonja's father believed it was better to train far, far away from one's rivals. That winter she intensified work on each of the eighty school figures from which the Olympic test would be chosen. Also, her father promoted small exhibitions at her training spot and several more formal ones in Bergen to get her used to performing before audiences.

Another event occurred in that summer between winning the world championship and the games at St. Moritz. She went to London and saw the idol of her dancing dreams perform—Pavlova. The experience rekindled Sonja's passion for the dance that had a profound influence on her free-skating style.

Back on the ice that fall, she worked to blend the design of the ballet solo with the elements of figure skating. Her skating instructor, Martin Stixrud, helped her choose the jumps and spins she would have to incorporate to show her skill to the judges. She arranged them in a sequence that would capture the mood of dancing.

All of the facets of her rigorous training fortified her well for St. Moritz.

Her high spirits carried her through to her first gold medal for figure skating at the Winter Olympics of 1928.

The next evening she opened the Olympic Ball and stepped completely on-to the merry-go-round of competitive skating where each swing into winter brought a new brass ring to reach for. It was a heady experience for a young person, and the rush of travel, the crowds, the glitter of performing, the celebrations and parties, the constant need to maintain training did not take away her love for skating. Professionalism was not an option then, and the only way to stay in skating was to stay in competition.

Once she stepped onto the merry-go-round in 1928 she stayed on to win the gold at Lake Placid in 1932 and again at Garmisch-Partenkirchen in 1936. In between there were other championships and countless exhibitions. She was introduced to the royal families of Europe and appeared before ever-growing crowds. She inspired an interest in the sport in other nations. She won five consecutive Norwegian championships and ten consecutive world championships.

The first year after St. Moritz was a capsule of the strenuous rounds that were to come. Within a month after the Olympics, the 1928 world champion-ship competition was held in London. The caravan of competitors left Switzerland and moved to the British capital to prepare for the second big contest of the year. This time the Henies were among them, Sonja destined for her second world championship. The evening before the competition, however, held more sparkle. A special exhibition was given before the British royal household. The occasion aroused such enthusiasm in Princess Elizabeth and Princess Margaret Rose that it was decided right then that they should receive ice skates of their own.

Next was Berlin for the opening ceremonies of a six-day bicycle race, and then home to Oslo, where she was to compete in the Norwegian national championship event representing her own club. The crowds were con-siderably larger than usual because an Olympic champion was in the com-petition. Summer brought an invitation from Prince Heinrick of Holland to open the Summer Olympic Games at Amsterdam.

At an exhibition in Sweden the fifteen-year-old performer learned how

easily a crowd can become a mob. Eager spectators closed around her upon her arrival at the rink, causing some terrifying moments until her father arrived with the officials. Again, upon their return to their hotel, the press of the crowds had to be brought under control by militia.

Another exhibition brought comic relief. In Copenhagen several days later, large crowds on the ice caused long cracks to develop. Hardly daring to watch where she was skating, she went on with her performance. Wild applause made her wonder whether the spectators liked her skating or the effect of the sprays of water that spurted out of the cracks as she skated over them.

Other exhibitions and other championships kept Sonja touring the continent in the 1928-29 season, with the high point being a unanimous decision for the 1929 world championship in Budapest. The round of performances and parties demanded of champions was hectic even for a person as young and healthy and well conditioned as Sonja. She had to adhere to her strict training schedule despite heavy social duties.

The winter of 1929-30 brought the world championship competition to Madison Square Garden in New York and Sonja Henie to the United States. Languages had been part of Sonja's studies, so that she was able to absorb her experiences in the United States and Canada more easily. There was a great deal of interest in her favorite ice skates and her skating costumes, and much was made of them by the newspapers. Americans seemed more interested in the things that made her an individual than in her technical skills and skating background. It was a new experience.

Prior to the championship there was an ice carnival at Madison Square Garden that ran for several nights and involved the championship contestants. The production was four hours long and used hundreds of skaters. The late hours were poor preparation for the skating competition, but the experience was a good opportunity to become familiar with American crowds and the new ice. The indoor gallery made possible a more intimate awareness of the spectators than did the vast outdoor grandstands surrounding open ice.

The challengers in 1930 were impressive, but Sonja held her defense of the title and won her fourth world championship. After the competition and throughout the ensuing tour the Henies were greeted by crowds of Norwegian-Americans. Many of them remembered Sonja's father as the world champion bicyclist and from other sporting competitions in which he had won 160 trophies of all sorts.

The Americans were also very interested in seeing the European skating style, and the U.S. Figure Skating Association promoted numerous exhibitions for the European caravan. By the time the group sailed from New York, everyone was exhausted. For the first time since 1924, it was decided that Sonja would not defend her Norwegian national title. The warmth of the people in the United States stayed with her, and seven years later she was to begin the process of becoming a U.S. citizen.

Despite the need to rest, the merry-go-round of world competition did not lose its charm for Sonja. Furthermore, she felt that she had not yet reached the peak of her form.

Her fifth world championship competition in March 1931 brought the realization that no crown is a permanent fixture. Young Hilda Holowsky from Vienna showed an enormous talent and won over the Berlin crowd. She placed an uncomfortably close second, edging out three far more experienced skaters.

Sonja had been training with Howard Nicholson, an American who was making a name as a master in figure-skating instruction and who had come to London to be near the world's ice centers. His methods gave a new lift to Sonja's work, and she felt the results showed in the reception she received in Vienna. She felt she was still growing in her effort to combine dancing and skating, but she also knew younger competitors were coming up through the ranks in Europe, England and America. They would make it hard for her to stay on top.

Winning the title at the Olympic Games at Lake Placid in 1930 against a strong rank brought a satisfying victory for Sonja. It helped counteract dif-

9

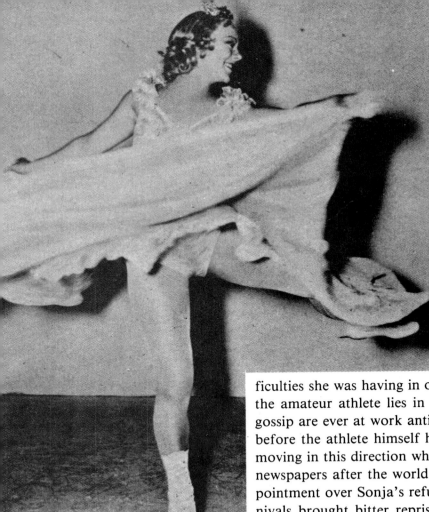

ficulties she was having in other areas of her career. One of the hazards for the amateur athlete lies in maintaining the amateur standing. Rumor and gossip are ever at work anticipating the move to professional standing long before the athlete himself has made the decision. The Henies were not yet moving in this direction when a storm over the issue broke in the Canadian newspapers after the world championship competition in Montreal. Disappointment over Sonja's refusal to appear at several of Canada's winter carnivals brought bitter reprisals in the press. Hurt and disillusioned, Sonja finished her stateside commitments and returned to Eruope.

Her welcome on the other side of the Atlantic was sincere and soothing, but the following summer she seriously considered retiring for the first time. In the end, however, the distractions of summer and the lure of a new season at hand pushed the thoughts aside. That fall her dream of combining dancing and skating was realized. She made her debut in Milan in an ice version of the swan solo from *Swan Lake*, and her effort was well received. A new era began for her in her skating style. Her solos thereafter were designed around the dance and the theater.

Fame continued to bring its burdens as well as its satisfactions. Whispers of temperament, romance and declining powers were an annoyance. Nervous strain, however, became a real factor, and Sonja decided that the 1935-36 season would be her last in competition. Looking back over her nine years since becoming a world champion in figure skating brought a quiet satisfaction. She knew she had run her course as an amateur. When she made her statement public, her future was sealed.

Her final season was her busiest, most demanding and most dramatic. The European championships were to be held in Berlin, the Olympics in Garmisch-Partenkirchen, the world championships in Paris. In between were scheduled exhibitions all over the Continent. Training in London was instructive. She felt like a veteran watching the young hopefuls, realizing their potential, seeing training methods she had originated becoming standard operating procedure.

10

As the exhibition route crisscrossed Europe, the sense of approaching climax mounted. Sonja Henie cared more about winning now than in any other winter of her life. She wanted to leave her competitive career while she was still at the top.

She felt at home in the Sports Palast in Berlin. Her nervousness faded. She formally announced her plan to retire. The newspapers began adding up her titles, causing the entire skating world to focus on her exit.

While she retained her title in Berlin, the competition showed her that she could not relax her efforts. The real climax of the season was the Winter Olympic Games. Countries spend four years preparing their finest, and the pageantry has no equal in the sports world. There were twenty-three stars from twelve countries entered in the figure-skating event that year. Other considerations of the competition began pressing in on her thoughts. Even the majestic Alpine peaks surrounding the stadium seemed to be focused on the little square of ice in the Olympic arena. The flame was lit, the brasses blared and the Olympic Games of 1936 were under way.

The school-figure competition yielded Sonja a slim lead. Cecilia Colledge, a fifteen-year-old from England, was a very close second. The free-skating final was the second-to-last event of the entire Olympic Winter Games. Sonja Henie was the final contestant. She followed her custom of sleeping until her father's phone call one hour before her turn on the ice. That way she avoided the nervous wait at the edge of the ice, and she could skate right out fresh and rested. She shut the spectators out of her mind and told herself that she "led in points, the ice was not too good, and [she] must be careful." With that she pushed off to the opening chords of her music. Four minutes later she was again an Olympic champion. It was her third and last time and an unequaled feat.

Cecilia Colledge did not enter the Paris competition, nor did many of the other skating stars. Sonja had her final victory as world champion and the final satisfaction of "going out on top."

Figure Skating

WHY NOT A TRIPLE JUMP?

Why not a triple jump?'' Dick Button asked himself that question as he began training for the 1952 Olympic Games.

In his previous years of competition Dick Button had presented variations on standard moves to make his five-minute free-skating programs original. Now, he decided, it was time for a completely new move. No one had ever done a triple jump in competition. Few considered such a thing possible.

However, new moves were being added to skaters' repertoires every year. Jumps and spins that were unheard of in the early Olympics had become standard. Dick Button himself introduced the double axel in 1948, the double loop/double loop in 1949, the triple-double-loop in 1950, and the double axel/double axel in 1951. After World War II, novice skaters found themselves competing in a sport that was changing at a rapid pace.

If Dick Button was to go forward in the sport and make a bid for another Olympic title, he would have to do something distinctive.

The decision to work on a triple jump had its roots in the summer of 1951. Planning the strategies for his free-skating program with his teacher, Gus Lussi, took place at Lake Placid, New York, in July and August. By fall the figures and movements Dick Button hoped would win another Olympic title were well established.

Each year of his career, Dick Button had tried to present a new jump, spin or combination. It was decided that 1952 required more than a variation on a standard move. Teacher and pupil began to consider triple revolutions. The triple jump captured Button's imagination. Several types of jumps were considered. A triple salchow seemed to be a good possibility for a while, but it lacked the eye appeal of higher jumps. It was finally decided that the triple loop jump would become the triple jump on which to begin.

Doing it was another matter, however. Button began daily work on a triple revolution. He was not successful but could not accept the possibility that he would not be able to do it. For relief he returned to simpler jumps, only to discover that his timing was seriously affected by this increase in rotation. He found he could not control even the most elementary jumps. Frantic, he

Richard Button, U.S.A.

Richard Button, U.S.A.

turned to his teacher where he received reassurance that his control would return. And so it did, but precious practice time was lost. School figures and the new free-skating program claimed the balance of the training session. College classes then took precidence, and work on the triple did not resume until winter vacation.

Once more on ice, Button nonchalantly made the preparatory moves he had worked out for a triple jump. Then he found himself whirling through the three revolutions and landing—poorly but cleanly. There it was. He had done it. Exhilaration filled him as he rushed to telegraph the news to Mr. Lussi. Much hard work remained to perfect the jump, but nothing could dampen his enthusiasm at that moment.

It is usually an advantage to keep new movements a secret until the figure skaters' performance before the judges. This was the strategy Button used earlier in his career when he invented and was the first to perform the Flying Camel, a combination jump spin which was for many years known as the Button Camel. In the case of a radical change there are valid reasons to do just the opposite. If not forewarned, the judges might not recognize a new jump. They might pass it off as an illusion. Consequently, the triple loop was publicized in advance of the games at Oslo in February.

Newsmen gathered at airports and sportsmen gathered at rinkside, all speculating on the probability of Button's accomplishing the feat in competition. Training moved to Germany and intensified. The falls were punishing

14

Richard Button, U.S.A.

Richard Button, U.S.A.

and the havoc to his timing was demoralizing. At an exhibition in Vienna, where he especially wanted to do well, he fell attempting the triple loop. Not wanting to leave a bad impression with a city that had favored him with ever-increasing audiences, he rescheduled his program for the following evening. The resolve to perform well lifted his program out of its slump and restored his confidence. The triple-loop jump was successful. He was ready for the ultimate test at Oslo.

The practice and pageantry that filled the opening of the 1952 Olympic Games left taut nerves and high spirits. Dick Button stood at the crowning effort of years of practice. Nervous and extremely aware of every element of the scene before him, he forced himself into the opening movements of his program. Cooly he thought through one axel, a double lutz. Now he had the feel of the ice. Would it work? The next jump would tell. There were the preparation steps. Momentary panic. Rotation. Feet crossed in air. Wind! Cold! Height! A fraction of a second and a clean steady landing and Dick Button knew as the applause rolled out to meet him that he had been the first to do a triple jump in competition!

Figure skating is the oldest Olympic winter sports event. In 1908 a complete figure-skating program was held at the IV Olympic Summer Games in London. There was competition again at the summer games in Antwerp in 1920, and since the I Olympic Winter Games at Chamonix in 1924, figure skating has been part of the standard program.

Sonja Henie, Norway

Cecilia Colledge, Great Britain

Herma Plank, Szabo, Au

Results, Figure Skating, Women

1908 (London)
1. Madge Syers, Great Britain
2. Elsa Rendschmidt, Germany
3. Dorothy Greenhough-Smith, Great Britain
4. Elna Montgomery, Sweden
5. G. Lycett, Great Britain

1920 (Antwerp)
1. Magda Julin-Mauroy, Sweden
2. Svea Norén, Sweden
3. Theresa Weld, U.S.A.
4. Phyllis W. Johnson, Great Britain
5. Margot Moe, Norway
6. Ingrid Gulbrandsen, Norway

1924 (Chamonix)
1. Herma Planck-Szabo, Austria
2. Beatrix Loughran, U.S.A.
3. Ethel Muckelt, Great Britain
4. Theresa Blanchard-Weld, U.S.A.
5. Andrée Joly, France
6. Cecil Smith, Canada

1928 (St. Moritz)
1. Sonja Henie, Norway
2. Fritzi Burger, Austria
3. Beatrix Loughran, U.S.A.
4. Maribel Vinson, U.S.A.
5. Cecil Smith, Canada
6. Constance Wilson, Canada

FIGURE SKATING—WOMEN

In the first Olympic figure-skating contest for women in 1908, the English set the pace. At that time Madge Syers was in a class of her own and even competed successfully with the men. At Chamonix in 1924 Herma Planck-Szabo from Austria was unanimously voted Olympic winner. This was followed by the great series of victories by Sonja Henie from Norway, which is not likely to be repeated in view of the ever-growing attractions of the ice shows.

Sonja Henie first entered international competition at the age of eleven in 1924 just for the exposure and experience, she said. In the 1924 Olympic Winter Games, which were held in Chamonix, France, Sonja finished last. She was, however, also fifth that same year in the world championships. In 1926 Sonja was second in the world championships in singles and fifth in pairs with Arne Lie, her only international competitive appearance in pairs.

Sonja won her first world title the following year, in 1927, at Oslo in her native country when she was fourteen years old. She went on to compile an

16

Barbara Scott, Canada

unequaled record of ten consecutive world championship titles, including two won in North America in 1930 and 1932. She won her last world title at Paris in 1936.

She won the first of three Olympic championships in 1928. Sonja successfully defended that title at Lake Placid in 1932 and again at Garmisch-Partenkirchen in 1936. She is the only woman to win gold medals in three consecutive Olympiads in any sport and the only woman to win more than one figure-skating gold medal in singles.

Sonja Henie was also the European women's champion six consecutive times, from 1931 through 1936, in an event that was established in 1930.

More recently, Olympic and world championship victories have become spring boards to a profitable career in ice shows. In 1948 at St. Moritz, the victory of Barbara Ann Scott from Canada heralded the shift from the domination of women's figure skating by the European countries. At Oslo in 1952

Jeanette Altwegg, Great Britain

1952 (Oslo)
1. Jeanette Altwegg, Great Britain
2. Tenley Albright, U.S.A.
3. Jacqueline du Bief, France
4. Sonya Helen Klopfer, U.S.A.
5. Virginia Baxter, U.S.A.
6. Suzanne Morrow, Canada

1956 (Cortina)
1. Tenley Albright, U.S.A.
2. Carol Heiss, U.S.A.
3. Ingrid Wendl, Austria
4. Yvonne Sugden, Great Britain
5. Hanna Eigel, Austria
6. Carole Jane Pachl, Canada

1960 (Squaw Valley)
1. Carol Heiss, U.S.A.
2. Sjoukje Dijkstra, Netherlands
3. Barbara Roles, U.S.A.
4. Jana Mrázková, Czechoslovakia
5. Joan Haanappel, Netherlands
6. Laurence Owen, U.S.A.

Jeanette Altwegg from England succeeded in bringing back the gold medal once more, but after that the great days of the Americans Tenley Albright and Carol Heiss started. Then, on February 15, 1961, American figure skating suffered a terrible loss when the entire U.S. team was killed in an air crash near Brussels on its way to the world championships in Prague, a catastrophe that led to the world championship event's being canceled. For the United States it meant that, in addition to the many lives, the development work of many years was lost. A new start had to be made.

18

Hayes Alan Jenkins, U.S.A.

Gillis Grafström, Sweden

Willy Böckl, Austria

FIGURE SKATING—MEN

Only the older generation still remembers that at one time Sweden played a dominating role in men's figure skating. This was particularly reflected in the impressive series of victories of Ulrich Salchow, ten times world champion, and of the triple Olympic winner Gillis Grafström. After the resignation of Vivi-Ann Hultén, who gained the bronze medal in the women's competition at Garmisch in 1936, Sweden dropped back as far as figure skating is concerned. After World War II Richard Button from America overshadowed all his predecessors with his athletic style of jumping.

Results, Figure Skating, Men

1960 (Squaw Valley)
1. David Jenkins, U.S.A.
2. Karol Divin, Czechoslovakia
3. Donald Jackson, Canada
4. Alain Giletti, France
5. Timothy Brown, U.S.A.
6. Alain Calmat, France

1956 (Cortina)
1. Hayes Alan Jenkins, U.S.A.
2. Ronald Robertson, U.S.A.
3. David Jenkins, U.S.A.
4. Alain Giletti, France
5. Karol Divin, Czechoslovakia
6. Michael Robert Booker, Great Britain

1952 (Oslo)
1. Richard Button, U.S.A.
2. Helmut Seibt, Austria
3. James Grogan, U.S.A.
4. Hayes Alan Jenkins, U.S.A.
5. Peter Firstbrook, Canada
6. Carlo Fassi, Italy

1948 (St. Moritz)
1. Richard Button, U.S.A.
2. Hans Gerschwiler, Switzerland
3. Edi Rada, Austria
4. John Lettengarver, U.S.A.
5. Ede Király, Hungary
6. James Grogan, U.S.A.

1936 (Garmisch-Partenkirchen)
1. Karl Schäfer, Austria
2. Ernst Baier, Germany
3. Felix Kaspar, Austria
4. Montgomery Wilson, Canada
5. Henry Graham Sharp, Great Britain
6. Jack Dunn, Great Britain

1932 (Lake Placid)
1. Karl Schäfer, Austria
2. Gillis Grafström, Sweden
3. Montgomery Wilson, Canada
4. Marcus Nikkanen, Finland
5. Ernst Baier, Germany
6. Roger Turner, U.S.A.

1928 (St. Moritz)
1. Gillis Grafström, Sweden
2. Willy Böckl, Austria
3. Robert v. Zeebroeck, Belgium
4. Karl Schäfer, Austria
5. Josef Sliva, Czechoslovakia
6. Marcus Nikkanen, Finland

1924 (Chamonix)
1. Gillis Grafström, Sweden
2. Willy Böckl, Austria
3. Georges Gautschi, Switzerland
4. Josef Sliva, Czechoslovakia
5. John Page, Great Britain
6. Nathaniel Niles, U.S.A.

1920 (Antwerp)
1. Gillis Grafström, Sweden
2. Andreas Krogh, Norway
3. Martin Stixrud, Norway
4. Ulrich Salchow, Sweden
5. Sakari Ilmanen, Finland
6. Nathaniel Niles, U.S.A.

1908 (London)
1. Ulrich Salchow, Sweden
2. Richard Johansson, Sweden
3. Per Thorén, Sweden
4. John Kieller Greig, Great Britain
5. A. March, Great Britain
6. Irving Brokaw, U.S.A.

1908 (London)
1. Nikolaj Panin, Russia
2. Arthur Cumming, Great Britain
3. G. N. E. Hall-Say, Great Britain

19

Maxi Herber/Ernst Baier, Germany

Andrée Brunet/Pierre Brunet, France

Results, Figure Skating, Pairs

1960 (Squaw Valley)
1. Barbara Wagner/Robert Paul, Canada
2. Marika Kilius/Hansjürgen Bäumler, Germany
3. Nancy Ludington/ Ronald Ludington, U.S.A.
4. Maria Jelinek/Otto Jelinek, Canada
5. Margret Göbl/Franz Ningel, Germany
6. Nina Zhuk/Stanislav Zhuk U.S.S.R.

1956 (Cortina)
1. Elisabeth Schwarz/Kurt Oppelt, Austria
2. Frances Dafoe/Norris Bowden, Canada
3. Marianna Nagy/László Nagy, Hungary
4. Marika Kilius/Franz Ningel, Germany
5. Carole Ann Ormaca/ Robin Greiner, U.S.A.
6. Barbara Wagner/Robert Paul, Canada

1952 (Oslo)
1. Ria Falk/Paul Falk, Germany
2. Karol Estelle Kennedy/ Michael Kennedy, U.S.A.
3. Marianna Nagy/László Nagy, Hungary
4. Jennifer Nicks/John Nicks, Great Britain
5. Frances Dafoe/ Robert Norris Bowden, Canada
6. Janet Gerhauser/ John Nightingale, U.S.A.

1948 (St. Moritz)
1. Micheline Lannoy/ Pierre Baugniet, Belgium
2. Andrea Kékessy/Ede Király, Hungary
3. Suzanne Morrow/ Wallace Diestelmeyer, Canada
4. Yvonne Sherman/ Robert Swenning, U.S.A.
5. Winnifred Silverthorne/ Dennis Silverthorne, Great Britain
6. Karol Kennedy/ Michael Kennedy, U.S.A.

FIGURE SKATING—PAIRS

In the pairs figure skating, those countries excelled which did not put up a particularly good performance at the men's and women's singles events. This was especially true of Germany and also of France, whose famous pair Andrée and Pierre Brunet won two Olympic gold medals and one bronze medal. Also outstanding were Finland, Belgium and Hungary.

1936 (Garmisch-Partenkirchen)
1. Maxi Herber/Ernst Baier, Germany
2. Ilse Pausin/Erik Pausin, Austria
3. Emilia Rotter/László Szollás, Hungary
4. Piroska Szekrényessy/ Attila Szekrényessy, Hungary
5. Maribel Vinson/George Hill, U.S.A.
6. Louise Bertram/Stewart Reburn, Canada

1932 (Lake Placid)
1. Andrée Brunet/Pierre Brunet, France
2. Beatrix Loughran/ Sherwin Badger, U.S.A.
3. Emilia Rotter/László Szollás, Hungary
4. Olga Orgonista/Sándor Szalay, Hungary
5. Constance Wilson-Samuel/ Montgomery Wilson, Canada
6. Frances Claudet/Chauney Bangs, Canada

1928 (St. Moritz)
1. Andrée Joly/Pierre Brunet, France
2. Lilly Scholz/Otto Kaiser, Austria
3. Melitta Brunner/Ludwig Wrede, Austria
4. Beatrix Loughran/ Sherwin Badger, U.S.A.
5. Ludovika Jakobsson/ Walter Jakobsson, Finland
6. Josy van Leberghe/ Robert van Zeebroeck, Belgium

1924 (Chamonix)
1. Helene Engelmann/ Alfred Berger, Austria
2. Ludovika Jakobsson/ Walter Jakobsson, Finland
3. Andrée Joly/Pierre Brunet, France
4. Ethel Muckelt/John Page, Great Britain
5. G. Herbos/Georges Wagermans, Belgium
6. Theresa Blanchard/ Nathaniel Niles, U.S.A.

1920 (Antwerp)
1. Ludovika Jakobsson/ Walter Jakobsson, Finland
2. Alexia Bryn/Yngvar Bryn, Norway
3. Phyllis W. Johnson/ Basi Williams, Great Britain
4. Theresa Weld/Nathaniel Niles, U.S.A.
5. Ethel Muckelt/S. Wallwork, Great Britain
6. G. Herbos/Georges Wagermans, Belgium

1908 (London)
1. Anna Hubler/Heinrich Burger, Germany
2. Phyllis W. Johnson/ James H. Johnson, Great Britain
3. Madge Syers/Edgar Syers, Great Britain

20

Ria Falk/Paul Falk, Germany

Maxi Herber/Ernst Baier, Germany

rianna Nagy/László Nagy,
ngary

Karol Estelle Kennedy/Michael Kennedy, U.S.A.

Micheline Lannoy/Pierre Baugniet, Belgium

Carol Heiss, U.S.A.

Carol Heiss, U.S.A.

SQUAW VALLEY—1960

Women's Figure Skating

For three days, from February 20 to 22, the entrants in the women's figure skating had to submit to the disciplines of compulsory figure skating before, on February 23, they could enjoy the relative relaxation of free skating.

There were twenty-six women skaters from thirteen countries entered in this four-day ordeal, but the experts spoke of only one favorite, Carol Heiss, four times world champion and winner of the silver medal at Cortina, where the unforgettable Tenley Albright won the gold.

Figure skating is one of those competitions in which the outcome depends on objective human judgment rather than on the impersonal precision of clocks or tape measures, and sometimes there are controversies about the judges' decisions. The task of deciding between "good," "better" an'd "best" is a thankless one.

The women's figure skating at Squaw Valley was an exception. There was no doubt about the decision, for Carol Heiss mastered her compulsory figures with the same excellence that she later displayed in her free skating.

When Carol's keenest rival, Sjoukje Dijkstra from Holland, whirled over the ice, the Americans watched her anxiously. Dijkstra started her program with an unusually high axel followed by a series of beautiful spins and jumps. The middle section of her four-minute program was an elegant combination of steps that afforded her some respite before her finale, in which she demonstrated strikingly the strength at her command. She ended with an exhibition of verve that brought the audience to its feet in a thunderous ovation. The public was sufficiently unbiased to acknowledge that Sjoukje Dijkstra was a front-rank performer, regardless of whether Carol Heiss was better or not.

Carol Heiss appeared on the ice, a pretty twenty-year-old blonde, her trim figure clad in a red dress and a glittering tiara holding back her hair. Her ap-

23

Carol Heiss, U.S.A.

Barbara Roles, U.S.A.

Sjoukje Dijkstra, Netherlands

pearance was accompanied by the cheers of her American supporters, who shouted her name over and over again.

Carol Heiss had selected music by Tchaikovsky, Delibes and Rossini to give an effective background to her nymphlike performance. At once her musical sensitivity asserted itself, and her steps and jumps conformed perfectly to the rhythm.

The young New York girl performed everything that was difficult in free skating. Fourteen years before, the then six-year-old Carol had begun training with her graying coach, Pierre Brunet, four times world champion and twice Olympic champion in the pairs figure skating. "You must train for ten years before you become a true skater," Brunet told her then. To bear out his prediction, Carol Heiss won her silver medal at Cortina in 1956, almost exactly ten years later.

Heiss was unchallenged for the gold medal. Her performance was mature, inspired, harmonious and accomplished. The judges awarded her from 5.5 to 5.9 points for contents and from 5.6 to 5.8 for performance. The Americans went wild with enthusiasm when her victory was announced.

RESULTS, FIGURE SKATING, WOMEN
1960 (SQUAW VALLEY)
(Compulsory, Feb. 20–22; free skating, Feb. 23. 26 skaters from 13 nations.)

	Ordinals	Total Points
1. Carol Heiss, U.S.A.	9	1490.1
2. Sjoukje Dijkstra, Netherlands	20	1424.8
3. Barbara A. Roles, U.S.A.	26	1414.9
4. Jana Mrazková, Czechoslovakia	53	1338.7
5. Joan Haanappel, Netherlands	52	1331.9
6. Laurence R. Owen, U.S.A.	57	1343.0
7. Regine Heitzer, Austria	58	1327.9
8. Anna Galmarini, Italy	79	1295.0
9. Karin Frohner, Austria	99	1266.0
10. Sandra Tewkesbury, Canada	78	1296.1

David Jenkins, U.S.A.

Hayes Alan Jenkins, U.S.A.

Men's Figure Skating

After the compulsory section America's David Jenkins, one of the favorites, ranked second behind Karol Divin of Czechoslovakia and was followed by Alain Giletti of France and Canada's Donald Jackson.

On February 26, the day of the free skating, the ice stadium was again crammed with spectators. Until then, men's figure skating had always been overshadowed by the women's event because the women added a touch of glamor that the men could not offer.

The eight thousand spectators were waiting for David Jenkins of America, winner of the bronze medal in Cortina. His elder brother, Hayes Alan Jenkins, had won in 1956 and then, after his fourth world championship, retired from skating. As David began, a hush fell. After his first jump and pirouette the applause swelled. Jenkins's program was without precedent for its brilliance and assurance. He jumped a triple lutz, a triple salchow and even two triple axels in almost uninterrupted succession. Never relaxing, he

Barbara Wagner/Robert Paul, Canada

seemed inexhaustible and wholly unaffected by the thinner air. His movements were harmonized and fluid. His free skating was repeated many times on television and people wondered how the greater medal winners of the past would have fared against him.

RESULTS, FIGURE SKATING, MEN
1960 (SQUAW VALLEY)

(Compulsory, Feb. 24–25; free skating, Feb. 26. 19 skaters from 10 nations. 18 skaters scored.)

	Ordinals	Total Points
1. David W. Jenkins, U.S.A.	10	1440.2
2. Karol Divin, Czechoslovakia	22	1414.3
3. Donald Jackson, Canada	31	1401.0
4. Alain Giletti, France	31	1399.2
5. Timothy T. Brown, U.S.A.	43	1374.1
6. Alain Calmat, France	54	1340.3
7. Robert L. Brewer, U.S.A.	66	1320.3
8. M. Schnelldorfer, Germany	75	1303.3
9. Tilo Gutzeit, Germany	86	1274.0
10. Donald McPherson, Canada	83	1279.7

Pairs Figure Skating

The European championships in Garmisch-Partenkirchen had produced much controversy. The results of the pairs figure-skating event at Squaw Valley on February 19 were awaited with particular interest. This event was probably the most elegant competition apart from the ski jumping.

The Canadians wagered on their entrants, Barbara Wagner/Robert Paul. The Germans set their hopes on either Marika Kilius/Hans Jürgen Bäumler or Margret Göbl/Franz Ningel. Some of the seven thousand spectators believed the Soviet pair Nina and Stanislav Zhuk had a good chance.

26

Barbara Wagner/Robert Paul, Canada

As expected, the Canadians received their well-earned gold medal and the spectators left the stadium knowing they had witnessed an outstanding day's skating.

The striking point about the pairs skating was the small number of nations entered and the large number of entries from several of them. Seven nations entered. It was suggestive that many countries were overawed by the brilliance promised by Canada, Germany and the United States. As it turned out, the Germans' approach—safety in numbers—earned them a silver medal and the fifth and seventh places. Canada concentrated its resources and won the gold medal and the fourth place.

RESULTS, FIGURE SKATING, PAIRS
1960 (SQUAW VALLEY)
(Free skating only, Feb. 19. 13 pairs from 7 nations.)

		Ordinals	Total Points
1.	Barbara Wagner/Robert Paul, Canada	7.0	80.4
2.	Marika Kilius/Hans J. Bäumler, Germany	19.0	76.8
3.	Nancy Ludington/Ronald Ludington, U.S.A.	27.5	76.2
4.	Maria Jelinek/Otto Jelinek, Canada	26.0	75.9
5.	Margret Göbl/Franz Ningel, Germany	36.0	72.5
6.	Nina Zhuk/Stanislav Zhuk, U.S.S.R.	38.0	72.3
7.	Rita Blumenberg/Werner Mensching, Germany......	53.0	70.2
8.	Diana Hinko/Heinz Dopfl, Austria	54.5	69.8
9.	Ludmila Belousova/Oleg Protopopov, U.S.S.R.....	60.5	68.6
10.	Maribel Owen/Dudley S. Richards, U.S.A.	69.0	67.5

Ludmilla Beloussova/Oleg Protopopov, U.S.S.R.

INNSBRUCK—1964

The first gold medal to be awarded in the Innsbruck games went to a Russian couple, Oleg Protopopov and his wife, Ludmilla Belousova, in the pairs figure-skating competition. They upset the favored West German pair while Ronnie and Vivian Joseph of Highland Park, Illinois, took a surprising fourth, losing the bronze medal to the Canadian team by a narrow margin.

Brother and sister Judianne and Jerry Fotheringill of Tacoma, at nineteen and twenty-one the oldest of the American pairs, finished seventh, one place ahead of teenagers Cynthia and Ronald Kauffmann of Seattle. Seventeen pairs competed. The Americans' showing was surprisingly good in spite of their lack of experience.

Fourteen-year-old Scott Allen of Smoke Rise, New Jersey, won the only American medal, taking the bronze for third place in the men's figure skating. Competing with the world's outstanding skaters through a breathtaking succession of jumps, spins and turns to highly accented or subtle music, the youngster trailed only Manfred Schnelldorfer of West Germany and Alain Calmat of France, who had been favored to win. Thomas Litz of Hershey, Pennsylvania, finished sixth and Monty Hoyt, Denver, tenth among the twenty-four competitors.

Peggy Fleming, U.S.A.

Sjoukje Dijkstra, twenty-two-year-old of the Netherlands, found the four-year wait for her gold medal worth it in the women's figure skating. She had finished second to Carol Heiss in 1960, but this year she leaped and spun on the ice to finish far ahead of the field.

The best score from the judges is 6. When the nine score cards were held up at the end of her four-minute program, none showed less than 5.8 for content and execution.

The three American entries were grouped in sixth, seventh and eighth places. U. S. champion Peggy Fleming of Pasadena led the way.

Peggy Fleming, U.S.A.

Peggy Fleming, U.S.A.

Peggy Fleming, U.S.A.

GRENOBLE—1968

This highly popular competition was staged in the beautiful Stade de Glace in midtown Grenoble, which was specially built for the occasion. What the spectators saw was skating of an extremely high standard. Many skaters demonstrated movements that broke completely with the traditional pattern and extended at the same time the technical limits to a degree one would not have believed possible. It was as if this sport of grace and skill, of physical accomplishment and the art of dancing, had sought for itself a new language. There might be some who regret this development, which would seem to be influenced by television and the prospects of rewarding professional careers in the ice revues. They may claim that these skaters have in mind first to please the crowd and only second the judges. They did both.

Women's Figure Skating

Peggy Fleming was the reigning queen on the ice. Her long and painstaking efforts to reach the top at last paid dividends. She stood on the prizewinners' rostrum flanked by Gabriele Seyfert, East Germany (silver), and Hana Maskova, Czechoslovakia (bronze).

Peggy Fleming was by far the most accomplished skater and the most popular. The way the marks were awarded showed how impressed the judges were by her performance. Yet she didn't use sentimental effects and didn't dance herself "into the heart" of the public. Her own personality, naturally expressed through her great technical command on the ice and the graceful movements of a ballerina, won for her.

Results, Figure Skating, Women
1968 (Grenoble)

(5 compulsory figures and free skating, Feb. 11. 31 skaters from 15 nations. Finishing order decided on the place marks of the majority of the judges.)

	Ordinals	Total Points
1. Peggy Fleming, U.S.A.	9	1970.5
2. Gabriele Seyfert, E. Germany	18	1882.3
3. Hana Maskova, Czechoslovakia	31	1828.8
4. Albertina Noyes, U.S.A.	40	1797.3
5. Beatrix Schuba, Austria	51	1773.2
6. Zsussa Almassy, Hungary	57	1757.0

31

Tim Wood, U.S.A.

Men's Figure Skating

Twenty-eight competed in the men's figure skating at Grenoble, among them such gifted and artistically endowed performers as the Austrian Emmerich Danzer, his fellow countryman Wolfgang Schwarz, the Frenchman Patrick Péra and the American Timothy Wood. While the first three appeared to have reached their peak at Grenoble, Wood still seemed to be improving. He was, according to the judges, only good enough for the silver medal. His potential looked bigger than what he showed in the ice stadium, technically and artistically. The system under which he worked seemed to be open to criticism.

Results, Figure Skating, Men
1968 (Grenoble)

(5 compulsory figures and free skating, Feb. 16. 28 skaters from 14 nations. Finishing order decided on the place marks of the majority of the judges.)

	Ordinals	Total Points
1. Wolfgang Schwarz, Austria	13	1904.1
2. Tim Wood, U.S.A.	17	1891.6
3. Patrick Péra, France	31*	1864.5
4. Emmerich Danzer, Austria	29*	1873.0
5. Gary Visconti, U.S.A.	52	1810.2
6. John Mischa Petkevich, U.S.A.	56	1806.2

*The highest number of place marks gets 3rd place.

Ludmilla Beloussova/Oleg Protopopov, U.S.S.R.

Pairs Figure Skating

Oleg Protopopov and his wife Ludmila were the feted winners in the pairs figure skating. They added new laurels to their Olympic triumphs of Innsbruck and the world championships of 1963 and 1966. Seeing the Protopopovs in action, one had the impression that they were technically so highly developed that they did not need the world of gimmicks.

The sixteen other pairs who competed against them must have realized that they stood no chance while trying to beat the Protopopovs in their own style. Thus the very opposite approach was taken—exuberant attack and a whole fireworks display of new kinds of flips, jumps and pirouettes that in their scope not only enlarged the existing repertory but also enriched it by an athletic virtuosity that set new standards for the future. Such bravura was exhibited particularly by the U.S.S.R.'s Tamara Moskvina and Alexei Michine, whose free skating contained some themes and variations more complex than one would have believed possible. Still, they gained only fifth place. Tatiana Joukchesternava and Aleksandr Gorelik won the silver medal.

Results, Figure Skating, Pairs
1968 (Grenoble)

(18 pairs from 9 nations, Feb. 14.)	Ordinals	Total Points
1. Ludmila Beloussova/Oleg Protopopov, U.S.S.R.	10	315.2
2. Tatiana Joukchesternava/Aleksandr Gorelik, U.S.S.R.	17	312.3
3. Margot Glockshuber/Wolfgang Danne, W. Germany	30	304.4
4. Heidemarie Steiner/Heinz-Ulrich Walter, E. Germany	37	303.1
5. Tamara Moskvina/Aleksei Michine, U.S.S.R.	44	300.3
6. Cynthia Kauffmann/Ronald Kauffmann, U.S.A.	58	297.0

33

Julie Lynn Holmes, U.S.A.

Karen Magnussen, Canada   Trixi Schuba, Austria   Janet Lynn, U.S.A.

SAPPORO—1972

The way out of the realms of anonymity in figure skating lasts years. There cannot, therefore, be any unknown champions. In Sapporo the world champions from 1971 collected the gold medals. However, it was exactly the performances on the ice that provided a lot of new talking points. In the Mikaho Ice Palace the ice was dyed blue for the compulsory figures, so that the tracks of the skaters were much more clearly visible. The pairs offered an abundance of ideas, which were prepared well enough for inclusion in a revue, and the men's free skating achieved a standard far above the level reached up to then.

Women's Figure Skating

The safest prediction for the gold medal at Sapporo was Trixi Schuba, and it proved to be a good one. Because of her superb compulsory figures, the phenomenally good free skaters Karen Magnussen and Janet Lynn did not stand the slightest chance of victory.

34

Janet Lynn, U.S.A.

Karen Magnussen, Canada   Trixi Schuba, Austria   Janet Lynn, U.S.A.

The Viennese girl's victory stirred up the discussion about evaluation once more—whether the proportion of 50 percent for the compulsory figures in the days of television is not archaic. Under the existing relation of compulsory figures to free skating, Trixi Schuba's gold medal went unchallenged. This was confirmed unanimously by the judges. It had been decided before the Olympiad to introduce a revised system of judging.

Julie Holmes, Karen Magnussen and Janet Lynn, all from North America, competed for the silver medal. With her second place in the compulsory figures, Julie Holmes had the most favorable starting position. However, her free skating let her down. The free-skating bombshell Karen Magnussen gained the silver, and Janet Lynn the bronze. The positions were decided by the compulsory figures.

Results, Figure Skating, Women
1972 (Sapporo)

(19 skaters from 14 nations. Feb. 4, 5 and 7.).	Ordinals	Total Points
1. Trixi Schuba, Austria	9.0	2751.5
2. Karen Magnussen, Canada	23.0	2673.2
3. Janet Lynn, U.S.A.	27.0	2663.1
4. Julie Holmes, U.S.A.	39.0	2627.0
5. Zsuzsa Almassy, Hungary	47.0	2592.4
6. Sonja Morgenstern, E. Germany	53.0	2579.4

Ondrej Nepela, Czechoslovakia

Sergei Tchetveroukin, U.S.S.R.   Ondrej Nepela, Czechoslovakia   Patrick Péra,

Kenneth Shelley, U.S.A.

Men's Figure Skating

Seventeen men presented their skating talents before the judges on the Olympic ice, and ten of them would have enriched any ice revue. The Czechoslovakian Ondrej Nepela presented himself as the perfect Olympic champion, executing compulsory figures and free skating with equal skill. The judges gave Tchetveroukin the best marks for the free skating and Péra received the bronze medal once more to round off his career.

Among the most impressive performances was that of the young American Kenneth Shelley. He caused amazement by appearing in two events (he skated with JoJo Starbuck in the pairs), and he attracted attention with an artistic free-skating program. Misha Petkevich, whose free skating had already been considered sensational since Grenoble, improved it at Sapporo, but he once more went home without a medal.

Results, Figure Skating, Men
1972 (Sapporo)

(17 skaters from 10 nations. Feb. 8, 9 and 11.)	Ordinals	Total Points
1. Ondrej Nepela, Czechoslovakia	9.0	2739.1
2. Sergei Tchetveroukin, U.S.S.R.	20.0	2672.4
3. Patrick Péra, France	28.0	2653.1
4. Kenneth Shelley, U.S.A.	43.0	2596.0
5. Misha Petkevich, U.S.A.	47.0	2591.5
6. Jan Hoffmann, E. Germany	55.0	2567.6

Irina Rodnina/Alexei Ulanov, U.S.S.R.

Ludmilla Smirnova/Andrei Suraikin, U.S.S.R.   Manuela Gross/Uwe Kagelmann, E. Germany

Irina Rodnina/Alexei Ulanov, U.S.S.R.

Pairs Figure Skating

Because of their personal disharmony, the Soviet couple Irina Rodnina and Alexei Ulanov did not display the superb performance that was expected. Rodnina-Ulanov, who dethroned the Protopopovs in 1969 at Garmisch, received six firsts at Sapporo and their Leningrad competitors only three. Ludmilla Smirnova and Andrei Suraikin, with their supercooled free skating, were not in a position to supplant the triple world champions. (The reason for the disagreement was confirmed later when Alexei Ulanov married Ludmilla Smirnova.) Storms of applause inspired the bronze medalists Gross-Kagelmann to give a really superb performance.

Results, Figure Skating, Pairs
1972 (Sapporo)

(16 pairs from 9 nations. Feb. 6 and 8.)	Ordinals	Total Points
1. Irina Rodnina/Alexei Ulanov, U.S.S.R.	12.0	420.4
2. Ludmilla Smirnova/Andrei Suraikin, U.S.S.R.	15.0	419.4
3. Manuela Gross/Uwe Kagelmann, E. Germany	29.0	411.8
4. JoJo Starbuck/Kenneth Shelley, U.S.A.	35.0	406.8
5. Almut Lehmann/Herbert Wiesinger, W. Germany	52.0	399.8
6. Irina Tcherniaeva/Vassili Blagov, U.S.S.R.	52.0	399.1

JoJo Starbuck/Kenneth Shelley, U.S.A.

37

Dorothy Hamill, U.S.A.

Dorothy Hamill, U.S.A.

INNSBRUCK—1976

A feature of both the figure-skating singles events was the glorious uncertainty of their outcome. Unlike so many previous contests, when the ultimate winners had been a foregone conclusion, the competitions were refreshingly open.

The addition of ice dancing to the Olympic schedule was amply justified. It fitted in as naturally as it had in other international skating championships for nearly a quarter of a century.

Women's Figure Skating

The 1976 Olympic Games will be long remembered by even lukewarm followers of winter sports because of the incandescent performance of nineteen-year-old Dorothy Hamill, who climaxed a six-year drive to the top by annexing the gold medal in the women's singles.

Her hot-pink skating costume and attractive coiffure were backdrops for a superb exhibition of "how it should be done" in the three parts of the sport—compulsory figures (she was second), a short free-skating program (she was first) and the final free-skating exhibition, where she earned loud acclaim from the jampacked indoor ice palace. Hundreds of bouquets showered on the ice when she concluded her program. The gold medal was hers in the hearts of the appreciative audience long before the winning scores were flashed on the huge scoreboard.

While Dorothy Hamill convincingly won the women's title, the fourth American to accomplish the feat, the silver medal went to Dianne de Leeuw, who had surpassed Dorothy in the 1975 world championships. Having learned her lesson twelve months earlier, Dorothy did not make any costly error in the short program. Known for her nervousness and superstitions, she appeared unusually relaxed considering the importance of the occasion. All her double jumps and spins looked graceful and effortless. "Floating" confidently in her jumps, she excelled with a superb layback spin and, of course, the Hamill camel. Every judge gave her 5.9 for artistic impression. Dianne,

Dorothy Hamill, U.S.A.

Dorothy Hamill, U.S.A.

39

Christine Errath, East Germany

Wendy Burge, U.S.A.

Dianne De Leeuw, Netherlands
Dorothy Hamill, U.S.A.
Christine Errath, East Germany

who skated last on the program and looked remarkably unruffled, nearly fell from a triple toe loop in an otherwise typically solid display.

Continuing ascendancy of American women in figure skating was emphasized at these games by two U.S. representatives in addition to the champion. Sixth-ranked Wendy Burge improved over her debut the previous year, and eighth-ranked Linda Fratianne was a very confident skater with excellent presentation.

Dianne De Leeuw, Netherlands

Results, Figure Skating
1976 (Innsbruck)

	Ordinals	Points
Women's Singles		
1. Dorothy Hamill, U.S.A.	9	193.80
2. Dianne de Leeuw, Netherlands	20	190.24
3. Christine Errath, E. Germany	28	188.16
4. Annet Poetzsch, E. Germany	33	187.42
5. Isabel de Navarre, W. Germany	59	182.42
6. Wendy Burge, U.S.A.	63	175.82

Toller Cranston, Canada

David Santee, U.S.A.

ıadimir Kovalev, U.S.S.R.   John Curry, Great Britain   Toller Cranston, Canada

Men's Figure Skating

The glorious men's victory of John Curry involved such a flawless long free-skating program that maxi 6.0 marks, implying perfection, were conspicuous by their absence. For explanation, notice the early position Curry had in the order. The judges were reluctant, as always, to produce the magical 6.0, since its early use allows no margin if a subsequent skater performs better.

Volkov was below his best in both short and long free-skating programs and, after leading in the figures, dropped to fifth. He ranked narrowly above David Santee, the discovery of the season. Terry Kubicka was acrobatically spectacular in the long free-skating program, featuring four triples and a back somersault—the only one ever done in championship competition—and ending with six Arabian jumps in succession.

Men's Singles

1. John Curry, Great Britain	11	192.74
2. Vladimir Kovalev, U.S.S.R.	28	187.64
3. Toller Cranston, Canada	30	187.34
4. Jan Hoffmann, E. Germany	34	187.34
5. Sergei Volkov, U.S.S.R.	53	184.08
6. David Santee, U.S.A.	49	184.28

41

Tai Babilonia/Randy Gardner, U.S.A.

Irina Rodnina/Alexandr Zaitsev, U.S.S.R.

Pairs Figure Skating

The standard of pairs skating rose considerably after Sapporo, with throw axels and double-twist lifts becoming as common as death spirals. As a result the event became far more spectacular for the audience to watch and far more difficult for the participants to perform. The pairs title was won comfortably by the Moscow husband-wife team Irina Rodnina and Aleksandr Zaitsev. Irina, seven times world champion, was defending the Olympic title she had won at Sapporo with her former partner, Alexei Ulanov. The winners included splendid overhead lifts and precisely timed solo jumps and spins, but scored no 6.0s because Zaitsev touched down on a double axel.

New U.S. champions Tai Babilonia and Randy Gardner outshone the Russian pair in free skating and finished fifth in the final standings. Tai and Randy's sequence of four pulled Arabian jumps in mind-boggling succession was a joy to behold. They were also the only pair who completed their side-by-side double axels.

Pairs

1. Irina Rodnina/Alexandr Zaitsev, U.S.S.R.	9	140.54
2. Romy Kermer/Rolf Oesterreich, E. Germany	21	136.35
3. Manuela Gross/Uwe Kagelmann, E. Germany	34	134.57
4. Irina Vorobieva/Alexandr Vlasov, U.S.S.R.	35	134.52
5. Tai Babilonia/Randy Gardner, U.S.A.	36	134.24
6. Kerstin Stolfig/Veit Kempe, E. Germany	59	129.57

Colleen O'Connor/Jimmy Millns, U.S.A.

Colleen O'Connor/Jimmy Millns, U.S.A.   Ludmilla Pakhomova/Alexandr Gorshkov, U.S.S.R.

Ice Dancing

The threatened Soviet monopoly of the medals in the premier ice-dancing competition of the Olympic Games was prevented by the Americans Colleen O'Connor and Jimmy Millns, who kept the bronze medal beyond reach of the fourth-place Natalia Linichuk and Gennadi Karponosov. Ludmilla Pakhomova and Aleksandr Gorshkov became the first Olympic ice-dance champions. Nobody could deny the perfect Moscow couple their right to the historic honor, for they had earned recognition as the world's outstanding performers in this most graceful branch of figure skating.

Ice Dancing

1. Ludmilla Pakhomova/Alexandr Gorshkov, U.S.S.R.	9	209.92
2. Irina Moiseeva/Andrei Minenkov, U.S.S.R.	20	204.88
3. Colleen O'Connor/Jimmy Millns, U.S.A.	27	202.64
4. Natalia Linichuk/Gennadi Karponosov, U.S.S.R.	35	199.10
5. Krisztina Regoczy/Andreas Sallay, Hungary	48	195.92
6. Matilde Cicia/Lamberto Ceserani, Italy	58	191.46

Linda Fratianne, U.S.A.

Top Contenders

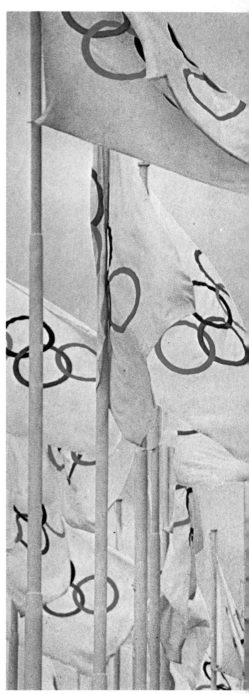

Linda Fratianne will be nineteen, and someone especially worth watching on our 1980 Winter Olympic figure-skating team at Lake Placid. Linda began skating when she was nine years old and at age fifteen in 1975 finished third in the Pacific Coasts women's title. In 1976 Linda won the Pacific Coasts title and the silver medal at the women's nationals. She was fifth at the women's world championship and eighth for the United States in the Winter Olympics at Innsbruck, Austria.

In 1977 Linda won the U.S. women's championship and went on to an outstanding win at the women's world championship. In 1978 she proved to be a tough competitor by again winning the U.S. championship, but lost in the world championship finals. Linda Fratianne is skating well in 1979 and shares her coach Frank Carroll's confidence that she will be a gold medal winner for the United States in 1980.

The 1979 U.S. national championships, January 30 to February 3, 1979, in Cincinnati, Ohio, were an astounding success. The largest crowd ever to witness an amateur figure-skating competition in the United States, more than 55,000 turned out to watch the week's events.

The four senior titles were all successfully defended by the 1978 winners. In fact, each champion earned unanimous first-place decisions from the judges, with a 7/1 majority across the board, and won each segment of each event.

The men's championship was dominated by Charlie Tickner, reigning world champion, who laid down some marvelous figures and received a thirty-second ovation after his short program with marks of 5.8 and 5.9. His free skating brought the crowd to its feet with his triple jumps, footwork and art. All blended together to win his third consecutive U.S. men's title.

It was not, however, Charlie's best performance, as he freely admitted. He said, "It wasn't what I would call a magical performance. I really had to go out and make it happen."

Charlie Tickner, U.S.A.

Charlie Tickner, U.S.A.

Charlie Tickner, U.S.A.

46

Allen Schramm, U.S.A.

Allen Schramm, U.S.A.

Scott Cramer, U

In second place was Scott Cramer. Scott free-skated to "Star Wars" and turned on the crowd, receiving marks ranging from 5.4 to 5.8. Right behind Scott was David Santee, 1976-1978 men's silver medalist from Park Ridge, Illinois. David opened his free skating with a nice double axel and a beautiful triple toe loop. He followed with a triple toe loop/double toe loop combination and left the crowd on its feet for a thirty-five-second ovation. David was second in the free skating. After the event he said the Cincinnati audience was "a special crowd, a knowledgeable crowd and receptive, too."

Another highlight of the men's event was the free skating of Allen Schramm. Schramm has a style and personality in his skating that are unmatched anywhere in the world. Skating to music that matched his pulsating, almost undulating style, Schramm ignited the crowd. "The Snake," as he has been called, is a great spinner and jumper while already a master at putting his elements together to best show off his talent. Allen had the crowd on their feet screaming for forty-five seconds, and they howled at the marks he received.

47   David Santee, U.S.A.

Charles Tickner—U.S.A.

Scott Cramer, U.S.A.

Jan Hoffman—East Germany

Robin Cousins—Great Britain

David Santee, U.S.A.

Lisa-Marie Allen, U.S.A.

Lisa-Marie Allen, U.S.A.

Carrie Rugh, U.S.A.

In the women's championship Linda Fratianne also swept through the field with a style that will be hard to beat. Linda's figures were by far the best of the field and her short program was right to the beat of the music, with spins that did not travel an inch. Linda's free skating began with a triple toe loop and then a triple salchow. Both were solid and fit in well with the program as she made her way to her third consecutive U.S. women's title.

In second place again was Lisa-Marie Allen, who stayed behind Linda every step of the way. Lisa-Marie was also eighteen and from California. Her long program was a pretty display of difficult moves—spinning in both directions, a double axel from an Ina Baur—bringing Lisa-Marie her second silver medal.

In third place was Carrie Rugh, sixteen, from El Segundo, California. Carrie, third in figures, fourth in the short program and sixth in the free skating, was on pins and needles at the end of the event before the final places were determined. Twelve-hundredths of a point behind Carrie was Sandy Lenz, and while Carrie waited for the results she said, "It was a very hard five minutes." She had not expected to go home wearing a medal. She felt very "happy, very lucky."

Carrie Rugh, U.S.A.

Tai Babilonia/Randy Gardner, U.S.A.

Tai Babilonia/Randy Gardner, U.S.A.

Tai Babilonia/Randy Gardner, U.S.A.

The U.S. pair championship belonged to Tai Babilonia and Randy Gardner, their fourth title. Tai and Randy won both the long and short programs, taking complete command of the ice whenever they skated. They opened their free skating with a throw triple salchow and displayed the best star lift of the competition. They executed perfectly—their footwork, lifts and timing brought the crowd to its feet.

Tai and Randy's scores were the highest they had ever received at a national championship. Randy said, "We were confident in the short, which built our confidence in the long. Now our goal is 1980." Coach John Nicks was also happy about the high marks indicating the full support for Tai and Randy.

Sheryl Franks/Michael Botticelli, U.S.A.

Vicki Heasley/Robert Wagenhoffer, U.S.A.

Vicki Heasley/Robert Wagenhoffer, U.S

Sheryl Franks/Michael Botticelli, U.S.A.

The surprise of the pair event were silver medal winners Vicki Heasley and Robert Wagenhoffer. They were third going into the free skating but dazzled both judges and the audience. They "grabbed" the crowd with their style and music and never let go. Robert, eighteen, from Fontana, California, and Vicki, seventeen, from West Covina, California, were "terribly surprised," Robert said. Vicki and Robert have been skating pairs for three years, coached by John Nicks (Tai and Randy's coach), and they also skate singles on the national level. He finished fifth in senior men's and she was fifth in junior women's.

In third place were Michael Botticelli and Sheryl Franks. Mike and Sheryl were also third in 1977 and 1978 and had hoped to capture second place. Their free skating was a solid routine including a very nice star lift. Mike said, "We had no major mistakes and I don't really know where second place went."

Stacey Smith/John Summers, U.S.A.

The dance championship was a beautiful event, dominated by Stacey Smith and John Summers, from Wilmington, Delaware. Winning both rounds of the event, Stacey, twenty-four, and John, twenty-one, avenged the defeats by silver medalists Carol Fox and Richard Dalley. Carol and Richard defeated Stacey and John twice in 1978, first at the world championships in Ottawa and later at the U.S. Olympic Committee's Sports Festival in Colorado Springs.

Stacey Smith/John Summers, U.S.A.

Stacey Smith/John Summers, U.S.A.

Stacey and John showed how much better they were than in July of 1978. They have matured and grown with their dancing, despite the strict enforcement of the dance regulations concerning lifts and spins. John said they and their coach, Ron Ludington, had torn apart their program looking for what might be considered illegal by the judges and had made changes wherever necessary. They were very happy with their free dance that changed tempo very well, switching into "Summertime" and a lovely section of complex footwork and dance maneuvers that slipped nicely into "It Ain't Necessarily So."

54

Carol Fox/Richard Dalley, U.S.A.

United States Figure Association 1979 World Team

In third place were Judy Blumberg and Michael Seibert. Judy, from Los Angeles, and Michael, from Indianapolis, created an energetic yet romantic free dance. It was precise and at the same time alluring. Third in both rounds of the event, Judy and Michael had been dancing together for only about a year. In 1978 Judy skated with Robert Engler and won the bronze medal in silver dance, while Michael skated with Kelly Morris, winning the U.S. silver dance title in 1977.

2

Speed Skating

HERO TODAY—GONE TOMORROW

Hero today, gone tomorrow," are the sweet-sour sentiments of Olympian Irving Jaffe. Jaffe was a gold medalist in both the 10,000-meter and 5000-meter speed-skating events in the 1932 Winter Olympics at Lake Placid, New York. With no job to go back to after the hero's parade down Fifth Avenue, Jaffe pawned his Olympic golds as well as four hundred other medals for two thousand dollars. He had a year to pay the loan back and reclaim his treasures, but the Depression got worse. The pawnshop was eventually torn down to make space for a skyscraper, and Jaffe was left with memories of glory that ended quickly.

Irving Jaffe's story has other twists. Four years earlier, in the 1928 games at St. Moritz, Switzerland, he was the unofficial winner of the 10,000-meter speed-skating race. The race was called off after the third heat, however, because of melting ice, and his triumph was not recognized. He was nineteen years old then. Lake Placid became his personal vindication. It was also an unprecedented sweep for the American team.

Skating came into Irving Jaffe's life when he was sixteen with a pair of mail-order skates four sizes too large. His mother felt he would "grow into them" and thus have them for a long time. Jaffe stuffed the skates with newspaper and wore several pairs of socks.

His first few races saw him finishing last. In his own words, he showed no more promise of becoming a future champ than most youngsters seen "sloshing along" every winter in New York City. The difference was that he liked it, and he got a job sweeping the ice in a local rink in order to skate free.

After borrowing skates that fit from a rink instructor, he made better progress. He began collecting medals in novice races. In the two years between that

Irving Jaffee, U.S.A.
Dives across the finish line

time and his debut in the Winter Olympics, he imposed a rugged training routine upon himself. It consisted of daily calisthenics, bicycle riding to develop legs and thighs, summer jobs that promoted physical training and roadwork with boxer friends. He sought out ponds in upstate New York that froze early. He skated with those better than himself in order to pick up pointers. He also skated longer distances than the races he was to enter so that the races would seem short. He added weights to skates during practice for similar reasons. He began winning championship after championship, and in 1928 was part of the U.S. Olympic team competing at St. Moritz and again in 1932 at Lake Placid. He had been a runner in a stock exchange to aid in the support of his parents and brother and sisters, but training for the Olympics demanded so much time that he lost the job.

Now he found himself the winner of the 5000-meter Olympic speed-skating race. Jack Shea, a sophomore at Dartmouth, had won the 500- and 1500-meter events. The American team was three for three. The 10,000 meters remained of the speed-skating events.

Tractors cleared an all-night snow from the track. Eight of the best distance racers in the world faced the icy-smooth racecourse in the early afternoon. Twenty-four laps later saw them still tightly bunched. Three yards separated the leaders from the rest of the group. At the final lap Norway's Ivar Ballangrud was at the pole with Jaffee alongside on the outside. On the final turn Jaffee outraced his opponent and sprinted into the straightaway, increasing his advantage to five yards. Throwing himself across the finish line, Jaffee lost balance and skidded to a close on his stomach.

Ballangrud followed across, with Frank Stack of Canada beating out another American, Eddie Wedge, by one yard for third.

Jaffee counted his Olympic victories as three.

58

Eric Heiden, U.S.A.

Edward Schroeder, U.S.A.

Leo Freisinger, U.S.A.

SPEED SKATING—MEN

Skating competitions had become international events even before skiing, largely because of the efforts of the International Skating Union (ISU), founded in 1892 in Scheveningen, Netherlands. The first speed-skating world championships already had been held in Amsterdam in 1889. Originally the world championship title was awarded for the four-race event—as a combined valuation of the traditional distances of 500 meters, 1500 meters, 5000 meters and 10,000 meters. At first there was even a clause stating that only a skater who had won three of those four distances could become world champion. If that requirement was not fulfilled, the world championship title was not awarded. Later, however, this harsh clause was replaced by a system of valuation by points.

In the Olympic Winter Games the four-race event in addition to the individual competitions was held only once, at Chamonix in 1924. In contrast to the world and European championships, where only good all-round skaters have the chance of success, the Olympic Games have become predominantly the field of the specialists in the various distances. It is here that they (like their counterparts in track events—the sprinter, the medium-distance runner, the long-distance runner) can demonstrate their particular abilities.

59

Kenneth Henry, U.S.A.

Kenneth Bartholomew, U.S.A.

Donald McDermott, U.S.A.   Kenneth Henry, U.S.A.   Arne Johansen, Norway
Gordon Audley, Canada

Kenneth Bartholomew, U.S.A.

Results, 500 Meters, Men

Speed Skating, 500 m., Men

Whereas the Norwegians have always been equally good over all four distances, the speed-skating sprint (500 meters) particularly suited the Americans. The first gold medal for this distance was won by Charles Jewtraw, and two more were won by John Shea and Kenneth Henry. In addition, American skaters won four silver and two bronze medals. Since Russian skaters appeared on the ice rink, however, they have made the speed-skating sprint their own. The Soviet Eugeny Grishin is the only skater so far who has become an Olympic winner twice in the 500-meter event, and each time he set a world's record.

1960 (Squaw Valley)	Time
1. Jewgenij Grishin, U.S.S.R.	40.2
2. William Disney, U.S.A.	40.3
3. Rafael Grach, U.S.S.R.	40.4
4. Hans Wilhelmsson, Sweden	40.5
5. Gennadij Voronin, U.S.S.R.	40.7
6. Alv Gjestvang, Norway	40.8

1948 (St. Moritz)	Time
1. Finn Helgesen, Norway	43.1
2a Kenneth Bartholomew, U.S.A.	43.2
2b Thomas Byberg, Norway	43.2
2c Robert Fitzgerald, U.S.A.	43.2
5. Kenneth Henry, U.S.A.	43.3
6a Sverre Farstad, Norway	43.6
6b Torodd Hauer, Norway	43.6
6c Delbert Lamb, U.S.A.	43.6
6d Frank Stack, Canada	43.6

1956 (Cortina)	Time
1. Jewgenij Grishin, U.S.S.R.	40.2
2. Rafael Grach, U.S.S.R.	40.8
3. Alv Gjestvang, Norway	41.0
4. Jurij Sergejew, U.S.S.R.	41.1
5. Toivo Salonen, Finland	41.7
6. William Carow, U.S.A.	41.8

1936 (Garmisch-P.)	Time
1. Ivar Ballangrud, Norway	43.4
2. Georg Krog, Norway	43.5
3. Leo Freisinger, U.S.A.	44.0
4. Shozo Ishihara, Japan	44.1
5. Delbert Lamb, U.S.A.	44.2
6a Allan Potts, U.S.A.	44.8
6b Karl Leban, Austria	44.8

1928 (St. Moritz)	Time
1a Clas Thunberg, Finland	43.4
1b Bernt Evensen, Norway	43.4
3a John O'Neil Farrell, U.S.A.	43.6
3b Roald Larsen, Norway	43.6
3c Jaakko Friman, Finland	43.6
6. Haakon Pedersen, Norway	43.8

1952 (Oslo)	Time
1. Kenneth Henry, U.S.A.	43.2
2. Donald McDermott, U.S.A.	43.9
3a Arne Johansen, Norway	44.0
3b Gordon Audley, Canada	44.0
5. Finn Helgesen, Norway	44.0
6a Kiyotaka Takabayashi, Japan	44.1
6b Hroar Elvenes, Norway	44.1

1932 (Lake Placid)	Time
1. John A. Shea, U.S.A.	43.4
2. Bernt Evensen, Norway	
3. Alexander Hurd, Canada	
4. Frank Stack, Canada	
5. William F. Logan, Canada	
6. John O'Neil Farrell, U.S.A.	

1924 (Chamonix)	Time
1. Charles Jewtraw, U.S.A.	44.0
2. Oskar Olsen, Norway	44.2
3a Roald Larsen, Norway	44.8
3b Clas Thunberg, Finland	44.8
5. Asser Vallenius, Finland	45.0
6. Axel Blomqvist, Sweden	45.2

60

Hjalmar Andersen, Norway

Willen Van De Voort, Netherlands

Roald Aas, Norway

Roald Aas, Norway   Hjalmar Andersen, Norway

Willen Van De Voort, Netherlands

Speed Skating, 1500 m., Men

In the 1500-meter event through 1960, the Norwegians as well as the Finns gave good performances. The great Finn Clas Thunberg won this race in both 1924 and 1928. More recently the Soviet Eugeny Grishin has been the champion skater of the 1500-meter, although he had to share his Olympic victories in 1956 at Cortina and in 1960 at Squaw Valley with another skater.

Results, 1500 Meters, Men

1960 (Squaw Valley)	Time
1a Roald Aas, Norway	2:10.4
1b Jewgenij Grishin, U.S.S.R.	2:10.4
3. Boris Stenin, U.S.S.R.	2:11.5
4. Jouko Jokinen, Finland	2:12.0
5a Per Olof Brogren, Sweden	2:13.1
5b Juhani Järvinen, Finland	2:13.1

1956 (Cortina)	Time
1a Jewgenij Grishin, U.S.S.R.	2:08.6
1b Jurij Mikhailov, U.S.S.R.	2:08.6
3. Toivo Salonen, Finland	2:09.4
4. Juhani Järvinen, Finland	2:09.7
5. Robert Merkulov, U.S.S.R.	2:10.3
6. Sigvard Ericsson, Sweden	2:11.0

1952 (Oslo)	Time
1. Hjalmar Andersen, Norway	2:20.4
2. Willem van der Voort, Netherlands	2:20.6
3. Roald Aas, Norway	2:21.6
4. Carl-Erik Asplund, Sweden	2:22.6
5. Kees Brockman, Netherlands	2:22.8
6. Lauri Parkkinen, Finland	2:23.0

1948 (St. Moritz)	Time
1. Sverre Farstad, Norway	2:17.6
2. Ake Seyffårth, Sweden	2:18.1
3. Odd Lundberg, Norway	2:18.9
4. Lauri Parkkinen, Finland	2:19.6
5. Gustav Harry Jansson, Sweden	2:20.0
6. John Werket, U.S.A.	2:20.2

1936 (Garmisch-P.)	Time
1. Charles Mathiesen, Norway	2:19.2
2. Ivar Ballangrud, Norway	2:20.2
3. Birger Vasenius, Finland	2:20.9
4. Leo Freisinger, U.S.A.	2:21.3
5. Max Stiepl, Austria	2:21.6
6. Karl Wazulek, Austria	2:22.2

1932 (Lake Placid)	Time
1. John A. Shea, U.S.A.	2:57.5
2. Alexander Hurd, Canada	
3. William F. Logan, Canada	
4. Frank Stack, Canada	
5. Raymond Murray, U.S.A.	
6. Herbert G. Taylor, U.S.A.	

1928 (St. Moritz)	Time
1. Clas Thunberg, Finland	2:21.1
2. Bernt Evensen, Norway	2:21.9
3. Ivar Ballangrud, Norway	2:22.6
4. Roald Larsen, Norway	2:25.3
5. Edward S. Murphy, U.S.A.	2:25.9
6. Valentine Bialas, U.S.A.	2:26.3

1924 (Chamonix)	Time
1. Clas Thunberg, Finland	2:20.8
2. Roald Larsen, Norway	2:22.0
3. Sigurd Moen, Norway	2:25.6
4. Julius Skutnabb, Finland	2:26.6
5. Harald Strom, Norway	2:29.0
6. Oskar Olsen, Norway	2:29.2

Kees Brockman, Netherlands   Sverre Haugli, Norway   Ivar Ballangrud, Norway

Speed Skating, 5000 m., Men

Through 1960, Norwegian skaters have won four gold medals, two silver medals and three bronze medals as well as placing well a number of times in the 5000-meter event. This distance suited Ivar Ballangrud particularly well. He won in 1928 and 1936 and placed at Lake Placid in 1932 despite group starts, a technique not used by the Europeans. He was among the world's best in three consecutive Olympic Winter Games.

Results, 5000 Meters, Men

1960 (Squaw Valley)	Time
1. Viktor Kosichkin, U.S.S.R.	7:51.3
2. Knut Johannesen, Norway	8:00.8
3. Jan Pesman, Netherlands	8:05.1
4. Torstein Seiersten, Norway	8:05.3
5. Valerij Kotow, U.S.S.R.	8:05.4˙
6. Oleg Goncharenko, U.S.S.R.	8:06.6

1956 (Cortina)	Time
1. Boris Shilkov, U.S.S.R.	7:48.7
2. Sigvard Ericsson, Sweden	7:56.7
3. Oleg Goncharenko, U.S.S.R.	7:57.5
4a Kees Broekman, Netherlands	8:00.2
4b Willem de Graaff, Netherlands	8:00.2
6. Roald Aas, Norway	8:01.6

1952 (Oslo)	Time
1. Hjalmar Andersen, Norway	8:10.6
2. Kees Broekman, Netherlands	8:21.6
3. Sverre Haugli, Norway	8:22.4
4. Anton Huiskes, Netherlands	8:28.5
5. Willem van der Voort, Netherlands	8:30.6
6. Carl-Erik Asplund, Sweden	8:30.7

1948 (St. Moritz)	Time
1. Reidar Liaklev, Norway	8:29.4
2. Odd Lundberg, Norway	8:32.7
3. Göthe Hedlund, Sweden	8:34.8
4. Gustav Harry Jansson, Sweden	8:34.9
5. Jan Langedijk, Netherlands	8:36.2
6. Kees Broekman, Netherlands	8:37.3

1936 (Garmisch-P.)	Time
1. Ivar Ballangrud, Norway	8:19.6
2. Birger Vasenius, Finland	8:23.3
3. Antero Ojala, Finland	8:30.1
4. Jan Langedijk, Netherlands	8:32.0
5. Max Stiepl, Austria	8:35.0
6. Ossi Blomqvist, Finland	8:36.6

1932 (Lake Placid)	Time
1. Irving Jaffee, U.S.A.	9:40.8
2. Edward S. Murphy, U.S.A.	
3. William F. Logan, Canada	
4. Herbert Taylor, U.S.A.	
5. Ivar Ballangrud, Norway	
6. Bernt Evensen, Norway	

1928 (St. Moritz)	Time
1. Ivar Ballangrud, Norway	8:50.5
2. Julius Skutnabb, Finland	8:59.1
3. Bernt Evensen, Norway	9:01.1
4. Irving Jaffee, U.S.A.	9:01.3
5. Armand Carlsen, Norway	9:01.5
6. Valentine Bialas, U.S.A.	9:06.3

1924 (Chamonix)	Time
1. Clas Thunberg, Finland	8:39.0
2. Julius Skutnabb, Finland	8:48.4
3. Roald Larsen, Norway	8:50.2
4. Sigurd Moen, Norway	8:51.0
5. Harald Ström, Norway	8:54.6
6. Valentine Bialas, U.S.A.	8:55.0

Hjalmar Andersen, Norway

Speed Skating, 10,000 m., Men

A review of the Olympic 10,000-meter competitions through 1960 shows a number of interesting characteristics. Here the Norwegians were not supreme. The Swedes, who could not match the Norwegians and the Finns in the other three distances, made a good showing in this competition with two Olympic winners, Ake Seyffarth and Sigvard Ericsson. Also, in this, the longest speed-skating distance, the Soviets, who were the most successful nation in speed skating at Cortina in 1956 and at Squaw Valley in 1960, could not make a decisive breakthrough. This is all the more surprising since the long-distance track events seemed to suit them particularly well.

Results, 10,000 Meters, Men

1960 (Squaw Valley)	Time
1. Knut Johannesen, Norway	15:46.6
2. Viktor Kosichkin, U.S.S.R.	15:49.2
3. Kjell Bäckman, Sweden	16:14.2
4. Ivar Nilsson, Sweden	16:26.0
5. Terence Monaghan, Great Britain	16:31.6
6. Torstein Seiersten, Norway	16:33.4

1956 (Cortina)	Time
1. Sigvard Ericsson, Sweden	16:35.9
2. Knut Johannesen, Norway	16:36.9
3. Oleg Goncharenko, U.S.S.R.	16:42.3
4. Sverre Haugli, Norway	16:48.7
5. Kees Broekman, Netherlands	16:51.2
6. Hjalmar Andersen, Norway	16:52.6

1952 (Oslo)	Time
1. Hjalmar Andersen, Norway	16:45.8
2. Kees Broekman, Netherlands	17:10.6
3. Carl-Erik Asplund, Sweden	17:16.6
4. Pentti Lammio, Finland	17:20.5
5. Anton Huiskes, Netherlands	17:25.5
6. Sverre Haugli, Norway	17:30.2

1948 (St. Moritz)	Time
1. Ake Seyffarth, Sweden	17:26.3
2. Lauri Parkkinen, Finland	17:36.0
3. Pentti Lammio, Finland	17:42.7
4. Kornel Pajor, Hungary	17:45.6
5. Kees Broekman, Netherlands	17:54.7
6. Jan Langedijk, Netherlands	17:55.3

1936 (Garmisch-P.)	Time
1. Ivar Ballangrud, Norway	17:24.3
2. Birger Vasenius, Finland	17:28.2
3. Max Stiepl, Austria	17:30.0
4. Charles Mathiesen, Norway	17:41.2
5. Ossi Blomqvist, Finland	17:42.4
6. Jan Langedijk, Netherlands	17:43.7

1932 (Lake Placid)	Time
1. Irving Jaffee, U.S.A.	19:13.6
2. Ivar Ballangrud, Norway	
3. Frank Stack, Canada	
4. Edwin Wedge, U.S.A.	
5. Valentine Bialas, U.S.A.	
6. Bernt Evensen, Norway	

1924 (Chamonix)	Time
1. Julius Skutnabb, Finland	18:04.8
2. Clas Thunberg, Finland	18:07.8
3. Roald Larsen, Norway	18:12.2
4. Fritjof Paulsen, Norway	18:13.0
5. Harald Ström, Norway	18:18.6
6. Sigurd Moen, Norway	18:19.0

Clas Thunberg, Finland

Four-Race Event, Men

As has been mentioned earlier, the four-race event in speed skating was part of the Olympic program in 1924 only. It ended with victory for the Finn Clas Thunberg, who, together with the Norwegian Ivar Ballangrud, was undoubtedly the greatest all-round master in the history of speed skating. Thunberg also holds the unofficial record for the most successful sportsman at any one Olympic Games. He returned to his home in Finland from Chamonix with three gold medals, one silver and one bronze medal, a success no winter sportsman has since achieved.

Results, Four-Race Event 1924 (Chamonix)

	500	1500	5000	10,000	Total
1. Clas Thunberg, Finland	1.5	1	1	2	5.5
2. Roald Larsen, Norway	1.5	3	2	3	9.5
3. Julius Skutnabb, Finland	4	2	4	1	11
4. Harald Ström, Norway	3	5	5	4	17 (203.64)
5. Sigurd Moen, Norway	5	4	3	5	17 (203.78)
6. Léon Quaglia, France	6	6	7	6	25

Speed Skating, Women

In 1932 speed-skating competitions for women were on the Olympic program at Lake Placid. However, these were only demonstration contests, and no Olympic medals were awarded for them. The United States and Canada took part in them. At Squaw Valley in 1960 these competitions were given full Olympic status. This was due largely to the initiative of the Soviet Union, where all women's competitions are more popular than in most other countries. A small number of entries was expected and, indeed, there were only twenty-three speed skaters from ten countries. In their decision to recognize women's speed skating as a full Olympic sport, the members of the IOC overlooked the fact that they had violated the Olympic Charter. It explicitly states that only "fields of sports practiced all over the world," practiced in at least twenty-five countries, may be included in the Olympic program. Actually, women's speed skating is still far from fulfilling this condition. Compared to men's speed skating, it is far less widespread.

64

Lidia Skoblikova, U.S.S.R.

SQUAW VALLEY—1960

One of the events held for the first time in the 1960 Winter Olympics was women's speed skating. As if to justify the decision, there were immediate entries from ten nations for this youngest of Olympic events.

All available information, as well as forecasts of most experts, suggested that Russia would carry off all the women's speed-skating events at Squaw Valley.

On February 20 the shortest of the women's races on ice was held, a distance of 500 meters. It was a surprise when Helga Haase from Germany made the fastest time after a duel with Donchenko of Russia. Jeanne Ashworth of the United States, also astonishingly fast, took third place. The first four places were separated by only 0.3 second, which gives an indication of the competition.

Soviet superiority asserted itself in the 1500-meter race, in which Lidia Skoblikova established a world record.

Klara Guseva claimed another victory for Russia in the 1000-meter event when she crossed the finish line only 0.2 second ahead of Helga Haase.

February 23 brought another sensational race. Lidia Skoblikova, with one gold medal in the 1500-meter, carried off the honors in the 3000-meter race. Her teammate, Valentina Stenina, took second place.

**Results, Speed Skating, Women
1960 (Squaw Valley)**

500 Meters

		Time
1.	Helga Haase, Germany	45.9
2.	Natalija Donchenko, U.S.S.R.	46.0
3.	Jeanne Ashworth, U.S.A.	46.1
4.	Tamara Rylova, U.S.S.R.	46.2
5.	Hatsue Takamizawa, Japan	46.6
6a	Klara Guseva, U.S.S.R.	46.8
6b	Elvira Seroczynska, Poland	46.8

1000 Meters

		Time
1.	Klara Guseva, U.S.S.R.	1:34.1
2.	Helga Haase, Germany	1:34.3
3.	Tamara Rylova, U.S.S.R.	1:34.8
4.	Lidia Skoblikova, U.S.S.R.	1:35.3
5a	Hatsue Takamizawa, Japan	1:35.8
5b	Helena Pilejczyk, Poland	1:35.8

1500 Meters

		Time
1.	Lidia Skoblikova, U.S.S.R.	2:25.2
2.	Elvira Seroczynska, Poland	2:25.7
3.	Helena Pilejczyk, Poland	2:27.1
4.	Klara Guseva, U.S.S.R.	2:28.7
5.	Valentina Stenina, U.S.S.R.	2:29.2
6.	Iris Sihvonen, Finland	2:29.7

3000 Meters

		Time
1.	Lidia Skoblikova, U.S.S.R.	5:14.3
2.	Valentina Stenina, U.S.S.R.	5:16.9
3.	Eevi Huttunen, Finland	5:21.0
4.	Hatsue Takamizawa, Japan	5:21.4
5.	Christina Scherling, Sweden	5:25.5
6.	Helena Pilejczyk, Poland	5:26.2

Roald Aas, Norway

SQUAW VALLEY—1960

The Squaw Valley site offered the enormous advantage of having most events situated close to each other so that it was possible to walk across the hard-packed snow from one contest to another in just a few minutes. Ice rinks, jumping hills and slalom course could be taken in at one glance. Never before had so many skiers been able to watch the speed skating, some of them having seen the events for the first time.

Speed Skating Oval Under Construction
Squaw Valley, 1960

The men's speed-skating results from the 1956 Winter Olympics had been phenomenal. The feeling at Squaw Valley in 1960 was that those records could not be bettered.

Nevertheless the Americans spared no expense or effort to provide a site comparable to Garmisch-Partenkirchen, which had to be abandoned during World War II. Squaw Valley saw the first artificial speed-skating rink in the world. It was 561 feet long and 231 feet wide, with a track width of 66 feet. It was quite independent of weather and temperature, and had snow-removal equipment standing by in case of a heavy snowfall. This is all the more remarkable in view of the fact that American Olympic participation is financed through donations.

Despite all these efforts, the artificial facility received some harsh criticism. During the training sessions the quality of the ice was under severe scrutiny. Since speed skaters flash across the ice at about 13 meters per second, the quality of the ice surface is of prime importance to every competitor.

When the events were run, however, the criticism proved to be unfounded. In the 500-meter sprint the Soviet Grishin missed breaking the 40-second mark by a waver. He did succeed in breaking this time after the Olympics, but this achievement could not be recognized because it was not made during an official competition. After Grishin crossed the finish line, seven skaters succeeded in covering the 500 meters in less than 41 seconds. American William D. Disney took second place in that race.

The next day, February 25, was the day of the men's 5000-meter event. It was also the day that Victor Kosichkin's accomplishments for Russia overshadowed everything else.

February 26 brought strong winds. The skaters in the 1500-meter race were hindered down one side of the track more than they were helped in the reverse direction. But a sensation was in store for the spectators when Roald Edgar Aas of Norway tied Grishin of Russia for first place with a time of 2:10.4 minutes. They both received a gold medal. Once before, in 1956, Grishin shared his victory, that time with his countryman Mikhailov. Aas had placed tenth in 1956, which showed how much progress he had made even though he was now thirty-two years old.

**Results, Speed Skating, Men
1960 (Squaw Valley)**

500 meters

		Time
1.	Grishin, U.S.S.R.	40.2
2.	Disney, U.S.A.	40.3
3.	Grach, U.S.S.R.	40.4
4.	Wilhemsson, Sweden	40.5
5.	Voronin, U.S.S.R.	40.7
6.	Gjestvang, Norway	40.8
7.	McDermott, U.S.A.	40.9
	Salonen, Finland	40.9
9.	Nagakubo, Japan	41.1
10.	Rudolph, U.S.A.	41.2
	Malyshev, U.S.S.R.	41.2
	van der Grift, Netherlands	41.2

1500 meters

		Time
1.	Aas, Norway	2:10.4
	Grishin, U.S.S.R.	2:10.4
3.	Stenin, U.S.S.R.	2:11.5
4.	Jokinen, Finland	2:12.0
5.	Jarvinen, Finland	2:13.1
	Brogren, Sweden	2:13.1
	Salonen, Finland	2:13.1
8.	Kouprianoff, France	2:13.3
9.	Kuhnert, Germany	2:13.6
10.	Gilloz, France	2:14.2

5000 meters

		Time
1.	Kosichkin, U.S.S.R.	7:51.3
2.	Johannesen, Norway	8:00.8
3.	Pesman, Netherlands	8:05.1
4.	Seiersten, Norway	8:05.3
5.	Kotov, U.S.S.R.	8:05.4
6.	Goncharenko, U.S.S.R.	8:06.6
7.	Nilsson, Sweden	8:09.1
	Tapiovaara, Finland	8:09.1
9.	Kouprianoff, France	8:10.4
10.	Gilloz, France	8:11.5

10,000 meters

		Time
1.	Johannesen, Norway	15:46.6
2.	Kosichkin, U.S.S.R.	15:49.2
3.	Backman, Sweden	16:14.2
4.	Nilsson, Sweden	16:26.0
5.	Monaghan, Great Britain	16:31.6
6.	Seiersten, Norway	16:33.4
7.	Dahlberg, Sweden	16:34.6
8.	Jarvinen, Finland	16:35.4
9.	Tapiovaara, Finland	16:37.2
10.	Zucco, U.S.A.	16:37.6

Dan Immerfall, U.S.A.   Valerly Muratov, U.S.S.R.

INNSBRUCK—1964

Terry McDermott, U.S.A.

"A perfect race . . . Off the line . . . After ten meters, begin to stroke . . . Legs under me . . . First turn . . . Work the turn . . . Backstretch . . . Low and long stroke . . . Technique . . . Last turn . . . Set it up . . . Work it hard . . . One hundred meters to go, the home stretch . . . Legs underneath me . . . Technique . . . Finish strong."*

That was his plan. He planned his event, the 500-meter speed-skating competition in the 1964 Winter Olympics, and he skated his plan. It worked so well that he, Terry McDermott, returned to the United States with the only gold medal won by an American at Innsbruck.

The 500-meter race is always exciting. The skaters are paired, and they sprint just as fast and hard as they can. Terry McDermott, however, had an unusual plan. The faster skaters prefer to skate in the first seeding. The ice is better, and the competition is better. Terry preferred to race against the clock; so he asked his coach to place him in the second seeding. When his turn finally came, all of the best sprint skaters had finished. The best time for the 500 meters was 40.6 seconds, set by the Soviet Eugeny Grishin and two others. They were all tied for first place. Grishin had won the gold medal for 500 meters in both 1956 and 1960.

Now it was McDermott's turn. Ready . . . Get set . . . Bang! He was off to a good start. Sprint. Then stroke hard. His coach, Leo Friesinger, waited on the backstretch to give Terry his time on the first split. "Ten seconds flat," Leo yelled. This was it. McDermott skated that perfect race he had practiced so many times before. When he looked over his shoulder after crossing the finish line, the electronic scoreboard read 40.3 seconds. That was an error. Terry McDermott's corrected time was 40.1 seconds. It was a world's record, an Olympic record, and the only American gold medal at Innsbruck.

Lydia Skoblikova of the Soviet Union was the whole story in women's speed-skating events. She won all four events, setting Olympic records in

*From "An Olympian Task Separates Friends," by Kim Chapin, *Chicago Tribune,* Feb. 2, 1979.

68

OLYMPIC STYLE SPEED SKATING

Olympic or European style skating consists of two skaters competing at one time on a 400 meter track. There are two separate lanes, divided by snow, on the track — the inside lane being shorter than the outside lane. In order that the racers each skate the same distance, they must change lanes each lap at the cross over point. A flagman stands there with a red and green flag and directs the leading skater to cross first. At the conclusion of the competition, the skaters are ranked on the basis of fastest time.

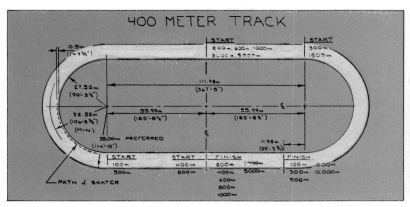

Lidia Skoblikova, U.S.S.R.

three. Jeanne Ashworth of Lake Placid and Janice Smith of Rochester, both of New York State, came the closest to medal honors for the Americans. Both showed considerable versatility, finishing high in three of the four events.

Skoblikova broke records in the 500-, the 1000- and the 1500-meter race. In winning four gold medals, a first in the Winter Games, she retained her championships of 1960 in the 1500- and 3000-meter races.

Ashworth was awarded fourth and Smith fifth in the 500-meter race, although both were timed in 46.2 seconds. Janice Lawler of Minneapolis took seventh.

Smith was seventh in the 1000 and Ashworth was eleventh. In tenth place was Barbara Lockhart of Park Ridge, Illinois. In the 1500-meter race Judith Morstein of Butte, Montana, took fifteenth. Lawler was nineteenth and Smith twenty-fourth.

Led by Richard (Terry) McDermott of Essexville, Michigan, the American men outdid their best previous performances. McDermott, using skates borrowed from his coach, gave the Americans their first gold medal of the Innsbruck competition, winning the 500-meter race in 40.1 seconds, an Olympic record.

Ed Rudolph of Northbrook, Illinois, finished sixth, ahead of Bill Disney, Rosemead, California (eighth), and Thomas Gray, Bloomington, Minnesota (fourteenth).

Russia's Ants Antson upset predictions to win the 1500-meter race ahead of Rudi Liebricht of the Netherlands.

Thirty-year-old Knut Johannsen led two younger Norwegian teammates to victory in the 5000-meter race, setting an Olympic record in the process. He had won a silver medal in the event four years before. Dick Hunt, La Crescenta, California, was twentieth; Wayne LeBombard, West Allis, Wisconsin, twenty-ninth; and Stanley Fail, Paramount, California, thirty-eighth.

A gold medal went to Sweden's Johnny Nilsson, the world record holder, whose favorable early start won him the 10,000-meter run. He was the only man to break 16 minutes.

69

Erhard Keller, W. Germany

GRENOBLE—1968

Men's Speed Skating

The 500-meter race consisted of forty-eight skaters racing in twenty-four pairs. Among them were the most illustrious names in this event—Terry McDermott of the United States, Eugeny Grishin of the U.S.S.R., both of whom had won gold medals at previous Winter Games, and West Germany's Erhard Keller, who then held the world record. In addition there were eleven other men who had at one time or other clocked under 40 seconds in the event. Therefore it was no surprise that it turned out to be a furious fight for the medals.

Keller's early time of 40.3 looked too good to be bettered by the later skaters, mainly because the rising temperatures of the sunny day caused the surface of the course to soften considerably. The 1967 winner, American Terry McDermott, was last in the field of fourteen pairs, with almost no chance of overcoming the conditions. He had a tremendous opening burst, covering the first 100 meters in 10.2 seconds, but he simply could not maintain such a pace. He finished in 40.5 seconds, good enough for a tie with Norway's Magne Thomassen for second place. Grishin finished fourth.

Results, 500 Meters

	Time
1. Erhard Keller, W. Germany	40.3
2. Magne Thomassen, Norway	40.5
2. Terry McDermott, U.S.A.	40.5
4. Eugeny Grishin, U.S.S.R.	40.6
5. Arne Herjuaunet, Norway	40.7
5. John Wurster, U.S.A.	40.7
5. Neil Blatchford, U.S.A.	40.7

Results, 5000 Meters

	Time
1. Fred Maier, Norway	7:22.4
2. Kees Verkerk, Netherlands	7:23.2
3. Petrus Nottet, Netherlands	7:25.5
4. Willy Guttormsen, Norway	7:27.8
5. Johnny Hoeglin, Sweden	7:32.7
6. Perjen Sandler, Sweden	7:32.8

70

Terry McDermott, U.S.A.   Erhard Keller, W. Germany   Magne Thomassen, Norway

The 5000 meters was the next contest instead of the scheduled 1500 meters. The organizers had decided that the sprinters should get a day of respite after their 500-meter exertions. Fred Anton Maier, the twenty-nine-year-old Norwegian world champion, saw his world record performance of 7:26.2 minutes bettered by Kees Verkerk, Netherlands, who reduced it by 3 seconds—only to beat Vererk's new record 20 minutes later by eight-tenths of a second. The Netherlander Nottet won the bronze medal, 2.3 seconds slower than Verkerk. Yet his time was, by seven-tenths of a second, faster than Maier's old world record.

The 1500-meter race was won by Verkerk of the Netherlands. Second best was Schenk, his fellow countryman, ahead of Eriksen of Norway.

The 10,000 meters, the last event of the competition, was skated under heavy wind conditions, which were a great nuisance to the skaters. Maier, the world record holder, blamed the weather for not having bettered his own best time. This was before Sweden's Hoeglin had his chance. He didn't break Maier's record, but beat him into second place. Rarely has there been better skating than Hoeglin's, which was marvelously paced and sustained over the long distance. Altogether Hoeglin provided the big sensation in the men's speed skating. All the Innsbruck gold medalists failed to repeat their successes. Only McDermott managed to win at least a silver medal.

Results, 1500 Meters

		Time
1.	Kees Verkerk, Netherlands	2:03.4
2.	Ard Schenk, Netherlands	2:05.0
3.	Ivar Eriksen, Norway	2:05.0
4.	Magne Thomassen, Norway	2:05.1
5.	Bjoern Tveter, Norway	2:05.2
5.	Johnny Hoeglin, Sweden	2:05.2

Results, 10,000 Meters

		Time
1.	Johnny Hoeglin, Sweden	15:23.6
2.	Fred Maier, Norway	15:23.9
3.	Perjen Sandler, Sweden	15:31.8
4.	Willy Guttormsen, Norway	15:32.6
5.	Kees Verkerk, Netherlands	15:33.9
6.	Johnny Nilsson, Sweden	15:39.6

Jennifer Fish, U.S.A.
Dianne Holum, U.S.A.
Mary Myers, U.S.A.

Dianne Holum, U.S.A.

Women's Speed Skating

Opening day of the speed-skating competition provided magnificent showings by the U.S. women's 500-meter sprinters. Mary Meyers, a junior at the University of Minnesota and the 1967 world champion skating with the second pair, immediately placed at the top of the scoreboard with 46.3 seconds. Seven pairs later Ludmila Titova, twenty-one-year-old all-events champion from the Soviet Union, sped to first place with 46.1 seconds. This eventually proved good enough for the gold medal, though the United States still challenged strongly. In the very next heat, sixteen-year-old Dianne Holum, a Northbrook, Illinois, high school student, burst into an all-out effort. Her time of 46.3 put her into a second-place tie with teammate Mary Meyers.

The final pair provided still more excitement. Soviet star Irina Egorova raced the United States' Jennifer Fish, an eighteen-year-old Baldwin-Wallace college freshman. To a crowd roaring with approval, Fish clocked 46.3 seconds to effect a triple U.S. deadlock for silver medal honors, the first time in history that three skaters from one nation achieved that feat.

Among the twenty-eight young women who competed in the skating rink of Parc Paul Mistral in the 500 meters, there were Mary, Dianne and Jenny from the United States. First it was Mary's turn. Her time was 46.3 seconds. Then came Dianne—and she also was clocked in 46.3 seconds. Finally, Jenny went on her way and when the electronic clock again stopped exactly at 46.3, it seemed as though the punch line had been delivered to an already delightful story. This highly unusual development created waves of excitement around the ice oval. Mary, Dianne and Jenny giggled and squealed like youngsters who had just pulled off their biggest prank. They had hoped for

Results, 500 Meters

	Time
1. Ludmila Titova, U.S.S.R.	46.1
2. Mary Meyers, U.S.A.	46.3
2. Dianne Holum, U.S.A.	46.3
2. Jennifer Fish, U.S.A.	46.3
5. Elisabeth van den Brom, Netherlands	46.6
6. Sigrid Sundby, Norway	46.7

Results, 1000 Meters

	Time
1. Carolina Geijssen, Netherlands	1:32.6
2. Ludmila Titova, U.S.S.R.	1:32.9
3. Dianne Holum, U.S.A.	1:33.4
4. Kaija Mustonen, Finland	1:33.6
5. Irina Egorova, U.S.S.R.	1:34.4
6. Sigrid Sundby, Norway	1:34.5

72

Jennifer Fish, U.S.A.   Dianne Holum, U.S.A.   Mary Myers, U.S.A.

Ludmila Titova, U.S.S.R.

one silver medal and now they had won three of them. The charming American three-stage rocket had blasted off with absolute perfection. Even the glitter of the gold medal, won in 46.1 seconds by the Russian Ludmila Titova, paled in comparison to the threefold silver lining of Mary's, Dianne's and Jenny's happiness. At this moment not one of the three Americans would have cared to switch places with Ludmila.

Only once before had there been a triple tie for second place in a speed-skating event—two U.S. men and a Norwegian gaining that distinction in 1948—but never before had three from the same nation accomplished that feat! Mary Meyers, Jennifer Fish and Dianne Holum, products of an intensive U.S. Olympic Committee development program, wrote their names indelibly in the Olympic annals. Dianne Holum also won a bronze medal by finishing third in the 1000-meter race, bringing to seven the total of medals for the U.S. entries.

In the 1000-meter race Ludmila Titova gained only the silver medal, the gold being won by Carolina Geijssen of the Netherlands. Dianne Holum was third, but this time she collected the bronze medal by herself.

The 1500 meters was won by Kaija Mustonen, Finland. Two teammates from the Netherlands took second and third, while Lidia Skoblikova, who had won this event in 1960 and 1964, was unable to do better than eleventh place.

The 3000-meter race reversed the previous Finland-Netherlands order. In this longest and last of the women's events, the Netherlands' Johanna Schut won the gold medal and Kaija Mustonen won the silver. Christina Kaiser of the Netherlands won the bronze medal, just as she had done in the 1500 meters. It is possible that if it hadn't rained so badly all through the race, Christina—or Stien, as she is called—would have done much better.

Results, 1500 Meters

		Time
1.	Kaija Mustonen, Finland	2:22.4
2.	Carolina Geijssen, Netherlands	2:22.7
3.	Christina Kaiser, Netherlands	2:24.5
4.	Sigrid Sundby, Norway	2:25.2
5.	Lasma Kaouniste, U.S.S.R.	2:25.4
6.	Kaija-L. Keskivitikka, Finland	2:25.8

Results, 3000 Meters

		Time
1.	Johanna Schut, Netherlands	4:56.2
2.	Kaija Mustonen, Finland	5:01.0
3.	Christina Kaiser, Netherlands	5:01.3
4.	Kaija-L. Keskivitikka, Finland	5:03.9
5.	Wilhelmina Burgmeijer, Netherlands	5:05.1
6.	Lidia Skoblikova, U.S.S.R.	5:08.0

73

Sapporo Speed Skating Rink

SAPPORO—1972

Men's Speed Skating

The peak event in the Makomanai Ice Stadium was the men's sprint. Four names were put forward as possible winners: world record holder Leo Linkovesi, Finland; former world record holder Hasse Borjes, Sweden; Valeri Muratov, U.S.S.R.; and Erhard Keller, West Germany. The defending German Olympic champion was held the favorite by many. For four years he had been preparing himself for this event, but before the race dashed off there were four false starts, three of them Keller's fault. At the fourth try Keller started slower than usual, a fact confirmed by his time for the first 100 meters—10.6 seconds. In spite of this poor start the strong-nerved German recovered his rhythm, skated increasingly faster and won with a time of 39.44.

The 1500 meters was the most fought-for race in speed skating. Among the thirty-nine participants were the Hollanders Ard Schenk, Kees Verkerk and Jan Bols, the Norwegians Roar Gronvold and Bjorn Tveter, and the Swede Goran Claesson. Each of them was worthy of a gold medal. In retrospect, however, the competition became a demonstration of style and strength. Ard Schenk beat Gronvold by 1.30 seconds.

In the 5000 meters everything conspired against Ard Schenk. He even had the unfavorable starting number of 1. During his race it snowed heavily. But Ard Schenk could not be denied victory. He lost his partner, the Italian Giovanni Gloder, after a few meters and raced with strong, long-reaching strides. Nevertheless his time was much slower than Fred Anton Maier's Olympic record in Grenoble in 1968 or his own world record of 7:12.00.

In the 10,000 the records tumbled one after another. Brilliant sunshine saw the Russian Valery Lavrouchkin take the lead with 15:20.08. Four years previously Johnny Hoeglin had won with the best Olympic time ever of 15:23.6. Sten Stensen of Norway was 13 seconds faster, and Kees Verkerk of the Netherlands continued with 15:04.70. For three hours Verkerk could dream of winning the Olympic gold medal. Then his countryman Ard Schenk took over and after 4000 meters had bettered Verkerk's time by 3.35 seconds. The silver medalist in the 1500 and 5000 meters, Roar Gronvold of Norway, had decided not to race in the 10,000.

Ard Schenk, Netherlands

Results, 500 Meters

		Time
1.	Erhard Keller, W. Germany	39.44
2.	Hasse Borjes, Sweden	39.69
3.	Valeri Muratov, U.S.S.R.	39.80

Results, 1500 Meters

		Time
1.	Ard Schenk, Netherlands	2:02.96
2.	Roar Gronvold, Norway	2:04.26
3.	Goran Claesson, Sweden	2:05.89

Results, 5000 Meters

		Time
1.	Ard Schenk, Netherlands	7:23.61
2.	Roar Gronvold, Norway	7:28.18
3.	Sten Stensen, Norway	7:33.39

Results, 10,000 Meters

		Time
1.	Ard Schenk, Netherlands	15:01.35
2.	Kees Verkerk, Netherlands	15:04.70
3.	Sten Stensen, Norway	15:07.08

74

Monika Pflug, W. Germany

Dianne Holum, U.S.A.

Dianne Holum, U.S.A.

Anne
Henning,
U.S.A.

Anne Henning, U.S.A.

Women's Speed Skating

The most convincing Olympic champion at Sapporo was a sixteen-year-old American schoolgirl, Anne Henning. She won the gold medal for the 500 meters twice over. Anne raced in the fifth pair against the Canadian Sylvia Burka, but as she changed lanes Sylvia impeded her. Despite the hindrance, Anne broke the Olympic record with a time of 43.73. However, the coach of the U.S. team filed a protest which was upheld. At the end of the racing Anne did a solo sprint over the 500 meters once more, and the chronometer showed a new best time ever of 43.33 seconds. A further proof of the American's superiority is shown by the fact that not one single competitor skated the 500 meters under 44 seconds.

Apart from Erhard Keller, there was no one who considered Monika Pflug among possible medal winners for the 1000 meters. She began her race disappointingly. Skating against the Swedish contender Ann-Sofie Jarnstrom, she was recalled twice by the starter for starting early. At the third try all went well, but her timing was not quite right. After 200 meters she registered a time of only 20.59 seconds, a lot slower than Keulen-Deelstra, Henning, Titova and Holum. By 600 meters, however, she was already in the lead with 54.74, and at 1000 meters the clock registered 1:31.40—a new Olympic record.

In the first of the women's speed-skating races, the 1500 meters, Dianne Holum saw her dream realized. She had narrowly missed winning a gold medal in Grenoble and had had to content herself with silver and bronze. In Sapporo she skated a superb race and secured the victory with the last lap—400 meters in 38.9 seconds. Silver and bronze were won by the Hollanders Baas-Kaiser and Keulen-Deelstra.

The longest distance for the women resulted in triumph for the housewives from the Netherlands. Stien Baas-Kaiser was the champion of the 3000 meters, while Atje Keulen-Deelstra was third. The twenty-year-old American Dianne Holum gained the silver medal. After a slow start she was 3 seconds behind Baas-Kaiser at the 1000-meter mark. She finished with a superb burst of speed and succeeded in relegating Keulen-Deelstra to third place.

Results, 500 Meters

	Time
1. Anne Henning, U.S.A.	43.33
2. Vera Krasnova, U.S.S.R.	44.01
3. Ludmilla Titova, U.S.S.R.	44.45
4. Sheila Young, U.S.A.	44.53

Results, 1000 Meters

	Time
1. Monika Pflug, W. Germany	1:31.40
2. Atja Keulen-Deelstra, Netherlands	1:31.61
3. Anne Henning, U.S.A.	1:31.62

Results, 1500 Meters

	Time
1. Dianne Holum, U.S.A.	2:20.85
2. Stien Baas-Kaiser Netherlands	2:21.05
3. Atje Keulen-Deelstra, Netherlands	2:22.05

Results, 3000 Meters

	Time
1. Stien Baas-Kaiser, Netherlands	4:52.14
2. Dianne Holum, U.S.A.	4:58.67
3. Atje Keulen-Deelstra, Netherlands	4:59.91

Peter Mueller, U.S.A.

Piet Kleine, Netherlands

Hans
Van Helden,
Netherlands

Sten Stensen, Norway

Peter Mueller, U.S.A.

INNSBRUCK—1976

Speed skating has become one of the most popular sports on the program for the Olympic Winter Games simply because the rules are easy to understand, the action takes place in front of the spectators at all times, the winners are determined on the basis of time and results can be compared with other international competitions, since all speed-skating contests are on a refrigerated ice rink, 400 meters in circumference. Thus speed skating is the single winter sport that has recognized national, world and Olympic records.

Speed skating brought additional focus on the well-trained U.S. athletes in the winter sports at Innsbruck. The highlight of the speed-skating competitions, where Olympic records set at Sapporo were being broken in wholesale quantities by the top skaters, was Sheila Young. For the first time a U.S. athlete won a gold, a silver and a bronze in the speed-skating events.

The President of the United States placed a personal call to Miss Young at the Olympic Village—the first President ever to phone congratulations to a U.S. gold medalist at the site of the games. In post-Olympic competition Sheila retained her world sprint speed-skating title, her third world title in four years.

Men's Speed Skating

Another high point for Americans was the men's 1000-meter event. Peter Mueller, who was engaged to teammate Leah Poulos, won the gold medal for the United States. It had been twelve years since the Americans could rejoice over a victory in the men's speed-skating category. The last time had been at Innsbruck in 1964 when Terry McDermott won the 500-meter race.

The 1000-meter race was one of two new events on the program for the XII Olympic Winter Games. Mueller had always been at his best in this event in other national and international competitions. Said the new gold medal holder, "For the first 200 meters I was pretty stiff, and my coach had told me to go out early. From 200 to 800 meters it went good and I closed down the 2½ laps around the ring in 1:19.32, only .32 second slower than I had mentally pictured the time it would take to win."

Eric Heiden, U.S.A.

Sten Stensen, Norway

"For the last 200 meters I was biting my nails," said his fiancee, Leah Poulos, herself an Olympic silver medalist. "But I knew he could do it and I wanted him to take a better medal than I did."

Mueller admitted that he had been a nervous wreck before the race and hadn't eaten in two days. Actually, Mueller had been fighting the flu, which felled a number of athletes in the Olympic Village. The evening of his triumph he was bedded down with a high temperature. The next day he was permitted to leave the sickbed long enough to attend his medal presentation and enjoy the adulation of the spectators in the Ice Palace.

Peter Mueller, U.S.A. Leah Poulas Mueller.

Results, Speed Skating, Men
1976 (Innsbruck)

500 Meters

	Time
1. Eugeny Kulikov, U.S.S.R.	39.17
2. Valery Muratov, U.S.S.R.	39.25
3. Dan Immerfall, U.S.A.	39.54
4. Matts Wallberg, Sweden	39.56
5. Peter Mueller, U.S.A.	39.57
6. Arnulf Sunde, Norway	39.78
6. Jan Bazen, Netherlands	39.78
8. Andrei Malikov, U.S.S.R.	39.85
9. Oloph Granath, Sweden	39.93
10. James Chapin, U.S.A.	40.09

1000 Meters

1. Peter Mueller, U.S.A.	1:19.32
2. Jorn Didriksen, Norway	1:20.45
3. Valery Muratov, U.S.S.R.	1:20.57
4. Aleksandr Safronov, U.S.S.R	1:20.84
5. Hans Van Helden, Netherlands	1:20.85
6. Gaetan Boucher, Canada	1:21.23
7. Matts Wallberg, Sweden	1:21.27
8. Pertti Nittylae, Finland	1:21.43
9. Horst Freese, W. Germany	1:21.48
10. Klaus Wunderlich, E. Germany	1:21.67

1500 Meters

1. Jan-Egil Storholt, Norway	1:59.38
2. Yuri Kondakov, U.S.S.R.	1:59.97
3. Hans Van Helden, Netherlands	2:00.87
4. Sergei Riabev, U.S.S.R.	2:02.15
5. Dan Carroll, U.S.A.	2:02.26
6. Piet Kleine, Netherlands	2:02.28
7. Eric Heiden, U.S.A.	2:02.40
8. Victor Coates, Austria	2:03.34
9. Klaus Wunderlich, E. Germany	2:03.41
10. Olavi Koeppae, Finland	2:03.69

5000 Meters

1. Sten Stensen, Norway	7:24.48
2. Piet Kleine, Netherlands	7:26.47
3. Hans Van Helden, Netherlands	7:26.54
4. Victor Varlamov, U.S.S.R.	7:30.97
5. Klaus Wunderlich, E. Germany	7:33.82
6. Dan Carroll, U.S.A.	7:36.46
7. Vladimir Ivanov, U.S.S.R.	7:37.73
8. Oerian Sandler, Sweden	7:39.69
9. Jan Egil Storholt, Norway	7:40.60
10. Colin Coates, Austria	7:41.96

10,000 Meters

1. Piet Kleine, Netherlands	14:50.59
2. Sten Stensen, Norway	14:53.30
3. Hans Van Helden, Netherlands	15:02.02
4. Victor Varlamov, U.S.S.R.	15:06.06
5. Oerjan Sandler, Sweden	15:16.21
6. Colin Coates, Austria	15:16.80
7. Dan Carroll, U.S.A.	15:19.29
8. Franz Krienbuehl, Switzerland	15:36.43
9. Olavi Koeppae, Finland	15:39.73
10. Amund Siobrend, Sweden	15:43.29

Sheila Young, U.S.A.

Sheila Young, U.S.A.

Sheila Young, U.S.A.

Tatiana Barabasch Averina, U.S.S.R.

Leah Poulos, U.S.A.   Sheila Young, U.S.A.
Tatiana Averina, U.S.S.R.

**Results, Speed Skating, Women
1976 (Innsbruck)**

500 Meters

		Time
1.	Sheila Young, U.S.A.	42.76
2.	Cathy Priestner, Canada	43.12
3.	Tatiana Averina, U.S.S.R.	43.17
4.	Leah Poulos, U.S.A.	43.21
5.	Vera Krasnova, U.S.S.R.	43.23
6.	Lubov Sadchikova, U.S.S.R.	43.80
7.	Makiko Nagaya, Japan	43.88
8.	Paula Halonen, Finland	43.99
9.	Lori Monk, U.S.A.	44.00
10.	Heike Lange, E. Germany	44.21

1000 Meters

1.	Tatiana Averina, U.S.S.R.	1:28.43
2.	Leah Poulos, U.S.A.	1:28.57
3.	Sheila Young, U.S.A.	1:29.14
4.	Sylvia Burka, Canada	1:29.47
5.	Monika Holzner, W. Germany	1:29.54
6.	Cathy Priestner, Canada	1:29.66
7.	Ludmila Titova, U.S.S.R.	1:30.06
8.	Heike Lange, E. Germany	1:30.55
9.	Makiko Nagaya, Japan	1:31.23
10.	Erwina Rys, Poland	1:31.59

For the first time in Olympic speed-skating history, the combined men's and women's U.S. forces were on the attack in all races. In the opening men's race, the 500-meter, Dan Immerfall, a University of Wisconsin music major, earned the bronze medal by the closest of margins over Sweden's Matts Wallberg and teammate Mueller. This race to decide second place was the highlight of the morning's program. Spongy ice had made unexciting racing. The Muratov-Immerfall pair skated after the intermission when conditions had improved. Said Immerfall, "I almost fell in the first 75 meters after I hit my right heel with my left skate. However, I picked it up [the pace] around the first turn and then slipped crossing over to the inner course. In the last 100 I did my fastest time of the race."

Women's Speed Skating

For seven years the Soviet speed-skating ace, Tatiana Averina, had sought victory in an important international competition. Averina, a world record holder in the 1000-meter and the 1500-meter, was third behind Sheila Young and Cathy Priestner of Canada in the short sprint race. Her moment of victory came on a foggy Saturday morning in the 1000-meter race at Innsbruck in 1976. This race brought together the best in the world—Young, Poulos

Andrea Mitscherlich, E. Germany

Leah Poulos, U.S.A.

Sheila Young, U.S.A.

Tatiana Averina, U.S.S.R.

Leah Poulos, U.S.A.

Galina Stepanskaya, U.S.S.R.

1500 Meters

1.	Galina Stepanskaya, U.S.S.R.	2:16.58
2.	Sheila Young, U.S.A.	2:17.06
3.	Tatiana Averina, U.S.S.R.	2:17.96
4.	Lisbeth Korsmo, Norway	2:18.99
5.	Karin Kessow, E. Germany	2:19.05
6.	Leah Poulos, U.S.A.	2:19.11
7.	Ines Bautzmann, E. Germany	2:19.63
8.	Erwina Rys, Poland	2:19.69
9.	Sylvia Burka, Canada	2:19.74
10.	Andrea Mitscherlich, E. Germany	2:20.05

3000 Meters

1.	Tatiana Averina, U.S.S.R.	4:45.19
2.	Andrea Mitscherlich, E. Germany	4:45.23
3.	Lisbeth Korsmo, Norway	4:45.24
4.	Karin Kessow, E. Germany	4:45.60
5.	Ines Bautzmann, E. Germany	4:46.67
6.	Sylvia Filipsson, Sweden	4:48.15
7.	Nancy Swider, U.S.A.	4:48.46
8.	Sylvia Burka, Canada	4:49.04
9.	Sijtje van der Lende, Netherlands	4:50.86
10.	Erwina Rys, Poland	4:50.95

and Monika Pflug Holzner, who at seventeen in 1972 was the surprising victor. This was strictly a competition among the top women speed skaters.

In the two and a half turns around the rink, Leah Poulos came close to skating a perfect race. When she posted a 1:28.57 clocking, it put her in front. In the very next pair, however, Averina was ahead of Poulos's pace over the first 200 meters. Averina clinched the gold medal with a time of 1:28.43. Poulos was second and Young third. Had the three top winners skated side by side, there would have been a mere sixteen inches between first, second and third places.

Leah Poulos had a great Olympic Games. She took a silver medal in the 1000 meters, a fourth in the 500 meters, and a sixth in the 1500 meters. Another notable performer came up with no medal awards in his final Olympic Games. Dan Carroll, a veteran of two games, placed in four races: fifth in the 1500-meter, sixth in the 5000-meter, seventh in the 10,000-meter and a disappointing twenty-eighth in the 1000-meter.

This Olympic team had been selected during trials covering two weekends in late December. Following selection, the entire squad went to Europe for a series of important competitions and additional training. Reports from Europe indicated that this was by far the most talented all-round squad ever entered by the United States.

79

Top Contenders

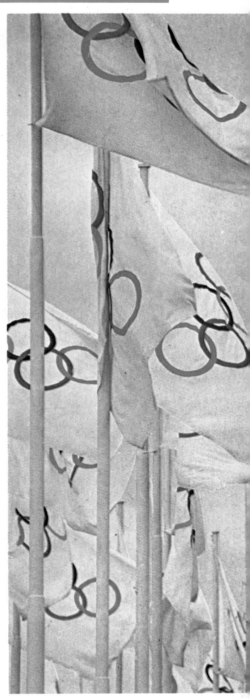

Can one family produce two Olympic Gold medal winners in the same year? Eric and Beth Heiden, brother and sister speed skaters from Madison, Wisconsin, believe it will happen.

In February 1979, Eric Heiden won his seventh and eighth world title championships. In the last three years he has won two junior, three senior and three sprint titles. At Oslo, Norway, Eric took the overall senior title, winning all four men's events—the 500, 1500, 5,000 and 10,000 meters. He also set the world record for total points. In Norway where speed skating is a major national sport, Eric was treated like a hero. He was featured in every newspaper. In spite of this popularity and pressure he went all out. Eric won the 500, the 1500 and 5,000. Then, saving his best for last, he skated the 10,000—6¼ mile race in an unbelievable 14:43.11. This was seven seconds better than the stadium record and 15.64 seconds ahead of the second-place skater. One week later in Inzell, West Germany, Eric Heiden again proved he is the best by winning the world sprint championship.

Beth Heiden is a champion of a different kind. Far smaller than her brother, she is the outgoing extrovert of the family. Eric wins with muscle and style; Beth wins with determination and heart.

In February 1979, Beth won the world speed skating womens title at The Hague. She won all four events at distances from 500 to 3,000 meters. Then a week later she joined her brother at Inzell, West Germany, to compete in the women's sprint championships. She skated better than the 1978 champion Lubov Sadchikova of the Soviet Union, but was surprised by another American, Leah Poulos Mueller. Mueller was the silver medalist at Innsbruck in 1976 and came back to win her second world sprint title. Beth Heiden was second and won the silver medal in Inzell.

With the 1980 Olympics so close, you can be sure that Eric and Beth Heiden are skating every day and planning to bring home the gold for the United States at Lake Placid.

Beth Heiden, U.S.A.

Peter Mueller, U.S.A.

Eric Heiden, U.S.A.

Kim Kostron, U.S.A.

Beth Heiden, U.S.A.

Craig Kressler, U.S.A.

Mike Woods, U.S.A.

Eugenij Kulikov, U.S.S.R.

Tatiana Averina, U.S.S.R.

Cindy Seikkula, U.S.A.
(Top Contender Speed)

th Heiden, U.S.A.

Dan Immerfall, U.S.A.

Nancy Louise Swider, U.S.A.

Eric Heiden, U.S.A.

85

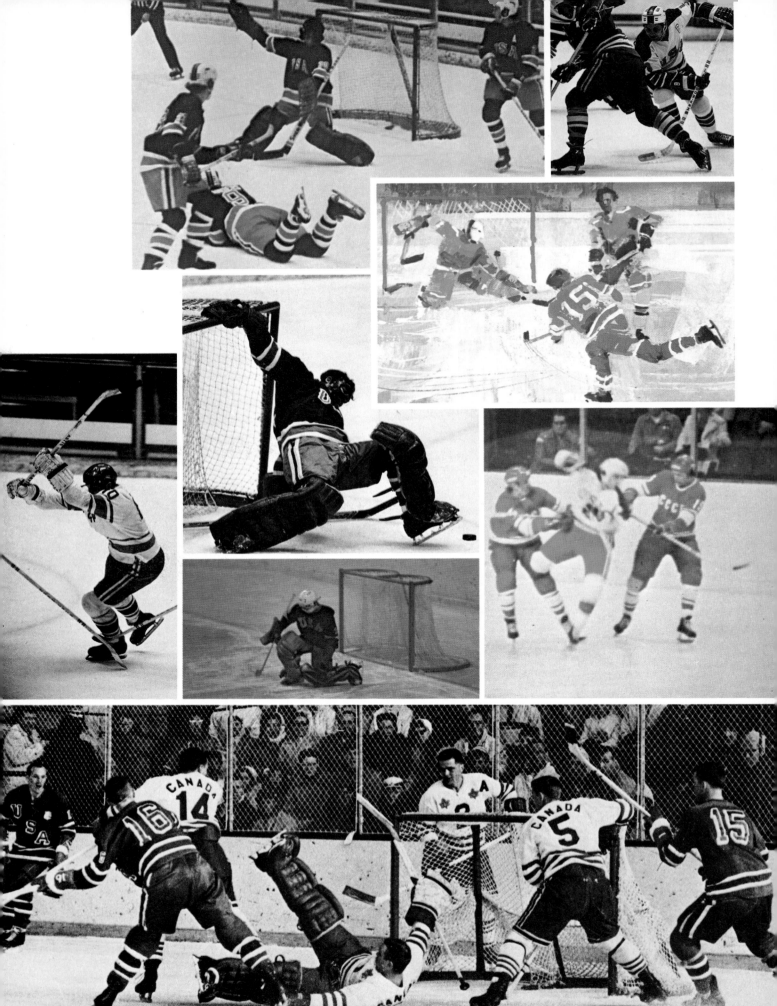

3

Ice Hockey

U.S. GOLD—A PREMIUM HOCKEY TEAM

Ice hockey presents its own special problems for the judges. Inherent in the game is forceful, rugged play. There is also the psychological aspect. Players who have been roughly handled by opponents are hard pressed not to avenge themselves. When the other man has lost his temper, even more control is needed. The end result of any real breach is, of course, the penalty bench.

In the 1960 Olympics there was a marked difference in standards among the ice hockey teams. The Finns, and especially the Japanese and the Australians, lacked the necessary experience. Only their courage was admired. All were eliminated in preliminary rounds. In the consolation match the Japanese forced a tie with the stronger Finns.

The six who reached the final round were Czechoslovakia, Germany, Canada, Sweden, the U.S.S.R. and the United States. The Germans were quite outclassed by stronger opponents and found their play transparent and without tactical finesse. The Swedes, in their traditional yellow and blue, did not live up to expectations. Their match with Russia was a dogged fight, but the next day, strained by their supreme effort, they could not hold their own against Czechoslovakia. A day later they led Canada 4 to 1 but were finally defeated 5 to 6 by their technically and tactically clever opponents. The Czechs were elegant to watch. Often a danger, they were not good enough to score more than five goals from the Soviets, who won 8-5. The Soviets were the favorites. Their play at Cortina was remembered. They were ideally suited to ice hockey, with its demand for perfect teamwork, occasional bursts of individual brilliance, thoroughness and admirable condition.

There was a keen rivalry. Canada, many times Olympic champion in the past, was in 1956 pushed back to third place by the U.S.S.R. and the United States. The Canadians wanted to avenge this. In their match with America they had a chance to begin, and it was one of the toughest fights of the Olympics. The Americans attacked impetuously, knowing their goal was defended by the brilliant McCartan. They won by a goal and ended Canada's chance for a gold medal for the third time in the Olympics.

Two days later the United States and the U.S.S.R. met. The stadium was packed. Early in the game there was nervous play. After the first period the

Squaw Valley Ice Arena

Soviet Team Congratulating Winners

1960 U.S.A. Olympic Ice Hockey Team

Final Standings
1960 (Squaw Valley)

	Points	Goals
1. U.S.A.	10	29-11
2. Canada	8	31-12
3. U.S.S.R.	5	24-19
4. Czechoslovakia	4	21-23
5. Sweden	3	19-19
6. Germany	0	5-45

Soviets led 2-1. In the last thirty-five seconds the score was 3-2 in America's favor, and Russia made an all-out effort. A sixth field player replaced the Soviet goalie and their goal was empty. The Americans knew that they would only have to hang on to their advantage. As the seconds ticked by, the red figures on the luminous dial of the stadium clock were counted aloud by the thousands of spectators. Time was over. America won by a goal. It was the United States' first victory in an Olympic ice hockey tournament. Canada, the former masters, won the silver medal and the U.S.S.R. the bronze.

88

United States Scores Winning Goal

OVERVIEW TO 1960

The Olympic Ice Hockey Tournaments

As in figure skating, there had been an Olympic ice hockey tournament before the introduction of the Olympic Winter Games. It was held in the Antwerp Ice Palace in 1920 from April 23 to 29. Seven countries entered. Canada, with a great show of skating and technical superiority, began a series of Olympic victories that continued through the games in Oslo in 1952 and were interrupted only once, by Great Britain at Garmisch-Partenkirchen in 1936. Canada's superiority was stopped in 1956 at Cortina when the Soviet Union scored a surprise victory. Four years later at Squaw Valley the Americans were victorious. At all Olympic Games Canada was represented by club teams only, sometimes strengthened in some positions. After World War II, however, other countries sent better-prepared national teams to the Olympic tournaments.

At the first Olympic tournament in Antwerp in 1920, only the Americans could offer any resistance to the Maple Leaf team and got away with a 0-2 defeat. In contrast, the European nations were thoroughly beaten, Czechoslovakia losing 0-15 and Sweden losing 1-12.

Four years later at Chamonix the superiority of the Canadians was even more obvious. In the semifinals Canada scored a goal ratio of 85-0. Czechoslovakia lost 30-0, Sweden 22-0 and Switzerland 33-0. In the finals Great Britain lost 19-2. Again the Americans stood up, losing 6-1. In all five matches the Canadians scored a goal ratio of 110-3, a superiority that is unique in Olympic sports.

At St. Moritz in 1928 Canada was exempted to the semifinals. With entries from eleven countries, three groups of semifinals had to be played. Switzerland, Sweden and Great Britain were the group winners, but in the finals they were beaten by Canada 13-0, 11-0 and 14-0. For the third time the Canadians had confirmed their reputation as the masters of ice hockey. Their total goal ratio of 38-0 was again most impressive.

At the III Olympic Winter Games at Lake Placid in 1932 the Americans nearly surprised everyone. Because of the traveling expenses from Europe, only two European teams were entered in the competition. This left Germany, Poland, Canada and the United States. The Organizing Committee decided that the four teams would also have to play return matches. In this memorable tournament the Canadians met serious resistance for the first time. It was not from the European countries, since Germany lost 1-4 and 0-5 and Poland lost 0-9 and 0-10, but from the Americans. The U.S. players had learned a lot since 1928 from matches with their neighbor, and even more from Canadian guest players. The first match between Canada and the United States was a narrow win for Canada, 2-1 after extra time. The return match was a 2-2 draw with three periods of extra time.

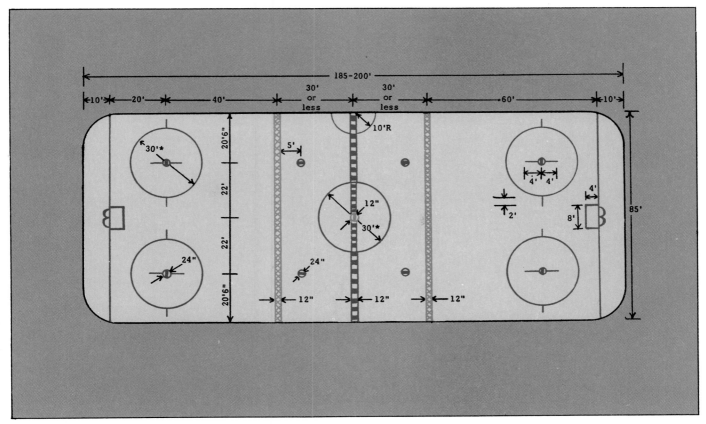

Ice Hockey Rink Specifications

Four years later in Garmisch-Partenkirchen fifteen countries entered the ice hockey tournament, still a record for entries. After the semifinals the two countries that had won first place in each of the four groups—Canada and Austria, Germany and the United States, Czechoslovakia and Hungary, Great Britain and Sweden—moved up into the intermediate round. Here the British team narrowly succeeded in beating the Canadians 2-1, and the Canadians lost their chance for the Olympic victory. They did move up, together with Great Britain, the United States and Czechoslovakia, into the finals, but there was no return match against Great Britain. According to the rules of the matches, the results from the intermediate round of participants in the finals automatically counted for the finals. The Canadians did beat the Americans, who had been considered their greatest competitors, 1-0. Olympic winner Great Britain took a 0-0 against the Americans in spite of three periods of extra time. The winning British team, incidentally, contained many Canadian-born players, some of whom had accepted British citizenship only shortly before.

At St. Moritz in 1948 the Czechs, who had moved into the top class of world hockey, held the Canadians to a 0-0 draw in the direct meeting, where the nine teams played in one group, each against the other. Because of the less favorable goal ratio, 80-16 against 69-5, they took the second-place silver

Czech Goalie

medal. The Olympic tournament was overshadowed by the fact that two American teams entered competition without the sanction of the I.O.C. One team was sent by the U.S.O.C., and the other by the AHA (American Amateur Hockey Association). Neither team was properly entered according to the rules. The AHA team was allowed to enter the games by the Swiss on an unofficial basis.

At the Olympic tournament in Oslo in 1952, the Canadians won again, scoring 3-3 against the United States, who, in turn, lost to Sweden 2-4. Sweden also held Canada to a 3-2 victory. Third place was hard fought between Sweden and Czechoslovakia, who had the same number of points and almost the same ratio of goals. A deciding match had to be played between the two countries for the bronze medal. The match took a dramatic turn two-thirds of the way through, with the Czechs leading 3-1. They seemed to have practically won the bronze when Sweden made a great effort and turned the contest into a 5-3 victory.

At Cortina in 1956 Canada lost its Olympic superiority. A year before, Canada had beat the Soviet team 5-0 in the Krefeld world championship final. Now, they lost in an upset against the United States with a clear 1-4.

92

Where's the Puck?

U.S.A. Beats Czechoslovakia 5-1

They still had a chance for the gold medal, however, if they could beat the Soviet Union by at least three goals. It didn't happen. The Soviets had a good team that had no weak points. With a 2-0 victory the Soviet Union became the winner, since they had also beaten the Americans 4-0. The Canadian team won the bronze medal, which was considered a failure in their home country. A great deal of controversy followed. It was felt that it was time for Canada to establish a national team made up of the best amateur players of the country, as was the practice with all other countries, instead of being represented by a club team.

Canada adhered to its tradition, however, and again nominated a club team for the Olympic tournament at Squaw Valley in 1960. It was the same team that caused the excitement at Cortina in 1956. The team did much better at Squaw Valley but did not quite fulfill all of their countrymen's hopes. They lost narrowly to the Americans 1-2 but had the satisfaction of winning 8-5 against the Soviet Union. They had the silver medal.

In their match against the Soviet Union the Americans had some tense moments but won 3-2. The gold medal seemed certain. On the last day the United States had to play Czechoslovakia, in a match that appeared to be a mere formality. The Czechs took an unexpected 4-3 lead. In the final third of

93

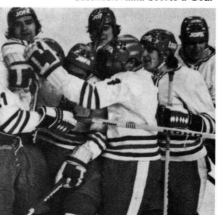

Czechoslovakia Scores a Goal

Soviet Player (16) Holding his Czech Opponent

Where's the Puck?

the match the Americans took hold, to storms of applause from the spectators. They turned out a 9-4 victory, the first American Olympic victory for ice hockey.

Olympic Medals in Ice Hockey

Since 1948 the Olympic ice hockey tournament has been played in championship fashion. Each team plays each other, at least in the finals. What this means is that there is no final match in ice hockey as, for example, there is in the Olympic football tournament, where each team that is beaten is automatically eliminated in cup fashion.

In ice hockey, probably the most strenuous of the team sports, the total team strength has been increased by the International Ice Hockey Federation to seventeen players—two goalkeepers, six back players and nine forward players. The International Olympic Committee awards seventeen medals for each of the first three places in gold, silver and bronze without asking whether the three teams in the best places have actually used all seventeen players in the course of the tournament. Thus the spare goalkeeper, who is usually a weaker player, is frequently not used, and also all six backs and all

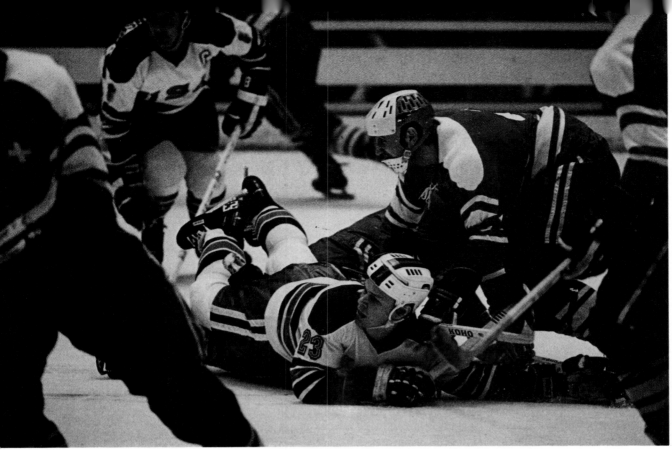

nine forwards are not always used. That is why in ice hockey it has happened that substitute players have been given Olympic medals and have not taken part in a single match of the tournament.

Number of Competitors in the Ice Hockey Tournaments through 1960

	1920 Antwerp	1924 Chamonix	1928 St. Moritz	1932 Lake Placid	1936 Garmisch	1948 St. Moritz	1952 Oslo	1956 Cortina	1960 Squaw Valley
Australia	—	—	—	—	—	—	—	—	17
Austria	—	—	12	—	12	17	—	17	—
Belgium	8	10	12	—	10	—	—	—	—
Canada	8	9	12	14	13	12	16	17	17
Czechoslovakia	8	11	12	—	13	16	17	17	17
Finland	—	—	—	—	—	—	17	—	17
France	7	12	11	—	11	—	—	—	—
Germany	—	—	11	10	12	—	15	17	16
Great Britain	—	10	12	—	12	14	—	—	—
Hungary	—	—	11	—	13	—	—	—	—
Italy	—	—	—	—	10	17	—	16	—
Japan	—	—	—	—	9	—	—	—	17
Latvia	—	—	—	—	11	—	—	—	—
Norway	—	—	—	—	—	—	17	—	—
Poland	—	—	11	10	11	17	16	17	—
Soviet Union	—	—	—	—	—	—	—	17	17
Sweden	10	10	12	—	13	16	17	17	17
Switzerland	7	11	12	—	12	17	17	17	—
U.S.A.	11	9	—	14	11	14	15	17	17
Participants	59	82	128	48	173	140	147	169	152
Countries	7	8	11	4	15	9	9	10	9

95

INNSBRUCK—1964

Russia's ice hockey team lived up to its favored status and took the Olympic championship, winning all seven games in the round-robin competition. Outscoring their rivals 54-10 in goals, the Soviets were 14 points ahead of Sweden, Czechoslovakia and Canada, all tied for second with identical five-won, two-lost records.

The U.S. teams, the upset winners in 1960 at Squaw Valley, won just two of their seven games. Sensational goal tending by Tom Yurkovich of Rochester, New York, and Pat Rupp of Detroit kept the Americans in contention in each contest despite the inexperience of the U.S. players. The 155-pound Rupp filled in for Yurkovich when the latter reinjured his left knee in the game against Canada. Rupp's 42 saves in that game prevented the Canadians from piling up many more points.

Yurkovich was first hurt in the first period against the Soviets when he lunged for a flying puck and tumbled onto the ice. Although in pain for the remainder of the game, he managed to make 58 saves, most of them spectacular. Injuries to defenseman Wayne Meredith of Minneapolis and assorted welts and bruises to several team members throughout the competition hampered the Americans.

Nevertheless the American team scored 29 goals in their seven games to place fifth among the eight teams in the A group.

GRENOBLE—1968

The ice hockey competition at Grenoble in 1968 provided one of the most exciting tournaments in memory. No dramatist could have plotted a bigger climax. Coming into the final matches, three teams were in the running for the gold medal—Russia, Czechoslovakia and Canada.
What made it even more exciting was that the final standings depended not only on how one match ended but also on the result of another match. All of this happened after the tournament's great sensation: the Czechs upset the Soviets 5-4 in the most memorable Olympic game in years. It was more than an ordinary athletic victory; it was a release of emotions for the Czechs, who had last conquered the Soviets seven years previously.

The next day the Czechs had what many thought would be a relatively easy match against Sweden, only to come away with a 2-2 draw, a natural letdown after their titanic effort the day before. Suddenly the Soviets had the way open and they took advantage of it by crushing the Canadians in the final, 5-0. Their teamwork was the key, although their speed and stickwork were almost equally impressive. There was little the Canadians could do.

U.S.A. and Canada Play to 1-1 Tie

Ice Hockey, 1968 (Grenoble)

Results of Games in Group A

	U.S.S.R.	Czech.	Can.	Swe.	Fin.	U.S.A.	West Ger.	East Ger.
1. U.S.S.R.	—	4-5	5-0	3-2	8-0	10-2	9-1	9-0
2. Czechoslovakia	5-4	—	2-3	2-2	4-3	5-1	5-1	10-3
3. Canada	0-5	3-2	—	3-0	2-5	3-2	6-1	11-0
4. Sweden	2-3	2-2	0-3	—	5-1	4-3	5-4	5-2
5. Finland	0-8	3-4	5-2	1-5	—	1-1	4-1	3-2
6. U.S.A.	2-10	1-5	2-3	3-4	1-1	—	8-1	6-4
7. West Germany	1-9	1-5	1-6	4-5	1-4	1-8	—	4-2
8. East Germany	0-9	3-10	0-11	2-5	2-3	4-6	2-4	—

Results of Games in Group B

	Yugo.	Jap.	Nor.	Rum.	Aus.	Fra.
9. Yugoslavia	—	5-1	3-2	9-5	6-0	10-1
10. Japan	1-5	—	4-0	5-4	11-1	6-2
11. Norway	2-3	0-4	—	4-3	5-4	4-1
12. Rumania	5-9	4-5	3-4	—	3-2	7-3
13. Austria	0-6	1-11	4-5	2-3	—	5-2
14. France	1-10	2-6	1-4	3-7	2-5	—

SAPPORO—1972

For a time in Sapporo it seemed as though the Olympic gold for ice hockey had lost its red-gold gleam for the Soviets and was taking on a blue-yellow shimmer for the Swedes as they drew 3-3 with the U.S.S.R. The final result was unchanged, however, and the Soviets once more became Olympic champions.

The tournament at Sapporo was extremely disappointing. The longer the tournament lasted, the louder became the call for the Canadians. The Canadians, five times Olympic champions, bronze medalists in Grenoble, did not compete because they were annoyed, as they had been before in the world championships. It was an ice hockey tournament without fire. Although there was no certainty about the medalists right up to the last day of the tournament, even the final day was disappointing. In the deciding game the U.S.S.R. beat the Czechs 5-2. It was an undramatic contest, with the U.S.S.R. already leading 4-0 before the Czechs closed up 2-4.

Some excitement was aroused when the U.S.S.R. played Sweden to a 3-3 draw, and one great surprise was the 5-1 victory of the United States over Czechoslovakia. An even greater surprise was the United States' silver medal. The Finns had helped by beating Sweden 4-3, thus ruining the latter's chances for a medal.

The opening game of the tournament set the tone when Sweden overwhelmed the United States 5-1. Then came the crucial test with Czechoslovakia, a team the United States had whipped a year earlier in world championship play. Curran was magnificent in this game, stopping 51 shots on goal as the United States tolled to a 5-1 triumph after the Czechs had opened the scoring in the first period.

The United States was whipped decisively 7-2 by the Soviets. With two games to play, the outlook was dim. The United States rallied and beat Finland 4-1. With a chance for a medal, the U.S. team outskated, outhustled and outshot Poland for a satisfying 6-1 victory, compiling a 4-0 lead in the first two periods as Sheehy, Boucha, Sarner and Irving all fired goals. In the third period, after Poland scored its only goal, the United States closed the contest with Sarner scoring again and Sheehy banging in the final tally.

The winning of the silver medal hinged on the final day's results. Finland scored its only triumph of the tournament over its foe Sweden, and the Soviet Union toyed with its nemesis Czechoslovakia while scoring a 5-2 victory.

Although the United States and Czechoslovakia had identical records of three victories and a pair of defeats, the silver medal was awarded the United States by virtue of its triumph over the Czechs.

United States Goalie Stops a Soviet Drive

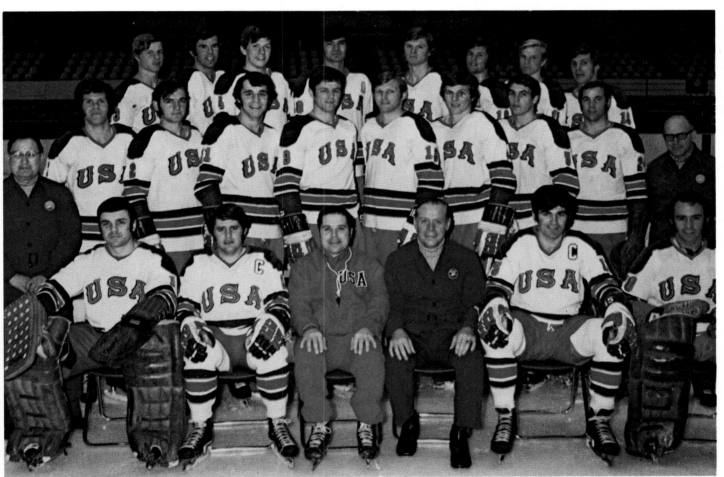

1972 U.S.A. Olympic Hockey Team

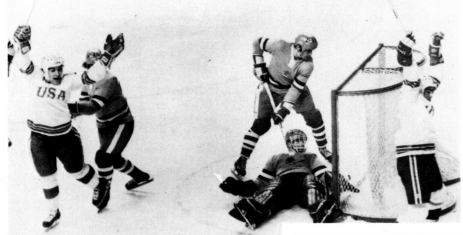

U.S.A. Scores in Qualifying Match
Against Yugoslavia

U.S.A. Scores Against Germany
at Innsbruck

West Germany Skates Past the U.S.A.

Fast Action in the Czechoslovakia-
West Germany Game

INNSBRUCK—1976

The West Germans were ecstatic. They had just won an Olympic bronze medal. They had beaten the U.S. team for that bronze.

The twenty Americans, whose average age was twenty-one, were the youngest U.S. team ever. For them, and for their coaches and managers, it was over. The six games in ten days were over. The breakfast here and the dinner there were over. The traveling and the hope for a medal were over. Even though the records of the two teams were identical, third place and the bronze medal were awarded on the basis of goals against each other in Olympic competition. The West Germans had been more productive in this area, and the medal was theirs.

In the beginning the U.S. hockey team needed a qualifying win against the Yugoslavs just to compete for any medal at all. They had beaten the Yugoslavs before, but this was Innsbruck, where emotions ran wild and the

U.S.A. Scores Against U.S.S.R. at Innsbruck

Czechs Down U.S.A. at Innsbruck

underdog suddenly became the equal. The winner of the qualifying game would face the top-seeded Soviet Olympic team, a team that was not missing any top players. After handling the Yugoslavs 8-4, the United States faced the Soviet team.

For the first two periods the Americans stayed with the Soviets. They skated with them, scored with them and checked with them. In the third the Soviets seemed to adjust to the determined Americans and left the ice the 6-2 victors. It was perhaps the Americans' best effort. They fought insurmountable odds and lost, and the effort was admirable. The coach expressed great pride in their determination.

Winners over the tough Finns, 2-1, the Czechs were next. The U.S. plan was the same, and the outcome was nearly the same, a 5-0 loss. The Finns were next.

Mixing It Up

Stop That Puck!

U.S.A. and Soviets Exchange Gifts

The Finns had beaten the highly regarded West Germans two days before and were ready for medal honors. The young U.S. squad turned the tables and beat the Finns 5-4. General Manager Berglund called it "one of the greatest moments in American Olympic hockey history. It resembled Squaw Valley when the United States won the gold in 1960."

Poland went down 7-2 and the contest was down to one game with West Germany. The winning team would be bronze medalist for the XII Winter Olympic Games, carrying with them the tangible reminder of their accomplishments for the rest of their lives.

The West German 4-1 victory turned out to be the surprise of the tournament.

Results, Ice Hockey
1976 (Innsbruck)

	G	W	L	For	Ag.	Pts.
U.S.S.R.	5	5	0	40	11	10
Czechoslovakia	5*	3	2	17	10	6
W. Germany	5	2	3	21	24	4
Finland	5	2	3	19	18	4
U.S.A.	5	2	3	15	21	4
Poland	5*	0	4	9	37	0

*Czechoslovakia forfeited 7-1 game with Poland. Czechoslovakia credited with loss, but Poland did not get victory. Czechoslovakia's goals were deleted from both teams' standings.

	U.S.S.R.	Czech.	Ger.	Fin.	U.S.A.	Pol.
U.S.S.R.	—	4-3	7-3	7-2	6-2	16-1
Czechoslovakia	3-4	—	7-4	2-1	5-0	*
W. Germany	3-7	4-7	—	3-5	4-1	7-4
Finland	2-7	1-2	5-3	—	4-5	7-1
U.S.A.	2-6	0-5	1-4	5-4	—	7-2
Poland	1-16	*	4-7	1-7	2-7	—

*Czechoslovakia forfeited game to Poland.

U.S.A. Passes It Away

American Congratulations

1976 U.S.A. Olympic Hockey Team

U.S.S.R. vs. Czechoslovakia

Top Contenders

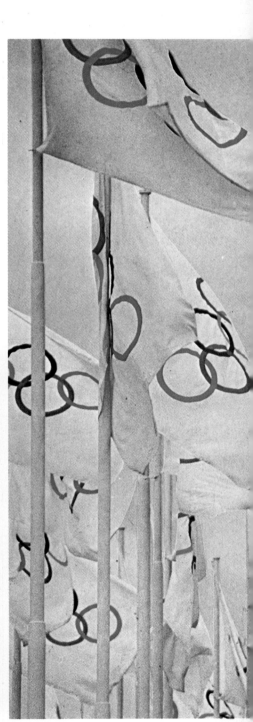

T he 1980 United States Olympic ice hockey team played a 55-game schedule, including 12 "home" games at the Metropolitan Sports Center in Bloomington, Minn., in preparation for the XIII Olympic Winter Games in Lake Placid. Ken Johannson was the general manager of the 1980 hockey squad.

The Metropolitan Sports Center was the headquarters for coach Herb Brooks' club. The home schedule began September 29 against the Minnesota North Stars of the National Hockey League. It marked the first time a U.S. international hockey team has played a NHL team.

The selection of the final U.S. squad will be determined in the fall of 1979, after subsequent matches evolve the top performers.

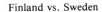

Finland vs. Sweden   U.S.A. vs. Canada

105

.A. Just Misses Tie-Breaking Goal Against Sweden

4

Alpine Skiing

CONTESTANT NUMBER ONE

About two hours after Anne Henning had won a bronze medal in the 1000-meter speed-skating final at Sapporo in 1972, Barbara Cochran was slowly walking up a Japanese mountain. She wore contestant banner number 1 over her ski jacket. A few minutes later, flying out of a dense cloud bank at the top of the course, she twisted and turned through the gates in a snowstorm at the bottom, to win the women's slalom. This gave the United States its first gold medal in Alpine skiing at the Olympics in twenty years.

Barbara, whose older sister, Marilyn, fell in the first of two runs, had a total time of 1:31.24 seconds. This gave the United States its third gold medal at Sapporo, the most America has won since Andrea Meade Lawrence was a double gold medalist in 1952.

Cochran had the fastest time on the first run—46.05 seconds. She then had the second-fastest time of 45.19 on the second run. These two runs gave her a winning margin of .02 second over Daniele Debernard of France, the silver medalist.

The Japanese referred to this woman skier from a farmhouse on the Winooski River in Vermont as *subarashii,* which means "beautiful and perfect." Barbara was one of four children coached by her father, Gordon (Mickey) Cochran. Though she was considered a possible medal winner, very few coaches or judges thought that she was capable of winning the gold. The field included a strong group of French women skiers led by Michèle Jacot, Britt Lafforgue, Danièle Debernard and Florence Steurer. After the first run Barbara led all skiers, although three of the French women were within a second of her lead time.

Quickly the weather started getting worse. It began to snow. As she climbed the second course slowly, she was intensely studying the snow at each gate. On this run she was starting fifteenth. This was a distinct advantage. The new soft snow on the course was being packed firm by each runner. Shrouded in snow and clouds at the top, she waited. "I tried not to think about my first run," she said later, "but I didn't want to worry too much about the second. So I just decided that I would do my best, and even if I fell I would have that good first run to remember."

Barbara Cochran, U.S.A.

107

Barbara Cochran, U.S.A.

It was now so foggy and snowy that Barbara could see only a few gates downcourse when she started. Already ahead of her, Debernard and Steurer had excellent times. Lafforgue had fallen near the end of an outstanding run that seemed worthy of the gold. Barbara flew downhill past thousands of Japanese grouped along the sides of the course, snow blurring their outline. As she skied through the finish gate her time was flashed electronically on the huge scoreboard. There was a brief pause, then a mighty shout of joy. The other American women racers ran over to congratulate and hug her. Barbara's brother Bobby and her boyfriend Rick Chaffee leaped over the fence holding back the crowd at the finish line. They hoisted her to their shoulders. She was laughing and crying at the same time. She had won the women's slalom at Sapporo by .02 second. Never before had an Olympic race been decided by such a narrow margin.

When Barbara was finally free from the mob of reporters, photographers and fans, she ran to the phone to call home. By now it was 2 A.M. in Vermont. Barbara's first comment to her mother was "Hi. It's me. I didn't think you'd mind." Her mom and dad were happy for her. They had watched her on live television. After Mickey Cochran watched his daughter win the gold medal he commented, "Well, it was almost perfect. But she did run it a little wide on the gates."

Nevertheless Barbara Cochran had proved to the world that she was number one!

Zeno Colò, Italy

Andreas Molterer, Austria

HISTORY OF ALPINE SKIING THROUGH 1960

It was not until Garmisch-Partenkirchen in 1936 that Alpine skiing was granted Olympic recognition. At first it was only for the Alpine combination: one total evaluation for downhill and slalom. The Olympic premiere was very impressive, and at the slalom races wonderful runs were witnessed by more than seventy thousand spectators, a figure never reached again at an Alpine skiing event.

Men's Downhill

The downhill race is the earliest competition of Alpine skiing. To get from a mountaintop down into the valley as quickly as possible was the first objective of the Alpine skiers. Courage, the distinct ability to stay up, an eye trained to recognize the shortest route and a mastery of the art of waxing are all factors playing a decisive part in downhill races, where top speeds up to 120 kilometers per hour are reached. It was only after World War II, at St. Moritz in 1948, that the downhill race was included in the Olympic Games as a separate competition. Ever since then it has been one of the highlights of the Winter Olympics; participants as well as spectators are seized by the frenzy of speed. The Frenchman Henri Oreiller, Zeno Colò of Italy, Toni Sailer from Austria and the Frenchman Jean Vuarnet were truly worthy Olympic winners.

Results of Men's Downhill through 1960

1960 (Squaw Valley)
1.	Jean Vuarnet, France	2:06.0
2.	Hans-Peter Lanig, Germany	2:06.5
3.	Guy Perillat, France	2:06.9
4.	Willy Forrer, Switzerland	2:07.8
5.	Roger Staub, Switzerland	2:08.9
6.	Bruno Alberti, Italy	2:09.1

1956 (Cortina)
1.	Anton (Toni) Sailer, Austria	2:52.2
2.	Raymond Fellay, Switzerland	2:55.7
3.	Andreas (Anderl) Molterer, Austria	2:56.2
4.	Roger Staub, Switzerland	2:57.1
5.	Hans-Peter Lanig, Germany	2:59.8
6.	Gino Burini, Italy	3:00.2

1952 (Norefjell, Oslo)
1.	Zeno Colò, Italy	2:30.8
2.	Othmar Schneider, Austria	2:32.0
3.	Christian Pravda, Austria	2:32.4
4.	Fredy Rubi, Switzerland	2:32.5
5.	William L. Beck, U.S.A.	2:33.3
6.	Stein Eriksen, Norway	2:33.8

1948 (St. Moritz)
1.	Henri Oreiller, France	2:55.0
2.	Franz Gabl, Austria	2:59.1
3a.	Karl Molitor, Switzerland	3:00.3
3b.	Rolf Olinger, Switzerland	3:00.3
5.	Egon Schöpf, Austria	3:01.2
6a.	Silvio Alvera, Italy	3:02.4
6b.	Carlo Gartner, Italy	3:02.4

Toni Sailer, Austria

Ernst Hinterseer, Austria

Men's Slalom

Also in the slalom, Olympic medals were first awarded in 1948. This is the event of the brilliant technicians and acrobats of skiing who must have complete mastery of their skis and their bodies. Also essential is a good "memory for figures," in order to find their way down through the many artificial obstacles (combinations of gates) in a smooth run. Through Toni Seelos, Austria played a pioneering role in the slalom in the thirties. The list of winners shows, besides Edi Reinalter from Switzerland, surprise winner of St. Moritz in 1948, only the Austrians Othmar Schneider, Toni Sailer and Ernst Hinterseer. A very good role in this "test of technicians" was also played by the Scandinavians with Stein Eriksen, Guttorm Berge and Stig Sollander. In his prime Stein Eriksen from Norway, the greatest stylist so far in Alpine skiing, was even superior to the Central European aces. In 1952, on familiar ground near Oslo, he started as the clear favorite, but was pushed into second place by the clever Austrian tactician Othmar Schneider.

Results of Men's Slalom through 1960

	1st Race		2nd Race		Total
	Time	Rank	Time	Rank	Time
1960 Squaw Valley					
1. Ernst Hinterseer, Austria	70.7	5	58.2	1	128.9
2. Matthias (Hias) Leitner, Austria	71.1	9	59.2	2	130.3
3. Charles Bozon, France	69.8	3	60.6	5	130.4
1956 Cortina					
1. Anton (Toni) Sailer, Austria	87.3	1	107.4	1	194.7
2. Chiharu Igaya, Japan	90.2	6	108.5	2	198.7
3. Stig Sollander, Sweden	89.2	5	111.0	3	200.2
1952 Oslo					
1. Othmar Schneider, Austria	59.5	3	60.5	2	120.0
2. Stein Eriksen, Norway	59.2	1	62.0	6	121.2
3. Guttorm Berge, Norway	61.1	6	60.6	3	121.7
1948 St. Moritz					
1. Edi Reinalter, Switzerland	67.7	3	62.6	1	130.3
2. James Couttet, France	67.5	2	63.3	4	130.8
3. Henri Oreiller, France	68.0	4	64.8	6	132.8

110

Christian Pravda, Austria

Stein Eriksen, Norway

Men's Giant Slalom

In the course of ever-increasing specialization, the giant slalom was introduced in the early fifties and also taken into the Olympic program in 1952. In return, the valuation of the combination was discontinued. By nature the giant slalom is like a downhill race, and in practice it is a downhill race under strict control though over shorter distances and with less difference of altitude.

In this contest the Austrian have shown their superiority, having won seven of the nine medals awarded in 1952, 1956 and 1960. Toni Sailer's victory at Cortina in 1956 is considered one of the greatest Olympic performances ever achieved. He beat his fellow countryman Anderl Molterer by no less than 6.2 seconds, a difference that would normally set two performances several classes apart.

Results of Men's Giant Slalom through 1960

1960 (Squaw Valley)
1. Roger Staub, Switzerland — 1:48.3
2. Josef (Pepi) Stiegler, Austria — 1:48.7
3. Ernst Hinterseer, Austria — 1:49.1

1956 (Cortina)
1. Anton (Toni) Sailer, Austria — 3:00.1
2. Andreas (Anderl) Molterer, Austria — 3:06.3
3. Walter Schuster, Austria — 3:07.2

1952 (Norefjell, Oslo)
1. Stein Eriksen, Norway — 2:25.0
2. Christian Pravda, Austria — 2:26.9
3. Toni Spib, Austria — 2:28.8

Men's Alpine Combined

Similar to the Nordic combined, the Alpine combined enjoyed a great reputation in the days when specialization had not progressed very far. The winner of the combined was considered the perfect all-round master who had to be equally versed in downhill and slalom. Thus at the Olympic premiere of Alpine skiing, only the Alpine combined was on the program. There were no medals yet for the specialists. Thus the Norwegians Laila Schou Nilsen and Birger Ruud, who ran the best times in the downhill race, had no chance of winning two gold medals. Twelve years later things had changed, for at St. Moritz in 1948 there was not only the Nordic combined but also individual contests in downhill and slalom. After 1948 the Alpine combined was discontinued in the Olympic Games. The giant slalom took its place.

Results, Men's Alpine Combined 1936, 1948

1948 (St. Moritz)
1. Henri Oreiller, France — 3.27
2. Karl Molitor, Switzerland — 6.44
3. James Couttet, France — 6.95

1936 (Garmisch-Partenkirchen)
1. Franz Pfnür, Germany — 99.25
2. Gustav Lantschner, Germany — 96.26
3. Emile Allais, France — 94.69

111

Trude Beiser-Jochum, Austria

Betsy Snite, U.S.A.

Results of Women's Downhill through 1960

1960 (Squaw Valley)
1. Heidi Biebl, Germany 1:37.6
2. Penelope (Penny) Pitou, U.S.A. 1:38.6
3. Traudl Hecher, Austria 1:38.9

1956 (Cortina)
1. Madeleine Berthod, Switzerland 1:40.7
2. Frieda Dänzer, Switzerland 1:45.4
3. Lucile Wheeler, Canada 1:45.9

1952 (Norefjell, Oslo)
1. Trude Jochum-Beiser, Austria 1:47.1
2. Annemarie Buchner, Germany 1:48.0
3. Giuliana Minuzzo, Italy 1:49.0

1948 (St. Moritz)
1. Hedy Schlunegger, Switzerland 2:28.3
2. Trude Beiser, Austria 2:29.1
3. Resi Hammerer, Austria 2:30.2

Women's Downhill

Trude Jochum-Beiser from Austria through 1960 was the only woman to have won Olympic victories in two consecutive Winter Games. To her victory in the Alpine combined in 1948 she added four years later a win in the downhill race. One of the best women downhill skiers in history was probably Madeleine Berthod from Switzerland. In Cortina in 1956 she beat all competitors by 4.7 seconds, an enormous lead in view of the fact that the total length of the course was not quite 1600 meters.

Women's Slalom

Past Olympic competitions in the women's slalom were in many ways remarkable. Almost always they brought great surprises, as neither Gretchen Fraser from America nor Renée Colliard of Switzerland nor Anne Heggtveit of Canada had been expected by the international experts to win. With two American victories and one Canadian victory, the women from North America did much better than in any other skiing competition.

Results of Women's Slalom through 1960

	1st Race		2nd Race		Total
	Time	Rank	Time	Rank	Time
1960 Squaw Valley					
1. Anne Heggtveit, Canada	54.0	1	55.6	2	109.6
2. Betsy Snite, U.S.A.	57.4	4	55.5	1	112.9
3. Barbi Henneberger, Germany	57.4	4	59.2	6	116.6
1956 Cortina					
1. Renée Colliard, Switzerland	55.6	1	56.7	1	112.3
2. Regina Schöpf, Austria	56.0	2	59.4	7	115.4
3. Eugenia Sidorova, U.S.S.R.	56.9	3	59.8	10	116.7
1952 Oslo					
1. Andrea Lawrence-Mead, U.S.A.	67.2	4	63.4	1	130.6
2. Ossi Reichert, Germany	66.0	1	65.4	2	131.4
3. Annemarie Buchner, Germany	67.6	8	65.7	3	133.3
1948 St. Moritz					
1. Gretchen Fraser, U.S.A.	59.7	1	57.5	2	117.2
2. Antoinette Meyer, Switzerland	60.7	4	57.0	1	117.7
3. Erika Mahringer, Austria	59.8	2	58.2	5	118.0

112

Slalom at Oslo, Norway, 1952

Trude Beiser-Jochum, Anne Marie Buchner, Germany

Andrea Mead Lawrence, U.S.A.

Ossi Reichert, Germany

Anne Marie Buchner, Germany

Andrea Mead Lawrence, U.S.A.

113

Andrea Mead Lawrence, U.S.A.

Watch those Gates!

**Results of Women's Giant Slalom
through 1960**

1960 (Squaw Valley)
1. Yvonne Rüegg, Switzerland   1:39.9
2. Penelope (Penny) Pitou, U.S.A.   1:40.0
3. Giuliana Chenal-Minuzzo, Italy   1:40.2

1956 (Cortina)
1. Ossi Reichert, Germany   1:56.5
2. Josefine (Puzzi) Frandl, Austria   1:57.8
3. Dorothea Hochleitner, Austria   1:58.2

1952 (Norefjell, Oslo)
1. Andrea Lawrence-Mead, U.S.A.   2:06.8
2. Dagmar Rom, Austria   2:09.0
3. Annemarie Buchner, Germany   2:10.0

**Results, Women's Alpine Combined
1936, 1948**

1948 (St. Moritz)
1. Trude Beiser, Austria   6.58   2:29.1
2. Gretchen Fraser, U.S.A.   6.95   2:37.1
3. Erika Mahringer, Austria   7.04   2:39.3

1936 (Garmisch-Partenkirchen)
1. Christel Cranz, Germany   97.06   5:23.4
2. Kathe Grasegger, Germany   95.26   5:11.0
3. Laila Schou Nilsen, Norway   93.48   5:04.4

Women's Giant Slalom

This competition is a good example of how close results have become since 1956. In 1952 the great Andy Lawrence-Mead won by a lead of 2.2 seconds. Four years later Ossi Reichert of Germany still won by a lead of 1.3 seconds. In Squaw Valley in 1960 it was only a tenth of a second that brought the gold medal to the Swiss surprise winner Yvonne Rüegg, ahead of Penny Pitou from America. Between first and sixth places there was a time difference of only eight-tenths of a second.

Women's Alpine Combined

For the women, as for the men, there were medals for the combined only at Garmisch-Partenkirchen in 1936 and at St. Moritz in 1948. On close examination of the results of those combined runs, the vast differences of time between the various places become apparent. That the famous Christel Cranz in the slalom could more than make up for arrears of 19 seconds out of the downhill race when she fell, seems incredible in view of the closenes of results today.

114

Haze is Bad

INNSBRUCK—1964

The slalom course at Innsbruck called for the skier to zigzag downhill through closely spaced gates in a test of control rather than speed. The rules require at least 65 gates for the men's 470-meter course; the women passed through at least 40 gates in 350 meters. In the giant slalom the gates were not so closely spaced, so the skier reached a much greater speed.

The downhill race is just what the name suggests—an all-out race against the clock over a course marked by a series of widely spaced gates. Some idea of the high speeds the skiers reach can be gathered from the fact that the Innsbruck downhill course dropped more than half a mile from start to finish. The American showing in the 1964 Olympics was a continuation of its effort four years previously. No individual Americans had been crowned champions in 1960, but their collective achievements were the finest in our history.

Jean Saubert, an Oregon State coed, tied for second place in the giant slalom and won a bronze medal in the slalom. Favored Christi Haas of Austria won the women's downhill competition, leading a sweep of the first three places for her nation. Starr Walton, Joan Hannah, Margo Walters and Saubert finished fourteenth, fifteenth, twenty-first and twenty-sixth.

Marielle and Christine Goitschel, two French sisters, traded places in the slalom events. Marielle took first in the giant slalom and second in the slalom. Christine reversed the order in both races. Saubert's time of 1:53.11 equaled that of second-place Christine in the giant slalom and was third in the other.

Egon Zimmerman took the lion's share of the men's Alpine events, winning the 3120-meter downhill race for Austria. He also took second to François Bonlieu of France in the giant slalom in a major upset. Austria's Pepi Stiegler won, as predicted, in the slalom. But he just edged American Billy Kidd, whose 60.31 run of the second course was the fastest of the event. Kidd took second and teammate Jim Heuga finished right behind, in third place. Wallace (Bud) Werner was eighth among fifty entries. Kidd led the American finishers, taking seventh, in the giant slalom, and Bill Marolt was twelfth among eighty finishers.

115

Alpine Course—Grenoble 1968

GRENOBLE—1968

Men's Downhill

The men's downhill course at Grenoble was 1 mile, 1400 yards long, with a vertical drop of 831 yards. It started at the Croix de Chamrousse and finished in Chamrousse, along the northwest slope of the mountain. Its gradient, with a 65-percent maximum and 29-percent average, made tremendous demands on the skiers' physical and mental resources. Guy Perillat of France was the first skier over the course. He raced in great style, taking the S bend magnificently and finishing with a time of 1:59.93—a very good performance by the French veteran, but how good nobody could tell, for lack of comparison. Soon one could tell, for none of the next eleven skiers managed to cover the course in under 2 minutes. Dätwyler of Switzerland was close, at 2:00.32, while the American Billy Kidd, the twelfth man down, had to favor an injured ankle and gave no serious challenge to Perillat's time. But after him came three Frenchmen, including Killy. Jean-Claude rose to the occasion, and, skiing in his inimitable manner, finished .08 second ahead of Perillat. No one could challenge this time; thus Killy added the Olympic gold medal in the downhill to his world championship, with Perillat taking the silver and Dätwyler, the bronze.

Results, Men's Downhill
1968 (Grenoble)

(88 participants from 29 countries. Chamrousse, Casserousse course. Start: 2252 meters. Finish: 1412 meters. Length of course 2890 meters. Feb. 9.)

1. Jean-Claude Killy, France	1:59.85		4. Heinrich Messner, Austria	2:01.03
2. Guy Perillat, France	1:59.93		5. Karl Schranz, Austria	2:01.89
3. Daniel Dätwyler, Switzerland	2:00.32		6. Ivo Mahlknecht, Italy	2:02.00

116

Jean-Claude Killy, France

The Course Looks Rough!

Jean-Claude Killy, France

Men's Giant Slalom

This race was taken in two legs on successive days, with the total time giving the results. The first *piste* was 1970 yards long, with a 492-yard drop. The second was 23 yards shorter and had 57 gates, 13 fewer than the first. The first day was blessed with ideal conditions, but the second was practically ruined by thick snowfall and fog. Once again it was Killy ahead of the field after the first day's run, and although he was beaten by Kidd the second day, he had built such a lead that the gold medal was easily his. Kidd makes a habit of concentrating on his final runs and had a fantastic race, particularly in view of the inconsistent nature of the course and his own bandaged ankle. His first day's time dropped him to fifth in the final standings.

Results, Men's Giant Slalom
1968 (Grenoble)

(102 participants from 33 countries. For the first time there were two courses. First course, Simond course. Start: 2090 meters. Finish: 1650 meters. Length of course: 1800 meters. 70 gates. Second course, Piste des Vallons. The start and finish were the same as in the first course. Length of course: 1780 meters. 57 gates. Feb. 12.)

	1st Run	2nd Run	Total
1. Jean-Claude Killy, France	1:42.74	1:46.54	3:29.28
2. Willy Favre, Switzerland	1:43.94	1:47.56	3:31.50
3. Heinrich Messner, Austria	1:45.16	1:46.67	3:31.83
4. Guy Perillat, France	1:44.78	1:47.28	3:32.06
5. Billy Kidd, U.S.A.	1:45.91	1:46.46	3:32.37
6. Karl Schranz, Austria	1:45.28	1:47.80	3:33.08

117

Vladimir Sabich 1968

Men's Slalom

The slalom eventually turned into a comedy of errors, but for Jean-Claude Killy—who else?—it had a happy ending. He gained his third gold medal, thus emulating Toni Sailor's feat at the 1956 games in Cortina. Just as the race began, the weather became even worse than it had been earlier, and instead of postponing the whole affair until the sun shone through again, the cardinal error was committed by allowing the race to continue. Thus the slalom was turned into an eerie show of fleeting shadows appearing and disappearing in the murky mist.

Ironically enough, the sun did make one appearance—during Killy's first run. The next set of errors involved two competitors: Haakon Mjön of Norway and Karl Schranz of Austria. Both of them beat Killy's time, only to find that they had missed two gates high on the course. Schranz's case was particularly strange: he told officials that he had to skid to a halt in order to avoid an observer who had suddenly crossed his path at gate 22. The officials accepted this and allowed Schranz to start over. He beat Killy's time, but was then disqualified for having missed gates 17 and 18 in the first run, before he was forced to stop at gate 22. But was the interloper responsible for his missing the gates? Why was Schranz allowed the extra run, if he missed gates before the intrusion occurred? Once he was allowed the extra run, should it have counted? These are questions too difficult for humans to answer. Austrians claimed first place for Schranz, but he was disqualified. Killy had won his third gold.

Results, Men's Slalom
1968 (Grenoble)

	1st Run	2nd Run	Total
1. Jean-Claude Killy, France	49.37	50.36	1:39.73
2. Herbert Huber, Austria	50.06	49.76	1:39.82
3. Alfred Matt, Austria	49.68	50.41	1:40.09
4. Dumeng Giovanoli, Switzerland	49.89	50.33	1:40.22
5. Vladimir Sabich, U.S.A.	49.75	50.74	1:40.49
6. Andrzei Bachleda Curus, Poland	49.88	50.73	1:40.61

118

U.S.A. Team, Grenoble

Women's Downhill

In this race the weather was fine and there were no disqualifications or protests, none of the things that marred the men's events. There was only the happiness of the winners and the disappointment of the losers.

With a course 2363 yards long and a vertical drop of 953 yards, the downhill had its start in Croix de la Chamrousse and its finish in the Skiing Stadium of Recoin. The event was won by a twenty-year-old Austrian girl, Olga Pall. She was .46 second faster than France's petite Isabelle Mir from the Pyrenees. Christl Haas, Austria, collected the bronze medal. The women's downhill used to be a purely Austrian affair, hence the delight of the French in Isabelle's success.

Results, Women's Downhill
1968 (Grenoble)

(41 participants from 14 countries. The Olympic course in Chamrousse. Start: 2525 meters. Finish: 1650 meters. Length of course: 2160 meters. Feb. 10.)

1. Olga Pall, Austria	1:40.87	4. Brigitte Seiwald, Austria	1:41.82
2. Isabelle Mir, France	1:41.33	5. Annie Famose, France	1:42.15
3. Christl Haas, Austria	1:41.41	6. Felicity Field, Great Britain	1:42.79

Women's Giant Slalom

This race was won by Canada's Nancy Greene. Her performance was 2.64 seconds better than that of France's Annie Famose. Nancy packed an incredible amount of attack and energy into her run and was, in her own words, "fighting all the way." The extremely long course—1761 yards with a 492-yard vertical drop—demanded stamina, technical skill and a good deal of courage. She was a highly popular winner.

Results, Women's Giant Slalom
1968 (Grenoble)

(49 participants from 18 countries. Gaboureaux course in Chamrousse. Start: 2101 meters. Finish: 1650 meters. Length of course: 1610 meters. 68 gates. Feb. 15.)

1. Nancy Greene, Canada	1:51.97	4. Florence Steurer, France	1:54.75
2. Annie Famose, France	1:54.61	5. Olga Pall, Austria	1:55.61
3. Fernande Bochatay, Switzerland	1:54.74	6. Isabelle Mir, France	1:56.07

119

Women's Slalom

The slalom at Grenoble was a battle between Nancy Greene, Marielle Goitschel of France and Annie Famose, the other French slalom champion. At first it looked, to everyone's surprise, as if the American foursome of Kiki Cutter, Rosie Fortna, Wendy Allen and Judy Nagel would spring a huge surprise, for in the first leg they had the four fastest runs—that was before the official results were known. Then the picture changed radically: Kiki, Rosie and Wendy were all disqualified, victims of their own dashing daredevil tempestuousness. The knowledge that she was the only American girl left must have upset Judy's well-known excitable nature, for she missed gate 10 on her second run and left the track. Nancy Greene had the fastest time in the second run, but it wasn't fast enough to catch Marielle Goitschel, whose 40.27 seconds in the first lag was, on the icy *piste,* an exceptionally good performance. Annie Famose won the bronze medal.

Results, Women's Slalom
1968 (Grenoble)

(49 participants from 18 countries. Chamrousse, slalom stadium. Start: 1806 meters. Finish: 1650 meters. Length of course: 425 meters; first course 56 gates, second course 57 gates. Feb. 13.)

	First Run	Second Run	Total
1. Marielle Goitschel, France	40.27	45.49	1:25.86
2. Nancy Greene, Canada	41.45	44.70	1:26.15
3. Annie Famose, France	42.21	45.68	1:27.89
4. Gina Hathorn, Great Britain	41.84	46.08	1:27.92
5. Isabelle Mir, France	42.14	46.08	1:28.22
6. Burgl Färbinger, W. Germany	42.70	46.20	1:28.90

Fransisco Fernandez Ochoa, Spain

Hank Kashiwa, U.S.A.   Bernhard Russi, Switzerland

The Beauty of Sapporo

SAPPORO—1972

Men's Downhill

Henri Duvillard and Bernhard Russi were regarded as the most likely winners of the men's downhill on the 2640-meter-long twisting slope on Mount Eniwa. The Swiss Russi started as number 4 in the race, whereas the Frenchman started at number 27, which is an unusually late position for a top skier. This was a winner-take-all move by the French. They had reckoned with new snow in the later group and speculated that a skier in this group would find better conditions. But the new snow did not play the game and their speculation failed. Russi, a perfect ski athlete, won in 1:51.43 minutes.

Not one single Frenchman was to be found among the first ten, but, in contrast, there were four Swiss in the first six. After the Swiss Russi and Collombin, the name Messner appears. A quiet man, Heinrich Messner had advanced as the Austrian hopeful. On this day he should have been in bed instead of hunting medals on Mount Eniwa. But Heini Messner presented himself to the starter, fought against both fellow competitors and the flu and was awarded the bronze medal.

**Results, Men's Downhill
1972 (Sapporo)**

1.	Bernhard Russi, Switzerland	1:51.43
2.	Roland Collombin, Switzerland	1:52.07
3.	Heinrich Messner, Austria	1:52.40
4.	Andreas Sprecher, Switzerland	1:53.11
5.	Erik Haker, Norway	1:53.16
6.	Walter Tresch, Switzerland	1:53.19

David Zwilling Turning

Werner Mattle, Switzerland

Roland Collombin, Switzerland

Men's Giant Slalom

The steepest giant slalom of all time was won by Gustavo Thoeni. At the end of the first run he lay third behind the Norwegian Erik Haker and the German Alfred Hagn. Following him were the Austrians Zwilling and Tritschler. The second run was begun by the skier with the fastest time the day before, nineteen-year-old Haker. He made mistakes that under normal circumstances he would never have made and finally fell. Gone was his dream of an Olympic victory. Thoeni had experienced Haker's misfortune himself two years previously during the world championship in Groeden, but in Sapporo he was another man; he was master of his role, remained on the attack despite Haker's fall and skied the second run perfectly.

After Haker had dropped out, someone else was unable to cope with the sudden vision of gold: the German Hagn. He played safe and lost every chance of a medal. The Austrian David Zwilling misjudged the situation as well. Although more experienced than Hagn, he also believed that he had to defend what he had not yet won—the bronze—and because of this he dropped back to seventh in the total list. The Swiss Bruggmann and Mattle reacted in exactly the opposite manner. They were not discouraged by tenth and eleventh places after the first run and managed to win the silver and bronze medals at the final count.

Results, Men's Giant Slalom
1972 (Sapporo)

(1st run—73 participants from 27 countries. Teineyama. Start: 952 m. Finish: 550 m. Length of course: 1034 m. Feb. 9/10, 1972.
2nd run—60 participants from 26 countries. Length of course: 1130 m. Feb. 10.)

	1st Run	2nd Run	Total
1. Gustavo Thoeni, Italy	1:32.19	1:37.43	3:09.62
2. Edmund Bruggmann, Switzerland	1:33.43	1:37.32	3:10.75
3. Werner Mattle, Switzerland	1:33.44	1:37.55	3:10.99
4. Alfred Hagn, W. Germany	1:31.78	1:39.38	3:11.16
5. Jean-Noel Augert, France	1:33.61	1:38.23	3:11.84
6. Max Rieger, W. Germany	1:33.86	1:38.08	3:11.94

122

Rolando Thoeni, Italy

Sapporo's Finish Line

Men's Slalom

In the slalom a Frenchman—Jean-Noel Augert, world champion—advanced to try for the gold. However, he was badly handicapped when he started the race, as he had had a bad fall during the classification race the day before and it was altogether doubtful if he would be able to race at all with his rib injury. The Austrian David Zwilling set the pace of the competition with the time of 57.30 seconds. The Spaniard Francisco Fernandez Ochoa caught attention with the time of 55.30. The Spaniard was a "foster child" of the French. He had often trained with them, and Augert had even given him tips.

On the second run Gustavo Thoeni rose to the occasion, whirled through the gates and registered the best time of all. But in the end it was the Spaniard Ochoa who placed the sensational full stop to the race: he was only .32 second slower than Thoeni and carried the gold medal off to Madrid. Rolando Thoeni achieved third place behind his cousin Gustavo. The Austrians were unable to hang on to their slalom tradition. The long line (Schneider, 1952; Sailer, 1956; Hinterseer, 1960; Stiegler, 1964) was not continued.

Results, Men's Slalom
1972 (Sapporo)

(1st run—73 participants from 25 countries. Teineyama. Start: 782 m. Finish: 554 m. Length of course: 530 m. Feb. 13.
2nd run—56 participants from 23 countries.)

	1st Run	2nd Run	Total
1. Francisco Fernandez Ochoa, Spain	55.30	53.91	1:49.27
2. Gustavo Thoeni, Italy	56.69	53.59	1:50.28
3. Rolando Thoeni, Italy	56.14	54.16	1:50.30
4. Henri Duvillard, France	55.92	54.53	1:50.45
5. Jean-Noel Augert, France	55.77	54.74	1:50.51
6. Eberhard Schmalzel, Italy	56.11	54.72	1:50.83

Karen Budge, U.S.A.

Women's Downhill

The Austrian Annemarie Pröll was expected to win the downhill. She had already won four of the five most important races during the winter leading up to the Olympic Games. She possessed the necessary self-confidence as well as strong nerves to go with it. When the French skier Françoise Macchi fell during training, one of her strongest competitors was no longer able to take part in the race.

Thus it had to be a decision between Pröll and Marie-Therese Nadig, Switzerland. It was in the upper part of the course that the Swiss girl skied the necessary hundredth of a second quicker that brought her victory. Thus, at seventeen, she became the youngest-ever gold medal winner of the Olympic downhill race. In the same race the young American Susan Corrock proved that her "nonstop" prerace best time was no accident by winning the bronze medal in 1:37.68.

Women's Giant Slalom

The giant slalom took place three days after the downhill. Annemarie Pröll had regained her confidence and wanted to take her revenge for her defeat in the downhill. She skied faultlessly, but even that was only good enough for silver. The victory in the downhill had acted as a stimulant for Marie-Therese—she proved to be simply unbeatable. In the previous season she had been completely unknown; in Sapporo she won two gold medals.

124

Barbara Cochran, U.S.A.

On the Course

Women's Slalom

The duel between Nadig and Pröll was not continued in the slalom. Here there was a dramatic contest between the American Barbara Cochran and the French girl Danièle Debernard. Young Danièle had to jump in for her injured team comrades Macchi, Lafforgue and Rouvier in order to give the French their long-desired prestige victory. Superb Michèle Jacot fell during the first run, Britt Lafforgue in the second after she had been lying third behind Cochran and Debernard at the end of the first run. This meant that by the second run one of the French girls trying to topple the twenty-one-year-old American had already fallen by the wayside.

Debernard had to catch up the .03 second she was behind Cochran after the first run. She managed 45.18 and the American, who started last in the second and decisive run, 45.19. Thus the seventeen-year-old Debernard was beaten and the girl from Richmond, Vermont, won the gold medal with a lead of .02 second. Never before had an Olympic race been decided by such a narrow margin. Florence Steurer, who was fourth in the giant slalom four years before at Grenoble, showed her perseverance and won the bronze. Annemarie Pröll played safe and gained fifth place, but her world champion's title did not compensate her for lost gold.

Results, Women's Slalom
1972 (Sapporo)

(1st run—42 participants from 13 countries. Teineyama. Start: 751 m. Finish: 567 m. Length of course: 450 m. Feb. 11. 2nd run—36 participants from 11 countries.)

	1st Run	2nd Run	Total
1. Barbara Cochran, U.S.A.	46.05	45.19	1:31.24
2. Danièle Debernard, France	46.08	45.18	1:31.26
3. Florence Steurer, France	46.57	46.12	1:32.69

Cindy Nelson, U.S.A.

INNSBRUCK—1976

Alpine skiing and Austria go together better than hot buttered rum and a roaring log fire after a day on the slopes. Austria had great hopes of capturing a lion's share of the medals in 1976 with its talented and deep skiers performing in their native Alps and before friendly crowds. If he had run for president the day after he won the men's downhill, Franz Klammer would have won with a record number of votes. Only three days later Austria was in mourning when Brigitte Totschnig, most successful of all racers in the pre-Olympic downhill competition, finished second.

There are compensations in every situation if you look for them. In the downhill the only non-Austrian who could win a gold medal and not make Austria mad was Rosi Mittermaier, West Germany. Three hours after she made her downhill rush at the Axamer Lizum slope, thousands of Olympic-goers were still chanting "Rosi, Rosi" and clamoring for the new heroine to make one more appearance on her hotel balcony. The victory came to Rosi after ten years of devotion to a sport that still occasionally leaves her afraid that a ski accident could cripple her for life. Those who understand and can interpret and interpolate speed and distance observed that if Rosi and Brigitte had raced side by side, the margin of victory would have been 15 yards.

But it was also a great day for the Americans. Discussing Cynthia Nelson's chances before the race, Hank Tauber, director of the U.S. Alpine effort, said, "It's the type of course where the finish places will fall to the best skier." Thus Tauber wasn't too surprised when Cindy won the bronze medal. Although the course was considered perfect for Cindy's skills, she did have prerace troubles solving the problems presented by the course. After the race Miss Nelson commented, "It was only the fourth time I've finished a complete run. I only finished three of seven training runs. There's a flat right before a series of S turns before the schuss to the finish. I lost my line and

126

Franz Klammer, Austria

had to make an extra turn to make a gate. If I'd skied a perfect race I would have won—but the same is true of Totschnig, too.''

The crowds were the largest in the history of the Olympic Games, many followers walking five or six miles to take up choice positions from which to catch a momentary glimpse of the speeding, schussing daredevils on the well-packed snow.

Pre-Olympic predictions were to prove almost meaningless. Who would have thought that the great Italian World Cup winner, Gustavo Thoeni, would not win a medal until the final event, the slalom, and that it would be silver in color? Alpine skiing is such a demanding sport that it is difficult for any skier to remain at the top for two Olympic Games. A comparison of 1972 and 1976 medalists shows that only three of sixteen medalists from Sapporo also won medals at Innsbruck—Gustavo Thoeni, Bernhard Russi and France's Danièle Debernard.

John Samuel, a British reporter, in describing Franz Klammer's downhill victory, commented, ''The downhill racing on the Patscherkofel produced results which could have been predicted by a computer. The top four in the World Cup standings at the time were tops in the Olympics, too. This Innsbruck downhill was the time when the Olympics did not bestow any of its customary favors on unknowns. Among the top ten finishers there were no surprises.''

Rosi Mittermaier commented after the downhill, ''After I finished, I was afraid to look at the scoreboard. Then my coach came and hugged me. This was the first downhill race my mother ever watched. She's always been afraid something would happen to me in downhill, particularly ever since my sister Evi, was badly injured.'' Three days later Rosi was back on the slopes at Axamer Lizum and, according to Rosi's sister, everyone from her hometown of Reit in Winkl was there except the aged and infirm.

127

Claudia Giordani, Italy Rosi Mittermaier, W. Germany Hanny Wenzel, Liech

Rosi Mittermaier, W. Germany

Slalom (two runs)
1. Rosi Mittermaier,
   W. Germany   1:30.54
2. Claudia Giordani, Italy   1:30.87
3. Hanni Wenzel, Liechenstein   1:32.20
4. Danièle Debernard, France   1:32.24
5. Pamela Behr, W. Germany   1:32.31
6. Linda Cochran, U.S.A.   1:33.24

Fred Tupper wrote in the *New York Times* after Rosi won her second gold medal, "Mama (as Rosi is known affectionately by the others on the international ski circuit) has done it again. Down icy tracks, for which she had been praying, the 25-year-old West German was second at the end of the first run and first in the second run for a combined time which was good enough to beat 20-year-old Claudia Giordani of Italy. Hanni Wenzel of Liechtenstein, sixth after the first run, ended up with the bronze medal. Two members of the United States team, Lindy Cochran and Mary Seaton, took sixth and tenth. The only American who was able to run both courses without any serious error was Cochran, a 22-year-old whose sister Barbara Ann had won the gold medal in the slalom four years ago. 'The second course was much better,' Lindy said after the race. 'The first course (51 gates set on a steep slope with a vertical drop of 800 feet) was icy and turny. But I think I skied well for me. Actually, I was delighted with the result.'"

As the men moved into the slalom and giant slalom events it was conceded that the Italians and Swiss would be battling for the medals, with Sweden's Ingemar Stenmark capable of sweeping both events. The long, difficult, steep course at Axamer Kizum was more than the usually unflappable Gustavo Thoeni could handle. He finished out of the money in fourth place and only .67 second ahead of Phil Mahre of the United States. The winner was Heini Hemmi, a twenty-seven-year-old who scored his first major international triumph in eight years of racing. "I was counting on some luck," Hemmi said. "I thought that on a very difficult course like this even a great champion like Thoeni could make a mistake and that's what finally happened."

The stark drama of the giant slalom had all the earmarks of a fiction story. With a crowd of twenty-five thousand looking on, Phil Mahre, starting

128

Rosi Mittermaier, W. Germany   Rosi Mittermaier, W. Germany   Kathy Kreiner, Canada   Daniele Debernara, France

sixth, took the early lead and appeared, with any luck, to be a medal winner. But Stenmark came with a flawless run to bump Phil to second. Then it was Hemmi's turn. He couldn't duplicate Stenmark's run, but the time advantage he had held from the day before was enough to put him into first place. When Hemmi crossed the finish line, Thoeni was already on the course. He registered a respectable halfway time, but in the final dozen gates on a particularly deep pitch he slid wide and had to fight to get back through the next gate. He never recovered and ended up a disappointing and temporary third. But the scene had not ended. Good, from Switzerland, running last in the first seed, held everything together to edge into second and collect the silver medal.

Although the results for the United States were encouraging—Phil Mahre fifth, Greg Jones ninth, Steve Mahre thirteenth and Cary Adgate twenty-first, Phil and Greg felt that the United States could do even better.

Two events remained on the Alpine program for 1976, the women's giant slalom and the men's slalom. The giant came first and it was the day Rosi Mittermaier was "going for all the marbles," a clean sweep of the three events never before accomplished by a woman. But it was not meant to be. By .12 second, Rosi missed the grand slam of Alpine skiing. With the world yelling encouragement, she finished second to Kathy Kreiner, an eighteen-year-old Canadian who had won only one major race in her life. After the race Rose said, "Lower down I made a mistake. I skied into a gate too directly. Actually, I'm very happy with the silver. I had not counted on such success." Lindy Cochran in twelfth place was the first of the four Americans to finish.

Giant Slalom (two runs)

1. Heini Hemmi, Switzerland		3:26.97
2. Ernst Good, Switzerland		3:27.17
3. Ingemar Stenmark, Sweden		3:27.41
4. Gustavo Thoeni, Italy		3:27.67
5. Phil Mahre, U.S.A.		3:28.20
6. Engelhard Pargatzi, Switzerland		3:28.76

Giant Slalom (single run)

1. Kathy Kreiner, Canada		1:29.13
2. Rosi Mittermaier, W. Germany		1:29.25
3. Daniele Debernard, France		1:29.95
4. Lisa-Marie Morerod, Switzerland		1:30.40
5. Marie Therese Nadig, Switzerland		1:30.44
6. Monika Kaserer, Austria		1:30.49

129

Piero Gros, Italy

Stenmark Ingemar, Sweden

And then the windup, the men's slalom with two runs on a single day. It was an intriguing challenge faced by Italy's Thoeni. He was sure he was the favorite, but perhaps preying on his mind was Olympic Alpine history: no skier had ever won gold medals in two Olympic Games. Gustavo had captured a gold at Sapporo in the giant slalom, and a silver in the slalom.

Slalom (two runs)
1. Piero Gros, Italy   2:03.29
2. Gustavo Thoeni, Italy   2:03.73
3. Willy Frommelt,
   Liechtenstein   2:04.28
4. Walter Tresch, Switzerland   2:05.36
5. Christian Neureuther,
   W. Germany   2:06.56
6. Wolfgang Junginger,
   W. Germany   2:07.08

Piero Gros, an Italian, got the gold medal in the slalom that he had predicted before the games he was going to get in the giant slalom. The course for the slalom was the trickiest—and steepest—faced by the slalomists in the current racing season. Gros's time at the intermediate mark was 34.01 seconds, by far the fastest of any racer. He continued just as fast, roaring down to the finish line. The crowd was already cheering as he flashed through the barrier for an elapsed time of 2:03.29 for the two runs.

Thoeni, two racers after Gros, was 1.18 seconds slower than his teammate and was relegated to second place. Along with the personal disappointment of Thoeni was the failure of Ingemar Stenmark of Sweden, the leader in the World Cup standings at that time. Ninth after the first run, Ingemar tumbled when a falling ski pole caught his trailing ski.

Piero Gros was completely candid in his postrace interview, saying, "I really never thought that I'd win gold. But I traveled to Innsbruck to bring a medal—at least one—home. After the first run I was as sure as I could be that I could never beat Thoeni. In my opinion at that time, Gustavo already had the gold medal in his pocket."

Thus on the next to closing day for the XII Olympic Winter Games the curtain was rung down on the six Alpine events. For months to come Alpine specialists will rehash the Innsbruck events. Really, it was more of a story than just Rosi and Franz—but they were wonderful, as were all the other medalists, along with some great skiers who didn't win a thing.

Franz Klammer, Austria

Piero Gros, Italy

Gustavo Thoeni, Italy

Heini Hemmi, Switzerland

131

Willy Frommelt, Liechtenstein

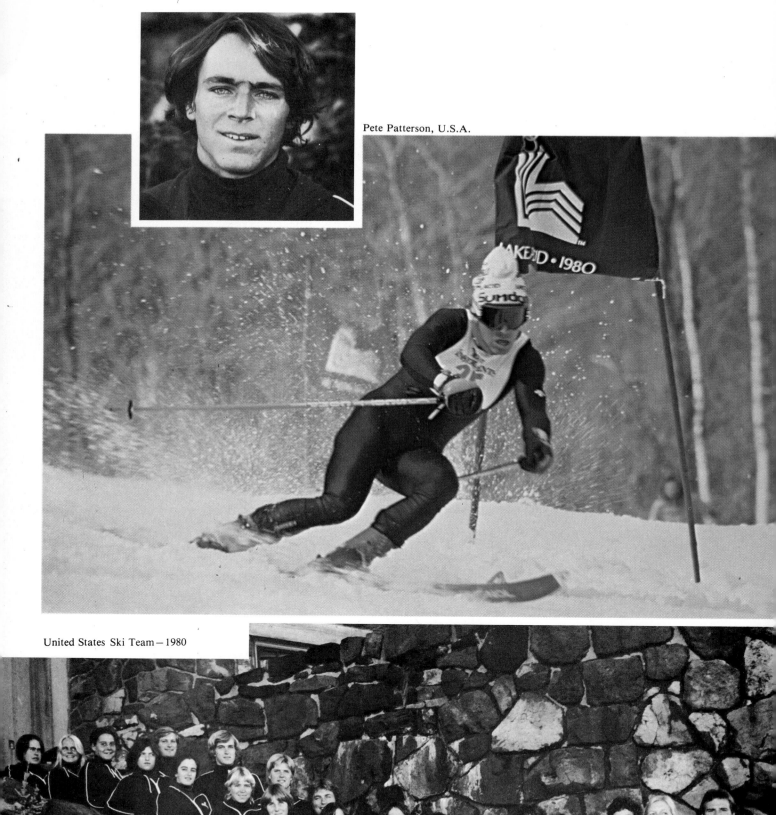

Pete Patterson, U.S.A.

United States Ski Team — 1980

Top Contenders

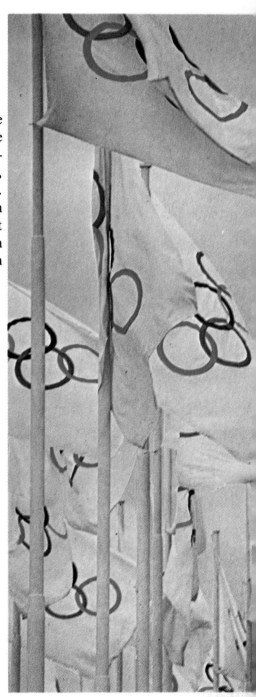

One of the final Alpine races before the 1980 Olympics was the downhill and giant slalom World Cup ski races at Whiteface Mountain, Lake Placid, in March 1979. At that time the twenty-one-year-old U.S. skiing star Phil Mahre, from White Pass, Washington, was in second place in the overall World Cup standings with 155 points. Mahre moved into second place behind Peter Lüscher of Switzerland in February 1979 after the World cup slalom and giant slalom competition at Are, Sweden. Three-time overall champion Ingemar Stenmark of Sweden was in third place with 149 points and Andreas Wenzel of Liechenstein in fourth place with 124 points.

The downhill portion of these World Cup races was won by Peter Wirnsberger from Austria. He was .03 second faster than Switzerland's Peter Müller. The race was a disappointment, however, for America's Mahre, who did not finish in the top twenty-five contestants.

Things got even worse for Phil the next day at the giant slalom. America's top Alpine skier dove through the starting gate and flew down the course. Halfway down the race he swung wide, bumping one gate, and then banged into the thirty-fifth gate at full speed and broke his left leg.

"It's bad luck," commented Ingemar Stenmark, who won the giant slalom with a total time of 2:38.93 (over 2 seconds ahead of Austria's Hans Enn). "He had a good chance to win the slalom cup, too. I'm sure he'll come back next year."

Phil Mahre, U.S.A.

Heidi Preuss, U.S.A.

Phil Mahre, U.S.A.

Cindy Nelson, U.S.A.

Christin Cooper, U.S.A.

Becky Dorsey, U.S.A.

Peter Patterson, U.S.A.

Cindy Nelson, U.S.A.

In addition to the World Cup leaders, one of the leading contenders during the competition at Whiteface Mountain was Franz Klammer of Austria, who captured the 1976 Olympic downhill gold medal at Innsbruck. Klammer had won the downhill title for the past four seasons but hit a slump in 1979 year and currently ranked twenty-second. But the famous Austrian ski star and national hero is far from retiring. He was in the Adirondack Mountains training for the World cup races in March 1979, but he knows that the 1980 Olympic Winter Games will be held on the same Alpine trails.

"I came over ahead of the other team members to look at the courses. Now I know what I must do for 1980. Winning a medal in 1980 is not the most important thing, but it would be nice," he said. Klammer won the downhill medal at Innsbruck in 1976 in a famous run when he pushed so hard he appeared to be on the verge of disaster.

Among the other top downhillers in the world are Peter Müller and Peter Lüscher of Switzerland and Ken Read and Steve Podborski of Canada. Lüscher's strongest discipline is the giant slalom. Sepp Ferstl of West Germany, who won the U.S. National downhill in February 1979, is another

Steve Mahre, U.S.A.

Viki Fleckenstein, U.S.A.

Tamara McKinney, U.S.A.

Abbi Fisher, U.S.A.

Heini Hemmi, Switzerland   Ingemar Stenmark, Sweden

Steve Mahre, U.S.A.

strong contender. In the giant slalom Stenmark is the powerhouse and leads the standings. Heini Hemmi of Switzerland ranks third in the world in that event. Other U.S. contenders include Cary Adgate, Boyne City, Michigan; Ron Biedermann, Stowe, Vermont; Steve Mahre, White Pass, Washington (Phil's twin brother); Andy Mill, Aspen, Colorado; and Pete Patterson, Sun Valley, Idaho.

In the women's downhill Annemarie Moser-Proll of Austria is the 1979 overall leader and heads the downhill standings. She will get her top American challenge from Cindy Nelson of Lutsen, Minnesota, who won the Olympic bronze medal at Innsbruck in the downhill. Nelson placed second in the national downhill championship in 1979 behind Irene Epple of West Germany. In addition, Marie-Therese Nadig of Switzerland and Evi Mitermaier of West Germany are expected to be strong contenders in the downhill events. In addition to Cindy Nelson, also on the strong U.S. Alpine A team are Christin Cooper, Sun Valley, Idaho; Becky Dorsey, Wenham, Massachusetts; Viki Fleckenstein, Syracuse, New York; Abbi Fisher, South Conway, New Hampshire; Jamie Kurlander, McAfee, New Jersey; and Susie Patterson, Sun Valley, Idaho.

Franz Klammer, Austria

135

5

Nordic Skiing

FIFTY-YEAR WAIT FOR MEDAL

With the introduction of the Olympic Winter Games in 1924 at the French resort of Chamonix in the heart of the Alpine ski country, the skiing program was restricted to Nordic events—cross-country runs, ski jumping, and the Nordic combined competition.

That this Nordic program embraces ten of the thirty-seven events scheduled for the Olympic Winter Games attests to its all-round acceptance. The United States is still considered in a development stage in these disciplines, even though Anders Haugen won a bronze medal in the Nordic combined competition fifty years after the close of the first Olympic Winter Games when an error in computation was discovered by the Norwegian National Olympic Committee.

Haugen was credited with a fourth-place finish in the ski-jumping portion of the Nordic event at Chamonix in 1924. He was given a score of 17.916 at the end of the games, just a shade behind the score of 18 given to Thorleif Haug of Norway in third place. A 1974 check of the final results indicated Haug's score was in error. So on September 12, 1974, accompanied by William Berry from the U.S. National Ski Hall of Fame, Anders Haugen received his medal in special ceremonies at the Norway Ski Museum.

The second medal won by an American in the Nordic events was captured by Bill Koch in 1976 at Innsbruck in the 30-kilometer cross-country race. He received the coveted silver only moments after the last runner crossed the finish line at Seefeld. The drought at last had been broken.

THE EVENTS IN NORDIC SKIING THROUGH 1960

Norway is to be considered the home of the Nordic types of skiing. With the Huseby races starting in 1879 and the Holmenkollen races in 1892, Norway has pioneered for skiing as a type of competition sport. The Holmenkollen races achieved worldfame, and as long as the Norwegians clearly dominated ski jumping and the Nordic combination, a victory at this event was valued higher than an Olympic victory.

Anders Haugen, Norway

137

L-R William Banks Berry, Robert Beattie, Anders Haugen

Originally special attention was given to the Nordic combination (17- to 18-kilometer cross-country race and jumping), and right into the 1930s the winner of this competition was in most countries considered the national champion. He was looked upon as a well-trained all-round master of cross-country running as well as of jumping. With increasing specialization, the individual contests achieved equal status with the combined. It was in 1900 that on Holmenkollen a 30-kilometer cross-country event was run. It was extended to 50 kilometers in 1902. Thus a standard program had been created which was retained until after World War II. It was only after 1950 that the International Skiing Federation introduced the splitting of cross-country skiing into 15-, 30- and 50-kilometer races.

In an age when the rapid progress of the automobile seems to eliminate the necessity for exercise, it is all the more astonishing to some people that long-distance athletic races are still being run. Moreover, they are among the most popular of athletic events. There is a certain type of people who refuse to yield to the comforts of technical progress and addict themselves to long-distance feats of endurance that require severe and disciplined training over many years. It is not surprising that in their enthusiasm skiers sometimes exceed their physical limitations and break down, unable to continue. Scientists who have studied this question sometimes express surprise that under the command of an iron will the human body can deliver as much as it does. But in every case there is a limit beyond which even the strongest will is of no avail.

It is no exaggeration to say that the strains involved in cross-country championship skiing are gigantic. It is hard to imagine the speeds that the best skiers can reach in covering 50 kilometers. Most take a fierce delight in the contest and apply themselves with a vigor and concentration that blot out the rest of the world during those hours. Without such devotion it would be impossible to hope for success in these competitions. Once on the track there is only the urge to press forward with a discipline that conserves enough strength to make sure the competitor lasts the distance. To tire before the finishing line means a hopeless loss of time.

Hallgeir Brenden, Norway

First-class times in cross-country skiing can be achieved only by the competitor who utilizes every trick of the trade. Each push of the poles is important; the manner of stride counts as much as instant adaptability to the course as its characteristics continually change. The rise and fall of the ground must be exploited rhythmically, as must be the fractional pause between strides—sometimes hardly perceptible, sometimes drawn out a little longer. It is this succession of short pauses that enables the skier to keep up a cracking pace for an hour or more.

A cross-country skier, to be acknowledged as an expert, must possess in his repertoire every imaginable means of changing direction on the sharp corners or the gently rounded bends. Step turns and swings must follow each other with as little time loss as possible. Stemming, or "snow ploughing," means the loss of precious seconds that can never be regained.

For many years cross-country races were not very popular in the United States, although even before 1869, immigrating golddiggers used to compete in races on unwieldly rough planks that they called skis. Their "racing skis" were up to twelve feet long and the winner could jingle a hundred-dollar prize in his pocket until he reached the gambling saloon.

From this era we have the story of "Snowshoe Thompson," born in Norway, of legendary strength and famous for a beard that refused to turn gray. Under the most rigorous conditions and hardships Thompson carried mailbags weighing more than seventy pounds to the mining camps when they were cut off from the outside world by high walls of snow. His toughness and endurance were incredible. In 1856 he is known to have frequently carried a heavy load over the ninety miles between Diamond Valley and Placerville. Today a tombstone with two crossed skis reminds us of Snowshoe Thompson. It seems that people accustomed to hard work have the endurance required by cross-country skiing.

Erik August Larsson, Sweden 1936—Gold

Hallgeir Brenden, Norway

18-Kilometer Cross-Country Race

Up to 1960 the most successful ski sprinter of the Olympic Games was Hallgeir Brenden from Norway, who in 1952, at the age of twenty-three, won in his native land and who repeated his Olympic victory four years later in Cortina. The great Olympic winners were Johan Gröttumsbraaten from Norway (1928) and the Swede Sven Utterström (1932), both of whom won with a lead of 2 minutes. The closest result up to 1960 was that of the 15-kilometer race in Squaw Valley, where the difference in time between the victorious Norwegian Brusveen and the Swede Jernberg, in second place, was only 3.1 seconds and where even the Finn Hakulinen, in third place, was only 7.5 seconds slower than the winner.

Results of 18-Kilometer Cross-Country through 1960

	Time
*1960 (Squaw Valley)**	
1. Haakon Brusveen, Norway	51:55.5
2. Sixten Jernberg, Sweden	51:58.6
3. Veikko Hakulinen, Finland	52:03.0
*1956 (Cortina)**	
1. Hallgeir Brenden, Norway	49:39.0
2. Sixten Jernberg, Sweden	50:14.0
3. Pavel Kolchin, U.S.S.R.	50:17.0

1952 (Oslo)
1. Hallgeir Brenden, Norway 1:01:34.0
2. Tapio Mäkelä, Finland 1:02:09.0
3. Paavo Lonkila, Finland 1:02:20.0
6. Martin Stokken, Norway 1:03:00.0

1948 (St. Moritz)
1. Martin Lundström, Sweden 1:13:50.0
2. Nils Östensson, Sweden 1:14:22.0
3. Gunnar Eriksson, Sweden 1:16:06.0

1936 (Garmisch-Partenkirchen)
1. Erik-August Larsson, Sweden 1:14:38.0
2. Oddbjörn Hagen, Norway 1:15:33.0
3. Pekka Niemi, Finland 1:16:59.0

1932 (Lake Placid)
1. Sven Utterström, Sweden 1:23:07.0
2. Axel T. Wikström, Sweden 1:25:07.0
3. Veli Saarinen, Finland 1:25:24.0

1928 (St. Moritz)
1. Johan Gröttumsbraaten, Norway
  1:37:01.0
2. Ole Hegge, Norway 1:39:01.0
3. Reidar Ödegaard, Norway 1:40:11.0

1924 (Chamonix)
1. Thorleif Haug, Norway 1:14:31.0
2. Johan Gröttumsbraaten, Norway
  1:15:51.0
3. Tapani Niku, Finland 1:26:26.0

Oddbjorn Hagen, Norway 1936 — Gold — Silver | Veikko Hakulinen, Finland

30-Kilometer Cross-Country Race

The International Skiing Federation decided to put a "medium distance" of 30 kilometers between the 18 and the 50 kilometers, and to reduce the former to 15 kilometers. The first 30-kilometer cross-country race was held at the world championships in Falun in 1954. Many skiers, such as the Finn Veikko Hakulinen and the Swede Sixten Jernberg, master all three distances equally well.

50-Kilometer Cross-Country Race

One of the best skiers in the 50 kilometers was the Swede Per Erik Hedlund, who in 1928 left his fellow countryman Gustaf Jonsson, who came second, 13:27 minutes behind. The hardest fights developed in 1932 and 1960, when there was only 20 seconds difference between the Finns in first and second places. The winning times differed tremendously—the longest time was needed by the Swede Hedlund in 1928 with 4:52.03 hours, the shortest by the Swede Jernberg in 1956 and 2:50.27. They cannot be compared with each other, as the type of ground as well as the snow and weather conditions play a considerable part and the distance of the course is not always measured exactly.

Results of 30-Km. Cross-Country

	Time
1960 (Squaw Valley)	
1. Sixten Jernberg, Sweden	1:51:03.9
2. Rolf Rämgård, Sweden	1:51:16.9
3. Nikolai Anikin, U.S.S.R.	1:52:28.2
1956 (Cortina)	
1. Veikko Hakulinen, Finland	1:44:06.0
2. Sixten Jernberg, Sweden	1:44:30.0
3. Pavel Kolchin, U.S.S.R.	1:45:45.0

Results of 50-Km. Cross-Country through 1960

	Time
1960 (Squaw Valley)	
1. Kalevi Hamäläinen, Finland	2:59:06.3
2. Veikko Hakulinen, Finland	2:59:26.7
3. Rolf Rämgård, Sweden	3:02:46.7
1956 (Cortina)	
1. Sixten Jernberg, Sweden	2:50:27.0
2. Veikko Hakulinen, Finland	2:51:45.0
3. Fiodor Terentyev, U.S.S.R.	2:53:32.0

1952 (Oslo)	
1. Veikko Hakulinen, Finland	3:33:33.0
2. Eero Kolehmainen, Finland	3:38:11.0
3. Magnar Estenstad, Norway	3:38:28.0
1948 (St. Moritz)	
1. Nils Karlsson, Sweden	3:47:48.0
2. Harald Eriksson, Sweden	3:52:20.0
3. Benjamin Vanninen, Finland	3:57:28.0

1936 (Garmisch-Partenkirchen)	
1. Elis Wiklund, Sweden	3:30:11.0
2. Axel Wikström, Sweden	3:33:20.0
3. Nils-Joel Englund, Sweden	3:34:10.0
1932 (Lake Placid)	
1. Veli Saarinen, Finland	4:28:00.0
2. Väinö Liikkanen, Finland	4:28:20.0
3. Arne Rustadstuen, Norway	4:31:53.0
1928 (St. Moritz)	
1. Per Erik Hedlund, Sweden	4:52:03.0
2. Gustaf Jonsson, Sweden	5:05:30.0
3. Volger Andersson, Sweden	5:05:46.0
1924 (Chamonix)	
1. Thorleif Haug, Norway	3:44:32.0
2. Thoralf Strömstad, Norway	3:46:23.0
3. Johan Gröttumsbraaten, Norway	3:47:46.0

Veikko Hakulinen, Finland

Tapio Mäkela, Finland—Silver

Relay Race, 4 × 10 Kilometers

The 4 × 10-kilometer cross-country skiing relay started in 1936. Of the five relay races held through 1960 the Finns won three and finished second twice. The most impressive victory, however, was that of the Swedes at St. Moritz in 1948, when they won by a lead of almost 9 minutes. Garmisch-Partenkirchen in 1936 and Squaw Valley in 1960 saw dramatic finishes between the Finns and the Norwegians. They were decided in the last few meters and were the highlights of those games. Here again, for the reasons already mentioned, the total times cannot be compared, although it is obvious that the times run have become shorter.

Results of 4 × 10-Km. Relay through 1960

	Total Time
1960 (Squaw Valley)	
1. Finland	
(Alatalo 35:03, Mäntyranta 34:45,	
V. Huhtala 35:01, Hakulinen 33:56.6)	2:18:45.6
2. Norway	
(Grönningen 35:07, Brenden 34:41,	
Östby 34:41, Brusveen 34:17.4)	2:18:46.4
3. U.S.S.R.	
(Shelyuchin 37:17, Vaganov 34:22,	
Kusnetsov 35:11, Anikin 34:31.6)	2:21:21.6
1956 (Cortina)	
1. U.S.S.R.	
(Terentyev 33:25, Kolchin 33:05,	
Anikin 34:23, Kusin 34:37)	2:15:30.0
2. Finland	
(Kiuru 34:56, Kortelainen 34:20,	
Viitanen 33:34, Hakulinen 33:41)	2:16:31.0
3. Sweden	
(L. Larsson 35:46, Samuelsson 34:22,	
P.E. Larsson 33:50, Jernberg 33:44)	2:17:42.0
1952 (Oslo)	
1. Finland	
(Hasu 35:01, Lonkila 35:22,	
U. Korhonen 35:47, Mäkelä 34:06)	2:20:16.0

	Total Time
2. Norway	
(Estenstad 36:52, Kirkholt 36:07,	
Stokken 35:37, Brenden 34:37)	2:23:13.0
3. Sweden	
(Täpp 36:19, S. Andersson 36:39,	
Josefsson 35:43, Lundström 35:32)	2:24:13.0
1948 (St. Moritz)	
1. Sweden	
(Östensson 36:16, Täpp 37:14,	
G. Eriksson 38:27, Lundström 40:11)	2:32:08.0
2. Finland	
(L. Silvennoinen 38:11, Laukkanen 38:16,	
Rytky 40:30, Kiuru 44:09)	2:41:06.0
3. Norway	
(Evensen 40:15, O. Ökern 38:37,	
Nyborg 41:39, Olav Hagen 44:02)	2:44:33.0
1936 (Garmisch-Partenkirchen)	
1. Finland	
(Nurmela 42:34, Karppinen 39:56,	
Lähde 39:49, Jalkanen 39:14)	2:41:33.0
2. Norway	
(Oddbjörn Hagen 41:32, Hoffsbakken 39:33,	
S. Brodahl 39:52, Iversen 40:42)	2:41:39.0
3. Sweden	
(Berger 42:49, E.A. Larsson 39:39,	
Häggblad 40:34, Matsbo 40:01)	2:43:03.0

142

Tapio Mäkela, Finland — Silver   Paavo Lonkila, Norway — Bronze

Special Ski Jump

The Norwegians maintained their supremacy in the special ski jump for many years. In the Olympic Games the Norwegian series of victories was not interrupted between 1924 and 1952. Three times (1924, 1932, 1948) the Norwegians were able to win all three Olympic medals and twice they gained double victories.

Ski jumping has always fascinated the uninitiated. Here man's performance is indeed birdlike—the graceful, fearless launching into space, the long drift and the seemingly gentle landing far down the jump. The finer points, once understood, are equally fascinating. Style may demonstrate a jumper's personality. The style may also show his sense of aerodynamics—his willingness to "make like a bird."

Tullin Thams of Norway initiated the "aerodynamic" era in 1924. The judges, used to the method of jumping in an upright position, were more shocked than enthusiastic as they watched the Norwegian sail through the air bent forward from the waist. Of course he won at the first Olympic Winter Games at Chamonix. The Ruud brothers—especially Birger, the younger— and other Norwegians kept up the new fashion. The movement spread and developed. It took many years for the change from the gliding "Icarus" with waving arms to the jumper flying in the so-called "drop of water" style, arms close to the body, shoulders far forward with the nose in line with the tips of the skis.

At the 1956 Olympics Antti Hyvärinen of Finland won the gold medal with an unforgettable performance. Then came his countryman Aulis Kallakorpi and Harry Glass of Germany.

The jumping at Squaw Valley was on the last day of the Winter Games. The weather is springlike and the snow conditions good. Thirty thousand fans surround the jump built by German architect Heini Klopfer. The jump is a natural, imbedded in the slope and flanked on both sides by protective woods. The jumper takes off with his back to the sun.

Almost all the favorites have drawn high starting numbers. In the first jump four men passed the 295-foot mark. The first to do so is the American Ansten Samuelstuen, followed by the Soviet Kamenski. Then Germany's Recknagel soars a mighty 306 feet in a perfect flying curve. He earns between 17.5 and 18.5 points out of a possible 20.

Now what do these distances mean? They mean much to the Olympic officials, concerned first and foremost with safety. The jumping shows that many are able and willing to exceed the critical 264 feet. Beyond this point the jumping becomes risky for even the best men. Serious injury awaits those jumping too far down the hill. After the first round there is a conference and the approach is shortened. From this moment everything depends on the most effective takeoff from the platform. The effect of the shortened takeoff is noticeable. The Norwegian Yggeseth loses 20 feet compared with his first jump. Kamenski loses 37 feet. Recknagel loses 29 feet, but he is still in the most commanding position. He wins the gold. The Finn Halonen wins the silver.

**Results of Special Ski Jump
through 1960**

	Distance (Meters)	Points			
1960 (Squaw Valley)			*1936 (Garmisch-P.)*		
1. Helmut Recknagel, Germany	93.5–84.5	227.2	1. Birger Ruud, Norway	75.0–74.5	232.0
2. Niilo Halonen, Finland	92.5–83.5	222.6	2. Sven Eriksson, Sweden	76.0–76.0	230.5
3. Otto Leodolter, Austria	88.5–83.5	219.4	3. Reidar Andersen, Norway	74.0–75.0	228.9
1956 (Cortina)			*1932 (Lake Placid)*		
1. Antti Hyvärinen, Finland	81.0–84.0	227.0	1. Birger Ruud, Norway	66.5–69.0	228.1
2. Aulis Kallakorpi, Finland	83.5–80.5	225.0	2. Hans Beck, Norway	71.5–63.5	227.0
3. Harry Glass, Germany	83.5–80.5	224.5	3. Kaare Wahlberg, Norway	62.5–64.0	219.5
1952 (Oslo)			*1928 (St. Moritz)*		
1. Arnfinn Bergmann, Norway	67.5–68.0	226.0	1. Alf Andersen, Norway	60.0–64.0	19.208
2. Torbjörn Falkanger, Norway	68.0–64.0	221.5	2. Sigmund Ruud, Norway	57.5–62.5	18.542
3. Karl Holmström, Sweden	67.0–65.5	219.5	3. Rudolf Burkert, Czechoslovakia	57.0–59.5	17.937
1948 (St. Moritz)			*1924 (Chamonix)*		
1. Peter Hugsted, Norway	65.0–70.0	228.1	1. Jacob Tullin Thams, Norway	49.0–49.0	18.960
2. Birger Ruud, Norway	64.0–67.0	226.6	2. Narve Bonna, Norway	47.5–49.0	18.689
3. Thorleif Schjelderup, Norway	64.0–67.0	225.1	3. Thorleif Haug, Norway	44.0–44.5	18.000

Nordic Skiing . . . Style Point Deductions

IN-RUN

Introduction

The FIS decided that inrun and takeoff styles are so individualistic that they are almost too difficult to judge properly. Therefore, scoring for style does not begin until the jumper reaches the lip of the takeoff.

However, for maximum exploitation of speed versus drag the jumper should adopt a relaxed half-crouched aerodynamic "egg" position adapted to the hill, the in-run and his body configuration. The takeoff is crucial, for it determines the success of the jump.

Penalty Points and Faults

Fall on the in-run ....20 points

Faults: Fall on in-run unless caused by force majeure, in which case a rerun is in order. A jury decision.

AIR FLIGHT

Introduction

The jumper must get into an aerodynamic flying position immediately after takeoff and maintain this position throughout the flight.

The body must be far forward with the back arched in the shape of an airplane wing section, arms at the side or stretched forward so that the hands can guide the flight like the ailerons of an airplane.

The skis should be held at a 10 to 30 angle to the relative wind. The angle should be less at the beginning of the flight and more toward the end. Skis must be close together and parallel, with the tips rising toward the end of the flight to maintain lift, then pressing forward into the classic telemark landing.

Penalty Points and Faults

Small deviations or faults which begin early
in flight and are immediately corrected ....½–2 points

Faults or deviations throughout the flight
or that occur in flight and are not corrected ....2–4 points

No telemark but soft with good balance ....2 points

No telemark and too low and too stiff ....3 points

No telemark, too low or too stiff, skis too
wide apart or remained in crouch position ....4 points

No telemark and unsteadiness in the out-
run in addition to the above........................6 points

REMEMBER:

If a jumper touches the snow with *one* or *both* hands and does not keep his balance, it is a fall.

Standing jumps are scored 20 to 6 points. Fallen jumps—12 to 0 points.

Judges are encouraged to use the full scale from 20 to 6 points for standing jumps and 12 to 0 points for fallen jumps.

Judging begins at moment of takeoff.

The personality of the jumper counts much in jumping.

The general impression of the jumper from the beginning to the end of his jump must determine his points.

The jumpers are entitled to uniform judging that makes full allowance for performance.

Judges are expected to have a comprehensive knowledge of style as well as the usual deviations.

Judges must understand the causes and effects of deviations.

The judge needs practice as well as the jumper.

LANDING

Introduction

Ideally, the jumper breaks his aerodynamic position just as the tails of his skis are about to touch the landing slope. He then presses forward with a definite landing action into a telemark landing to absorb the shock of transition from flight to the landing slope.

The jumper must go from air flight to the landing slope in one continuous smooth controlled movement.

Faults to Take into Consideration

1. Premature preparation for landing
2. Body not far enough forward on landing
3. Stiff landing
4. Body too bent on landing
5. Landing too low
6. Landing with feet even (without telemark)
7. Unsteadiness instantly connected
8. Unsteadiness on landing and on the landing slope

Penalty Points

Telemark with variations ....½–2 points

Major and minor faults not corrected ....2–4 points

Touching the snow with one hand and re-
gaining balance ....2–4 points

Touching the snow with both hands and
regaining balance ....8 points

Fall on landing or as result of handing ....10 points

Faults: Bent knees, hips or back
Poor body position
Skis high, low, wide, waving or crossed
Unsteadiness

Nordic Combined

The most traditional Nordic skiing contest, and the one which originally enjoyed the greatest reputation, is undoubtedly the Nordic combined. The objective is to show as balanced a performance as possible for the cross-country race and the jump. Today, in the age of specialization, it has been forgotten that for many years only the winner of the Nordic could win the title of national champion.

That is why the series of victories of the Norwegians in the Nordic combined is even more impressive than that in the ski jump. In 1924, 1928, 1932 and 1936 all medals for the Nordic combined were won by Norwegians. At Squaw Valley in 1960 Georg Thoma from Germany, with his victory in the Nordic combined, created one of the greatest sensations in any Olympic Winter Games. At first the cross-country race was held before the jump, but the two competitions have been reversed—the combination jump first—since 1952. The reason was that it was found that the good runners, after gaining a great lead, no longer went to the extremes of their possibilities in the jumps that followed. Now they can no longer afford not to do their best, because they jump first.

Results, Nordic Combined
through 1960

	Ski Jump	Cross-Country	Total Points
1960 (Squaw Valley)			
1. Georg Thoma, Germany	221.5	236.452	457.952
2. Tormod Knutsen, Norway	217.0	236.000	453.000
3. Nikolai Gusakov, U.S.S.R.	212.0	240.000	452.000

Ski Jump	Distance	Points
1. Thoma, Germany	62.0–69.0–67.5	221.5
2. Kochkin, U.S.S.R.	64.0–64.5–67.0	219.5
10b. Gusakov, U.S.S.R.	62.5–64.5–66.0	212.0

15-Km. Cross-Country	Time	Points
1. Gusakov, U.S.S.R.	58:29.4	240.000
4. Thoma, Germany	59:23.8	236.452
5. Knutsen, Norway	59:31.0	236.000

146

Simon Slåttvik, Norway   Heikki Hasu, Finland

UFFICIALE
OFFICIEL
OFFICIAL

VII GIOCHI OLIMPICI INVERNALI CORTINA D'AMPEZZO 1956

Results of Nordic Combined
through 1960

	Total Points	18/15 Km. Time	Race Rank	Race Points	Jump Distance	Jump Rank	Jump Points
1960 (Squaw Valley)							
1. Georg Thoma, Germany	457.952	59:23.8	(4)	236.452	62.0–69.0–67.5	(1)	221.5
2. Tormod Knutsen, Norway	453.000	59:31.0	(5)	236.000	61.5–64.5–67.0	(4)	217.0
3. Nikolai Gusakov, U.S.S.R.	452.000	58:29.4	(1)	240.000	62.5–64.5–66.0	(10b)	212.0
1956 (Cortina)							
1. Sverre Stenersen, Norway	455.000	56:18.0	(1)	240.000	65.0–73.0–74.0	(2)	215.0
2. Bengt Eriksson, Sweden	437.400	1:00:36.0	(15)	223.400	72.5–72.5–68.0	(3)	214.0
3. Franciszek Gron-Gasienica, Poland	436.800	57:55.0	(7)	233.800	66.5–72.5–71.5	(10)	203.0
1952 (Oslo)							
1. Simon Slåttvik, Norway	451.621	1:05:40.0	(3)	228.121	67.5–67.0–66.5	(1)	223.5
2. Heikki Hasu, Finland	447.500	1:02:24.0	(1)	240.000	63.0–63.0–61.0	(5)	207.5
3. Sverre Stenersen, Norway	436.335	1:09:44.0	(9)	213.335	67.0–68.0–69.5	(2)	223.0
1948 (St. Moritz)							
1. Heikki Hasu, Finland	448.80	1:16:43.0	(1)	240.00	57.0–61.5–64.0	(8b)	208.8
2. Martti Huhtala, Finland	433.65	1:19:28.0	(2)	224.15	62.0–61.0–61.5	(6)	209.5
3. Sven Israelsson, Sweden	433.40	1:21:44.0	(4)	211.50	67.5–66.0–67.0	(1)	221.9
1936 (Garmisch-Partenkirchen)							
1. Oddbjörn Hagen, Norway	430.30	1:15:33.0	(1)	240.00	42.0–46.0	(16a)	190.3
2. Olaf Hoffsbakken, Norway	419.80	1:17:37.0	(2)	227.80	47.0–45.5	(13)	192.0
3. Sverre Brodahl, Norway	408.10	1:18:01.0	(3)	225.50	40.0–47.0	(28)	182.6
1932 (Lake Placid)							
1. Johan Gröttumsbraaten, Norway	446.00	1:27:15.0	(1)	240.00	51.0–50.0	(6)	206.0
2. Ole Stenen, Norway	436.05	1:28:05.0	(2)	235.75	48.0–52.0	(12)	200.3
3. Hans Vinjarengen, Norway	434.60	1:32:40.0	(4)	213.00	54.0–62.0	(2)	221.6
1928 (St. Moritz)							
1. Johan Gröttumsbraaten, Norway	17.833	1:37:01.0	(1)	20.000	49.5–56.0	(8)	15.667
2. Hans Vinjarengen, Norway	15.303	1:41:44.0	(2)	17.750	59.5–61.0	(19)	12.856
3. John Snersrud, Norway	15.021	1:50:51.0	(9)	13.125	60.5–52.0	(3)	16.917
1924 Chamonix)							
1. Thorleif Haug, Norway	18.906	1:14:31.0	(1)	20.000	42.5–44.0	(1)	17.812
2. Thoralf Strömstad, Norway	18.219	1:17:03.0	(3)	18.750	46.0–45.5	(2)	17.687
3. Johan Gröttumsbraaten, Norway	17.854	1:15:51.0	(2)	19.375	44.5–39.5	(8)	16.333

147

Mirja Hietamies, Finland   Siiri Rantanen, Finland   Lydia Wideman, Finland

Women's 5-Kilometer Cross-Country

Following the trend toward specialization, a second cross-country race for women was held at the skiing world championships in Zakopane in 1962. Then the IOC moved that the women's 5-kilometer cross-country race be included in the Olympic program for 1964 at Innsbruck.

Women's 10-Kilometer Cross-Country

With the introduction of a 10-kilometer women's cross-country race at the Oslo games, followed four years later by a 3 *ff* 5-kilometer relay race, Scandinavian and Soviet wishes were realized. In Central Europe and North America women's cross-country events did not have much popularity and did not win much universal interest. At the Olympic premiere in 1952 it was the triple victory of the Finnish women that made the greatest impression. At Squaw Valley in 1960 the Soviet women took the first four places.

Results, Women's 10-Km. Cross-Country through 1960

1960 (Squaw Valley)

	Time
1. Maria Gusakova, U.S.S.R.	39:46.6
2. Liubov Baranova-Kosyreva, U.S.S.R.	40:04.2
3. Radia Yeroshina, U.S.S.R.	40:06.0

1956 (Cortina)

1. Liubov Kosyreva, U.S.S.R.	38:11.0
2. Radia Yeroshina, U.S.S.R.	38:16.0
3. Sonja Edström, Sweden	38:23.0

1952 (Oslo)

1. Lydia Wideman, Finland	41:40.0
2. Mirja Hietamies, Finland	42:39.0
3. Siiri Rantanen, Finland	42:50.0

Women's 3 × 5-Kilometer Relay Race

In view of the superiority of the Soviet women in the individual cross-country events, it was curious that in 1956 and in 1960 they did not win the relay races. They won the silver behind the Finnish women at Cortina and behind the Swedes at Squaw Valley. They were unfortunate in 1960, in that the first Soviet runner fell and broke a ski, thereby losing 1:26 minutes to the first Swede.

Results, Women's 3 × 5-Km. Relay through 1960

Total Time

1960 (Squaw Valley)

1. Sweden (Johansson 21:31, Strandberg 21:45, Ruthström-Edström 21:05.4)	1:04:21.4
2. U.S.S.R. (Yeroshina 22:57, Gusakova 21:18, Baranova-Kosyreva 20:47.6)	1:05:02.6
3. Finland (Rantanen 22:57, Ruoppa 21:51, Pöysti 21:39.5)	1:06:27.5

1956 (Cortina)

1. Finland (Polkunen 23:22, Hietamies 22:20, Rantanen 23:19)	1:09:01.0
2. U.S.S.R. (Kosyreva 22:58, Kolchina 22:38, Yeroshina 23:52)	1:09:28.0
3. Sweden (Johansson 24:10, A.L. Eriksson 23:36, Edström 22:02)	1:09:48.0

148

John Bower, U.S.A., Combined Nordic

INNSBRUCK—1964

Cross-country skiers face much the same difficulties as cross-country runners. They ski through wooded areas, constantly battling gravity. Trails are so laid out that they spend equal time climbing, descending and running on the flat. Climbs totaling 932 meters are required in the 30-kilometer course at Innsbruck. This is the most grueling event of the Winter Olympics.

America did not enter in the women's cross-country events, which were again dominated by the Soviets. Claudia Boyarski led the U.S.S.R. to the top three places in the 10,000-meter race. She also won as expected in the 5000-meter. The relay event of three 5000-meter runs was taken by the Soviet trio Alevtina Kolchina, Eudokia Mekshilo and Claudia Boyarski, who completed the event in half the time of the nearest competitor, Sweden.

The Scandinavians dominated the men's Nordic events. Finland's Eero Mäntyranta won both the 15,000- and 30,000-meter cross-country runs. In the 15,000 the U.S. entries—Michael Gallagher, Michael Elliott, Karl Bohlin and Richard Taylor—finished thirty-eighth, forty-first, forty-seventh and forty-ninth respectively.

In the 30,000 meters, Americans Elliott, Taylor, Larry Damon and James Shea placed thirtieth, forty-second, forty-sixth and forty-eighth.

Sweden's Sixten Jernberg won the 50,000-meter (31-mile) cross-country event, finishing minutes ahead of a countryman. It was his third gold medal in three Olympics. Damon was twenty-eighth and Taylor thirty-fourth.

Jernberg, Kark Asph, Janne Stefansson and Assar Rönnlund, in a rousing finish, upset Finland to win the relay event—four 10,000-meter runs. The American team of Gallagher, Elliott, Shea and John Bower finished thirteenth among fifteen teams, 21 minutes behind the winners.

Veikko Kankkonen of Finland upset Norway's Toralf Engan to win the 70-meter (small-hill) jump, but Engan reversed positions in the special 90-meter jump event. Kankkonen won on his final jump, showing flawless form. His second and third jumps were noted the best of the field.

John Balfanz of Minneapolis took tenth place in the 70-meter jump. He was followed by teammates Gene Kotlarek of Duluth in fourteenth place and Ansten Samuelstuen, Boulder, Colorado, twenty-fourth. Kotlarek was twenty-fourth in the longer jump. David Hicks of Duluth was twenty-ninth, Samuelstuen thirty-third and Balfanz forty-first among fifty-two entries.

The Nordic combined event, consisting of a jump and a 15,000-meter race, was won by Norway's Tormod Knutsen, who led the 70-meter jumpers and finished fourth in the 15,000-meter race. John Bower finished fifteenth and Jim Shea was twenty-seventh for the Americans.

John Bower, U.S.A., Combined Nordic

Robert Gray, U.S.A.

GRENOBLE—1968

The long-distance ski races, which originated in the Scandinavian mountains and which the Nordic skiers have made their own, were contested in a 15-square-mile area of the Vercors group of mountains, which the French organizers named "the Norway of the Alps." The little village of Autrans became the center of Olympic interest. The competitors were housed there, and the events had their organization headquarters nearby.

15,000-Meter Cross-Country

This race posed a number of problems for the competitors. Dense fog in parts of the course, a rising temperature, which had its effects on the snow, and the abnormally high degree of humidity in the air were some of them. The first three-fifths of the course was generally uphill, while the final part was downhill. Harald Grönningen, the thirty-three-year-old Norwegian who won the event, was lucky to have a low starting number. He was fifth to start and had no difficulty overtaking the first four, thus having the clear track for himself. Eero Mäntyranta, Finland, who gave Grönningen the expected duel, was less lucky. He had to start twenty-ninth. The outcome of the race was very close. Only 1.9 seconds separated the victorious Gronningen from the Finn, thus reversing the order of four years earlier. No one outside Scandinavia was among the first eight.

Results, 15,000-M. Cross-Country

(75 participants from 25 countries. Start and finish: ski stadium. Highest point: 1304 m. Lowest point: 1056 m. Gradient differential: 248 m. Feb. 10.)

	5 km.	10 km.	Finish
1. Harald Gronningen, Norway	16:57.1	35:06.5	47:54.2
2. Eero Mantyranta, Finland	17:06.4	34:56.9	47:56.1
3. Gunnar Larsson, Sweden	17:25.5	35:30.1	48:33.7

150

Franco Nones, Italy—Gold

30,000-Meter Cross-Country

This race provided a huge sensation. It was won by Franco Nones, the twenty-seven-year-old customs official from the Fieme Valley in the Dolomites. For the very first time a gold medal in a Nordic event was won by a non-Scandinavian. To prove that Italy's success was no fluke, fifth-place Giulio de Florian, another skier in the race, finished well ahead of many Scandinavians.

The race proceeded under ideal conditions that suited Nones very well. He was in top condition and had undergone extensive training in preparation for this distance, to which the Scandinavians were not overdevoted. Nones began the race at a pace that nobody believed he could keep up. Events like these are always decided in the last few miles, and this seemed to apply more than ever. The course was very tough, especially in its uphill section after the first eight miles. Yet Nones forged ahead and so did Eero Mäntyranta, who was the favorite to win the race. The Finn kept making up time and before the halfway stage he was clocked only 2 seconds slower than Nones. From then on the course sloped into its downhill section, and the Italian coasted home.

Results 30,000-M. Cross-Country
1968 (Grenoble)

(66 participants from 22 countries. The 30-km. course consists of 2 legs of 10 and 20 km. respectively. Start and finish: ski stadium. Highest point: 1331 m. Lowest point: 1056 m. Gradient differential: 275 m. Feb. 7.)

	20 km.	Finish
1. Franco Nones, Italy	1:07:40.4	1:35:39.2
2. Odd Martinsen, Norway	1:08:12.7	1:36:28.9
3. Eero Mäntyranta, Finland	1:07:44.6	1:36:55.3

151

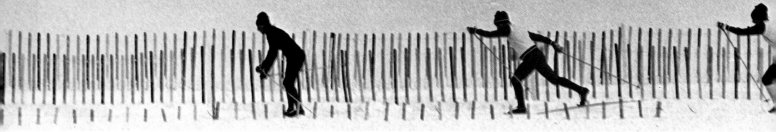

Cross Country Start

50,000-Meter Cross-Country

This race was distinguished by the fact that there was only one Scandinavian among the first three finishers. Nordic honor was upheld by Ole Ellefsäter of Norway, who won the gold medal. Vedenin of the U.S.S.R. took the silver and Haas of Switzerland, the bronze. The expected victory by Mäntyranta, who started as the favorite, did not take place. It was obvious that the exertions of the previous races had left him without sufficient reserves of strength for this marathon. It is true that the winners of the men's Nordic events were mainly in a mature age group, as it seemed that thirty was the age best suited to the long distance, but the thirty-year-old Finn was a little too old to repeat the feats he had been capable of only a few years earlier.

The race consisted of covering the 25-kilometer circuit twice. Ole Ellefsäter was already in a commanding position after the first leg. As the race continued, the time margin between him and Vedenin became less and less, but Vedenin could not better him.

Results, 50,000-M. Cross-Country
1968 (Grenoble)

(51 participants from 18 countries. The course consists of one 25-km. leg, which was lapped twice. Start and finish: ski stadium. Highest point: 1304 m. Lowest point: 1056 m. Gradient differential: 248 m. Feb. 17.)

	25 km.	40 km.	Finish
1. Ole Ellefsater, Norway	1:11:39.5	2:03:11.3	2:28:45.8
2. Vatscheslav Vedenin, U.S.S.R.	1:13:30.8	2:04:11.3	2:29:02.5
3. Josef Haas, Switzerland	1:13:28.1	2:04:28.0	2:29:14.8

4 × 10,000-meter Relay

This race gave Norway another gold medal, for the first time ever in this event. Each man on its team—Odd Martinsen, Paal Tyldum, Harald Grönningen and Ole Ellefsater—clocked the fastest time over his distance. Their victory was never in doubt. The Swedish team came second, the Finnish third. Finland owed its success to Mäntyranta's marvelous run. As last man in his team, he overtook Vedenin in the last stages of the race for third place.

Results, 4 × 10,000-M. Relay
1968 (Grenoble)

(15 teams from 15 countries. Start and finish: Ski stadium. Highest point: 1230 m. Lowest point: 1056 m. Gradient differential: 248 m. Feb. 14.)

		Individual Time	Total Time
1. Norway	Martinsen	31:57.3	
	Tyldum	32:13.8	
	Grönningen	32:05.2	
	Ellefsäter	32:17.2	2:08:33.5
2. Sweden	Halvarsson	32:37.0	
	Andersson	32:26.4	
	Larsson	32:24.4	
	Rönnlund	32:45.4	2:10:13.2
3. Finland	Oikarainen	33:00.7	
	Taipale	33:16.0	
	Laurila	32:16.3	
	Mäntyranta	32:23.7	2:10:56.7

152

Toini Gustafsson, Sweden

Women's 5000 and 10,000 Meters

Both of these races were won by Toini Gustafsson, the twenty-nine-year-old teacher from Sweden. In the 5000 meters Toini had luck on her side. Galina Kulakova, U.S.S.R., broke a ski and Marjatta Kajosmaa, Finland, had a bad fall in the last downhill section. However, the Swedish skier showed her true and great qualities in the following 10,000-meter race when she had to cope with tricky snow conditions. The way she waxed her skis was as correct as her racing was immaculate. Berit Mödre of Norway won the silver and Inger Aufles, also of Norway, won the bronze.

Results, Women's Cross-Country
1968 (Grenoble)

5 kilometers
(34 participants from 11 countries. Start and finish: ski stadium. Highest point: 1156 m.
Lowest point: 1056 m. Gradient differential: 100 m. Feb. 13.)

1. Toini Gustafsson, Sweden	16:45.2	4. Barbro Martinsson, Sweden	16:52.9
2. Galina Kulakova, U.S.S.R.	16:48.4	5. Marjatta Kajosmaa, Finland	16:54.6
3. Alevtina Kolchina, U.S.S.R.	16:51.6	6. Rita Achina, U.S.S.R.	16:55.1

10 kilometers
(34 participants from 11 countries. Start and finish: ski stadium. Highest point: 1195 m.
Lowest point: 1056 m. Gradient differential: 139 m. Feb. 9.)

	5 km.	Finish
1. Toini Gustafsson, Sweden	18:55.0	36:46.5
2. Berit Mördre, Norway	19:18.4	37:54.6
3. Inger Aufles, Sweden	19:12.2	37:59.9

Women's 3 × 5-Kilometer Relay

The Norwegian women came into their own in this race by taking first place ahead of Sweden. The U.S.S.R. had to be content with the bronze medal.

Results, Women's 3 × 5-Km. Relay
1968 (Grenoble)

(8 teams from 8 countries. Start and finish: ski stadium. Held over the same course as the Women's 5-km. cross-country. Feb. 16.)

		Individual Time	Total Time
1. Norway	Inger Aufles	19:08.8	
	Babben Enger Damon	19:19.5	
	Berit Mördre	19:02.5	57:30.0
2. Sweden	Britt Strandberg	19:46.7	
	Toini Gustafsson	18:56.7	
	Barbro Martinsson	19:07.6	57:51.0
3. U.S.S.R.	Alevtina Kolchina	19:32.8	
	Rita Achina	19:31.2	
	Galina Kulakova	19:09.6	58:13.6

Nordic Combined

This race consisted of three jumps from the Autrans "normal" jump platform, of which the two best jumps were counted, and a 15-kilometer cross-country race. There were forty-one competitors. The Scandinavians were expected to win, since they had collected twenty-two of the total of twenty-seven medals from nine previous Olympic Games. This time Sweden dropped out altogether and Finland and Norway finished in the second twenty. Germany had made great strides in the event, as was shown by Franz Keller's victory. Alois Kälin made it a close race, however. Had the event consisted only of the jump, Keller would have had nothing to worry about. Kälin was a magnificent long-distance skier and covered the 15-kilometer part of the race faster than Keller. He was not fast enough to overcome his low-point position due to the jumping.

154

The final yards of the race became a thriller, with Keller in the lead; but Kälin, who had started three and a half minutes after him, came closer and closer. It would have taken only 2.3 seconds for Kälin to win the event. As it was, Keller took the gold medal and Kälin the silver.

Results, Nordic Combined
1968 (Grenoble)

(41 participants from 13 countries. Jump from the ordinary platform. Each competitor has 3 jumps, with the 2 best on points counting. Feb. 10. 15-km. cross-country in Autrans. Highest point: 1270 m. Lowest point: 1056 m. Gradient differential: 214 m. Feb. 11.)

	Ski Jump	Cross-Country	Total Points
1. Franz Keller, W. Germany	240.10	208.94	449.04
2. Alois Kälin, Switzerland	193.20	254.79	447.99
3. Andreas Kunz, E. Germany	216.90	227.20	444.10

Ski Jump	Distance	Points	Total Points
1. Keller, W. Germany	73.0	118.1	
	77.5	122.0	
	77.0	81.3	240.1
10. Kunz, E. Germany	72.5	109.3	
	72.0	105.8	
	74.0	107.6	216.9
24. Kälin, Switzerland	61.0	73.1	
	71.0	97.8	
	69.5	95.4	193.2

15-Km. Cross-Country	5 km.	10 km.	15 km.	Points
1. Kälin, Switzerland	16:26.6	33:55.3	47:21.5	254.79
3. Kunz, E. Germany	17:16.8	35:28.2	49:19.8	227.20
13. Keller, W. Germany	17:29.9	36:35.5	50:45.2	208.94

Special Jump from the 70-Meter Platform

This event at Autrans was won by Czechoslovakia's Jiri Raska. His first jump of 79 meters gave him an advantage he never relinquished. Two Austrians took the silver and bronze medals.

Results, Special Jump, 70 Meters
1968 (Grenoble)

(58 participants from 17 nations. Ordinary Autrans platform. 2 jumps for each competitor. 5 judges eliminating highest and lowest markings. Critical point: 70 m. Feb. 11.)

	Meters	Points	Total Marks
1. Jiri Raska, Czechoslovakia	79.0	115.2	
	72.5	101.3	216.5
2. Reinhold Bachler, Austria	77.5	107.8	
	76.0	106.4	214.2
3. Baldur Preiml, Austria	80.0	113.8	
	72.5	98.8	212.6

Special Jump from the 90-Meter Platform

This event, held at St. Nizier, became an exciting duel between Raska and Vladimir Beloussov of the Soviet Union, with the Soviet contender defeating the Czech by only a half meter on both jumps. Lars Grini of Norway collected the bronze medal. Scandinavia had only one finisher in the top group. Björn Wirkola of Norway finished twelfth, despite the fact that he had been the pregames favorite. It represented a decline for the Nordic countries, which had taken both gold medals in the special jumps at the 1964 Winter Games in Innsbruck.

Results, Special Jump, 90 Meters
1968 (Grenoble)

(58 participants from 17 nations. The big Saint-Nizier platform. 2 jumps for each competitor. 5 judges eliminating highest and lowest markings. Critical point: 90 m. Feb. 18.)

	Meters	Points	Total Marks
1. Vladimir Beloussov, U.S.S.R.	101.5	118.0	
	98.5	113.3	231.3
2. Jiri Raska, Czechoslovakia	101.0	116.3	
	98.0	113.1	229.4
3. Lars Grini, Norway	99.0	111.5	
	93.5	102.8	214.3

Galina Kulakova, U.S.S.R. — Three Golds

SAPPORO—1972

Women's 5- and 10-Kilometer Cross-Country

The Soviet skiers who went home from Grenoble without gold medals succeeded in Sapporo. The lion's share of the triumph went to Galina Kulakova, a twenty-nine-year-old schoolteacher who became the most successful female athlete in Sapporo with her three gold medals. A superb skier, Kulakova first won the 10-kilometer cross-country hands down in front of her teammate Alevtina Olunina and the Finn Marjatta Kajosmaa. In the 5-kilometer race Kajosmaa took revenge on the world champion Olunina, but Kulakova still managed to beat her by 5 seconds.

Results, Women's Cross-Country
1972 (Sapporo)

5 kilometers
(43 participants from 13 countries. Gradient differential: 90 m. Feb. 9.)
1. Galina Kulakova, U.S.S.R.   17:00.50
2. Marjatta Kajosmaa, Finland   17:05.50
3. Helena Sikolova, Czechoslovakia   17:07.32

10 kilometers
(42 participants from 11 countries. Gradient differential: 103 m. Feb. 6.)

	5 Kilometers	10 Kilometers
1. Galina Kulakova, U.S.S.R.	16:39.46	34:17.82
2. Alevtina Olunina, U.S.S.R.	16:47.81	34:54.11
3. Marjatta Kajosmaa, Finland	16:51.20	34:56.45

A Lonely Road

Women's 3 × 5-Kilometer Relay

The Soviet skiers took the lead soon after the start of the relay and skied a superior race. Kulakova took over the final lap and proved once more that she was in a class of her own with a time of 15:26.04. The thirty-four-year-old Finn Kajosmaa was second fastest over the distance and it was thanks to her abilities that Finland won the silver medal.

Results, Women's 3 × 5-Km. Relay
1972 (Sapporo)

(11 teams. Gradient differential: 43 m. Feb. 12.)

		Individual Time	Total Time
1. U.S.S.R.	Lubov Moukhatcheva	16:49.20	
	Alevtina Olunina	16:30.91	
	Galina Kulakova	15:26.04	48:46.15
2. Finland	Helena Takalo	17:04.93	
	Hilkka Kuntola	16:41.67	
	Marjatta Kajosmaa	15:32.77	49:19.37
3. Norway	Inger Aufless	17:36.75	
	Aslaug Dahl	16:34.87	
	Berit Mördre-Lammedal	15:39.87	49:51.49

158

Sven-Ake-Lundback, Sweden   Paal Tyldum, Norway

Men's 15-Kilometer Cross-Country

Sixty-two athletes presented themselves to the starter of the 15-kilometer cross-country; no other Nordic competition was fought for to such an extent. Nearly a dozen were possible champions. The victory of the twenty-four-year-old Swede Sven-Ake Lundbäck did not come as a surprise. From the very beginning Lundbäck increased his lead over Simashov of the U.S.S.R. After the first 5 kilometers it was already 27 seconds and from then on he was in control of the race. Ivar Förmo, twenty years old, thrilled the experts, who prophesied a great future for the young Norwegian. In a sensational finish he beat the Finn Juha Mieto by .06 second to gain the bronze.

Vatcheslav Vadenin, U.S.S.R.

Results, 15-Km. Cross-Country
1972 (Sapporo)

(62 participants from 19 countries. Gradient differential: 130 m. Feb. 7.)

	5 km.	10 km.	15 km.
1. Sven-Ake Lundbäck, Sweden	14:43.35	30:51.88	45:28.24
2. Fedor Simashov, U.S.S.R.	15:10.88	31:30.30	46:00.84
3. Ivar Förmö, Norway	15:07.72	31:24.34	46:02.68

Men's 30-Kilometer Cross-Country

The 30-kilometer cross-country proved to be a contest between the great old men of cross-country skiing. The Finn Eero Mäntyranta, triple gold medal winner, was taking part in his fourth Olympic Games. In spite of his thirty-four years he still wanted to have a try at winning another medal. The thirty-seven-year-old German Walter Demel succeeded in finishing fifth. The gold was won by thirty-one-year-old Vatschelav Vedenin of the U.S.S.R.

Results, 30-Km. Cross-Country
1972 (Sapporo)

(59 participants from 18 countries. Gradient differential: 119 m. Feb. 4.)

	20 km.	30 km.
1. Vatscheslav Vedenin, U.S.S.R.	1:05:39.72	1:36:31.15
2. Paal Tyldum, Norway	1:05:50.18	1:37:25.30
3. Johs Harviken, Norway	1:06:02.05	1:37:32.44

The Start of the 4 × 10 Kilometer Relay

Men's 50-Kilometer Cross-Country

This skiing marathon turned out to be a triumph for the Norwegians. Only Vedenin prevented a triple Norseman victory. The story of the 50 kilometers was the effort of a twenty-four-year-old Swiss, Werner Geeser. He was the fastest starter to cover the first 25 kilometers and was leading at the end of 40 kilometers. But then he broke down. With the long strides of a sprinter, the Norwegian Paal Tyldum spurted past the Swiss and won the gold.

Results, 50-Km. Cross-Country
1972 (Sapporo)

(40 participants from 12 countries. Gradient differential: 127 m. Feb. 10.)

	25 km.	40 km.	50 km.
1. Paal Tyldum, Norway	1:20:27.33	2:10:58.61	2:43:14.75
2. Magne Myrmo, Norway	1:19:58.81	2:11:01.27	2:43:29.45
3. Vatscheslav Vedenin, U.S.S.R.	1:19:26.59	2:11:23.21	2:44:00.19

Men's 4 × 10-Kilometer Cross-Country Relay

For the second time in the history of this relay it was won by the Soviets. They had a fast finisher in Vedenin and he registered the time of 30:21.37 minutes for his lap. In the unbelievably exciting race, the U.S.S.R. and Nor-

160

way battled for the victory. Sweden and Switzerland fought a duel for third place that was no less exciting.

Everett Dunklee, U.S.A.

Results, 4 × 10-Km. Cross-Country
1972 (Sapporo)

(14 teams. Gradient differential: 109 m. Feb. 13.)

		Individual Time	Total Time
1. U.S.S.R.	Vladimir Voronkov	31:12.52	
	Yuri Skobov	30:55.42	
	Fedor Simashov	32:18.63	
	Vatscheslav Vedenin	30:21.37	2:04:47.94
2. Norway	Oddvar Braa	31:10.38	
	Paal Tyldum	30:58.11	
	Ivar Förmö	31:16.78	
	Johs Harviken	31:31.79	2:04:57.06
3. Switzerland	Alfred Kälin	31:54.76	
	Albert Giger	31:40.14	
	Alois Kälin	31:13.11	
	Eduard Hauser	32:12.05	2:07:00.06

Nordic Combined

This event has always been a purely Norwegian domain. The first non-Norwegian champion was the Finn Heikki Hasu, who won in St. Moritz in 1948. At least he was a Scandinavian. But in 1960 a German, Georg Thoma, actually managed to win and in 1968 still another German, Franz Keller, repeated the triumph.

In Sapporo the experts expected the Finn Rauno Miettinen to do well. The start appeared very promising for him. The ski-jump section of the Nordic combined was won by Hideki and Nakano, Japan, followed by Miettinen. He was thus in an extremely good starting position. The East German coaches, however, worked out that their man, Ulrich Wehling, only needed to be 1:01 minutes faster than the Finn over the 15 kilometers cross-country in order to win. And Wehling, a high school boy of nineteen, even managed to be 1:52 minutes faster than his closest adversary.

Results, Nordic Combined
1972 (Sapporo)

	Ski jump	Cross-Country	Total Points
1. Ulrich Wehling, E. Germany	200.9	212.440	413.340
2. Rauno Miettinen, Finland	210.0	195.505	405.505
3. Karl-Heinz Luck, E. Germany	178.8	220.000	398.800

	1st	2nd (meters)	3rd
Ski Jump			
2. Rauno Miettinen, Finland	73.5	77.5	79.0
3. Ullrich Wehling, E. Germany	78.0	76.5	77.5
17. Karl-Heinz Luck, E. Germany	69.5	74.0	67.0

15-km. Cross-Country	5 km.	10 km.	Total
1. Karl-Heinz Luck, E. Germany	15:25.2	34:00.9	48:24.9
3. Ullrich Wehling, E. Germany	15:47.7	34:37.4	49:15.3
15. Rauno Miettinen, Finland	16:27.2	35:52.3	51:08.2

Walter Demel, W. Germany

161

The Special Jump—70 Meters

The Japanese have never been as close to a triple-medal triumph as they are with the special jump from the 70-meter slope. The first Japanese to jump is Akisugo Konno. He lands at the 82.5-meter mark. The second Japanese to jump, Seiji Aochi, lands at 83.5 meters. A short time later the number 81 appears with the name Takashi Fujisawa. Three Japanese with over 80 meters. And the one carrying all the hopes has yet to come. Number 45, Kasaya, will be jumping very soon.

Dramatic technique, of course, has to play its role by insisting that the Norwegian, Ingolf Mork, jump first. Everyone knows that he will be the one, if any, to thwart the Japanese hopes. Only 78 meters for Mork. The first judge is the only one to give him 18 points for his beautiful flight. It is the Japanese judge Fumio Asaki, who supported the Norwegian without regard for Japan's hopes and ambition. This is the man who took the Olympic oath of fairness for all umpires during the opening ceremony.

An artificial pause. There are delays in clearing the tower. Glances at the wind sock. Then Yukio Kasaya soars out. Right up to an invisible premarked line. 84 meters. Four times 19 points for his posture. The spectators can read one another's expressions: there is surely no one else who can jump so beautifully and for such a distance. Not even Mork, not even Raska, the Olympic champion from Grenoble, and not even the Russian veteran Tsakadze.

Four Japanese hold the first four places after the first series of jumps. One good reason for the spectators to unpack from their black wrappings the hot rice balls that look rather like doughnuts—the hors d'ouevre of the huge triumphal feast.

In the second series of jumps Kasaya achieves 79 meters. Now no one can take the medals away from him, Konno and Aochi. Then the blond Viking Mork shoulders the man from Sapporo. Mork has practiced only six times on this jump, Kasaya nearly a hundred. But the Norwegian lifts Kasaya above him as if to show the audience of 40,000 that there cannot be the slightest doubt about this victory. Then, after the honoring of the champions, they go. The 90-meter hill awaits them. At this moment they have not the slightest notion that a young Pole called Fortuna will destroy the second part of their dream with a mighty jump of 111 meters.

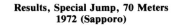

Results, Special Jump, 70 Meters
1972 (Sapporo)

(56 participants from 16 countries. Feb. 6.)

	Meters	Points	Total Marks
1. Yukio Kasaya, Japan	84.0	126.6	
	79.0	117.6	244.2
2. Akitsugu Konno, Japan	82.5	120.2	
	79.0	114.6	234.8
3. Seiji Aochi, Japan	83.5	123.3	
	77.5	106.2	229.5

Wojciech Fortuna, Poland

Yukio Kasaya,
Reaching Golden Heights

L-R Akitsuga Konno—Silver
Yukio Kasaya—Gold, Seiji Aochi—Bronze

The Special Jump—90 Meters

The Japanese reckoned with a repeat performance of their great initial success when it came to the special jump from the 90-meter platform. But after the first series of jumps only Kasaya still had hopes for a medal, and after the second series of jumps these hopes were blown away by the wind. After the first jump the order of succession was Wojciech Fortuna in front of Kasaya and Wolf. The Pole was thrilled after his first jump and disappointed after his second. His first was 111 meters, but his second was only 87.5 meters, a result of the dreadful wind conditions. This made him feel sure that he had lost the gold medal. But Kasaya managed only 85 meters, which meant that for the first time a Pole was Olympic champion in the ski jump. The Swiss jumper, Walter Steiner, found better conditions for his second jump and he took advantage of them. He went farther than his fellow competitors with 103 meters and thus jumped from thirteenth place to second.

Results, Special Jump, 90 Meters
1972 (Sapporo)

(52 participants from 15 countries. Feb. 11.)

	Meters	Points	Total marks
1. Wojciech Fortuna, Poland	111.0	130.4	
	87.5	89.5	219.9
2. Walter Steiner, Switzerland	94.0	101.6	
	103.0	118.2	219.8
3. Rainer Schmidt, E. Germany	98.5	106.4	
	101.0	112.9	219.3

INNSBRUCK—1976

Women's 5-Kilometer Cross-Country

Helena Takalo, twenty-eight-year-old Finnish housewife who brought her husband Teuvo along as a private coach, scored what may be the upset of the Olympics when she defeated the cream of the Soviet runners in the 5-kilometer cross-country race. Helena is a grocery store clerk from the northern Finland town of Pyhäjärvi. She was one of the favorites in this event and was seeking Finland's first triumph since 1952 in the women's cross-country. Takalo received word from her husband at the 3-kilometer mark that she was still in contention in a lightning-fast race. She rose to the occasion, stepped up the pace and vowed to overtake the early leader, Raisa Smetanina. The elapsed time for these two runners showed Helena 15:48.69, Raisa 15:49.73. This was the fastest 5 kilometers in the history of women's Olympic and Federation of International Skating world championships.

Women's 10-Kilometer Cross-Country

In the longer race over 10 kilometers, less than 25 seconds separated the medalists. Again it was Smetanina vs. Takalo. This time the Soviet ace won by the narrowest of margins, .87 second, with Kulakova trailing by another 24 seconds. Smetanina built up an 11-second lead at the midpoint of the race and appeared to be in better physical condition. Takalo refused to fold. She made a bold spurt on an uphill section of the course and gained 5 seconds. Her final burst came in the last 250 meters, but she fell short of nipping her Soviet competitor.

164

Helena Takola, Finland—Gold

Raisa Smetania, U.S.S.R.—Silver—Gold

Women's 4 × 5-Kilometer Relay

The Nordic nations had reason to regret a 1973 decision to change from a three-lap to a four-lap relay. Soviet depth may have decided the issue and contributed to the Soviet victory by 57 seconds over Finland. Lack of a fourth strong runner among the Finnish, East German and Swedish teams made it easy for the Soviets. It was the U.S.S.R. and Finland for first and second, with Barbara Petzold and Veronika Schmidt wresting third place for East Germany from Sweden for the bronze.

4 × 5-km. relay race	
1. U.S.S.R. (Nina Baldicheva, Zinaida Amosova, Raisa Smetanina, Galina Kulakova)	1:07:49.75
2. Finland	1:08:36.57
3. E. Germany	1:09:57.95
4. Sweden	1:10:14.68
5. Norway	1:11:09.08
6. Czechoslovakia	1:11:27.83

Men's 15-Kilometer Cross-Country

The Soviets gave signs of completely taking over the Nordic cross-country racing by placing three in the first four. Gold went to Nikolai Bashukov, a twenty-two-year-old soldier who had set the pace in the early stages of the 30-kilometer race, fading before the onslaught of Bill Koch, United States, and his more durable teammates. Finland's Arto Koivisto saved Scandinavia's honor by winning the bronze. Koch's sixth place was a tribute to his ability to come back—to come back after the many interviews and other distractions to which any newfound hero is exposed after placing second in the 30-kilometer race. Bogged down in twelfth place after two-thirds of the race, Koch made use of good wax and natural skill to turn in the fastest last 5 kilometers of any runner.

MEN	
15-km. cross-country	Time
1. Nikolai Bashukov, U.S.S.R.	43:58.47
2. Eugeny Beliaev, U.S.S.R.	44:01.10
3. Arto Koivisto, Finland	44:19.25
4. Ivan Garanin, U.S.S.R.	44:41.98
5. Ivar Förmö, Norway	45:29.11
6. Bill Koch, U.S.A.	45:32.22

Bill Koch, U.S.A. — Silver

Bill Koch, U.S.A. — Silver

Sergei Saveliev, U.S.S.R.

Men's 30-Kilometer Cross-Country

30-km. cross-country

1. Sergei Saveliev, U.S.S.R.		1:30:29.38
2. Bill Koch, U.S.A.		1:30:57.84
3. Ivan Garanin, U.S.S.R.		1:31:09.29
4. Juha Mieto, Finland		1:31:20.39
5. Nikolai Bashukov, U.S.S.R.		1:31:33.14
6. Gert-Dietmar Klause, E. Germany		1:32:00.91

In this race the hierarchy of cross-country skiing was turned head over heels. For the record, the Scandinavians failed to win a medal; instead an American, Bill Koch, made it to the silver. Koch was not a complete unknown among the foreigners—but no one had selected Koch to be the one who challenged the Soviets. The Scandinavians and East Germans, who did so well in the 1974 world championships, all were behind the top three, although Finland's top man, Juha Mieto, was within 11 seconds of the bronze.

Koch's success was particularly impressive because he was within 30 seconds of the victor, Sergei Saveliev, U.S.S.R. Koch gave much credit to his coach and to an older U.S. Olympian, Bob Gray, with whom Koch had trained but who was bypassed in the team selection. "When I was a kid, [Gray] was the one who encouraged me. He kept inspecting my skis and kept giving me helpful hints," said Koch.

Clothes may help make the businessman a success; Nordic cross-country skiers do rely on nourishment received during the race. Koch was fed Coca-Cola and a mixture, simply known as "erg," that contains glucose, salt and minerals.

166

Klause Gert-Dietmar, E. Germany—Silver

Ivar Formo, Norway—Gold

Ben Södergren, Sweden—Bronze

Ivar Formo, Norway

Men's 50-Kilometer Cross-Country

As the premier event of the Nordic program opened, the snows were falling—real Scandinavian weather for once. This is the single event on the Nordic program that the Scandinavians have won every time. At the midpoint in the race it was difficult to get a good focus on it: Bill Koch had caught up with Vasily Rotshev of the U.S.S.R., who had started 30 seconds earlier and was in first place. Koch had a narrow 8-second lead over East Germany's Klause and 29 seconds over Norway's last hope, Ivar Förmö. The six-foot Förmö hadn't given up. He had been exactly Koch's age, twenty, when he won a bronze at Sapporo in the 15-kilometer race. At the 40-kilometer mark Garanin appeared to be the only Soviet runner with a chance to win; Rotshev and Koch had worn out each other in a head-to-head duel and dropped more than 7 minutes behind Förmö. And when Förmö crossed the finish line first, his countrymen were already singing his praises loudly.

50-km. cross-country
1. Ivar Förmö, Norway   2:37:30.05
2. Gert-Dietmar Klause,
   E. Germany   2:38:13.21
3. Ben Södergren, Sweden   2:39:39.21
4. Ivan Garanin, U.S.S.R.   2:40:38.94
5. Gerhard Grimmer,
   E. Germany   2:41:15.46
6. Per Knut Aaland, Norway   2:41:18.06

Ulrich Wehling, E. Germany—Gold

Men's 4 × 10-Kilometer Cross-Country Relay

4 × 10-km. relay race
1. Finland (Matti Pitkänen, Juha
   Mieto, Pertti Teurajärvi,
   Arto Koivisto)   2:07:59.72
2. Norway   2:09:58.36
3. U.S.S.R.   2:10:51.46
4. Sweden   2:11:16.88
5. Switzerland   2:11:28.53
6. U.S.A.   2:11:41.35

Finland upheld the fading Scandinavian Nordic skiing superiority by winning the 4 × 10-kilometer relay in a race that had everything but the kitchen sink, including a near-successful bid for the bronze medal by the United States. Norway and the U.S.S.R. finished second and third, and the United States was sixth—49 seconds away from third. Koch actually succeeded in moving the United States into third during the third lap.

Nordic Combined

Nordic combined   Points
1. Ulrich Wehling, E. Germany
   (225.5 jumping,
   197.89 cross-country)   423.39
2. Urban Hettich, W. Germany 418.90
3. Konrad Winkler, E. Germany 417.47
4. Rauno Miettinen, Finland 411.30
5. Claus Tuchscherer,
   E. Germany   409.51
6. Nikolai Nogovitzin, U.S.S.R. 406.44

Since 1972 Ulrich Wehling, from East Germany, has been the Olympic and FIS world champion, and at Innsbruck he again won. He was the only Sapporo individual victor to retain his laurels at Innsbruck. In the jumping competition on the first day it appeared that Wehling had built up an insurmountable lead. But the 15-kilometer race put a lot of pressure on the defending champion. The person who applied the pressure was Urban Hettich, a West German. First in the cross-country running, Hettich was good enough in this phase of the combination, on the basis of his 48 minutes and 1.55 seconds, to gain the silver medal.

168

Jochen Danneberg, E. Germany—Silver

Anton Innauer, Austria—Silver

Karl Schnabl, Austria—Gold

The Special Jump

Four years earlier at Sapporo, Japan placed 1-2-3 in the jumping off the 70-meter hill. It was an improbability that any nation would match such a performance in the Innsbruck games. In the 70-meter competition East Germany went 1-2 as Hans-Georg Aschenbach leapt with the longest of the first jumps and the second longest of the other jump, to defeat teammate Jochen Danneberg and Austria's Karl Schnebl. Although the Americans made no dent in the front ranks, they greatly improved their international rankings when Jim Denney finished twenty-first with two jumps of more than 75 meters.

In spite of Aschenbach's triumph off the smaller hill, the closing event on the program, the 90-meter ski jump, was more dramatic than the wildest tales by authors of sports fiction. More than 60,000 eyewitnesses gathered at Bergisel for the windup, which had been billed as a dual meet between Austria and East Germany. The East Germans had won the day off the smaller hill; the confident Austrians had to make amends to regain public acclaim. Austrian ski jumpers, Austrian Olympic officials and the populace in general were deeply concerned that morning, for the Austrian national anthem had not been played since the first day of Alpine competition when Franz Klammer had won the downhill and become instantly "Mr. Austrian Sports Hero."

The first eight places in this premier event were divided equally between the two adversaries. Austria placed men 1, 2, 5 and 6; East Germany finished 3, 4, 7 and 8. For the home folks it was the greatest of all days for Austria at the Olympic Winter Games—a gold medal for Schnabl, one silver, followed by two more within the top six.

Ski jump, 70-m. hill	Points
1. Hand-Georg Aschenbach, E. Germany (84.5-m., 82.0-m. jumps)	252.0
2. Jochen Dannenberg, E. Germany	246.2
3. Karl Schnabl, Austria	242.0
4. Jaroslav Balcar, Czechoslovakia	239.6
5. Ernst von Grüningen, Switzerland	238.7
6. Reinhold Bachler, Austria	237.2

Ski jump, 90-m. hill	
1. Karl Schnabl, Austria (97.5-m., 97.0-m. jumps)	234.8
2. Toni Innauer, Austria	232.9
3. Henry Glass, E. Germany	221.7
4. Jochen Dannenberg, E. Germany	221.6
5. Reinhold Bachler, Austria	217.4
6. Hans Wallner, Austria	216.9

169

Walter Malmquist, U.S.A.

Eugeny Belieav, U.S.S.R.   Nikolai Bajukov, U.S.S.R.   Arto Koivisto, Finland

Alison Owen-Spencer   Bill Koch, U.S.A. — Silver   Chris McNeill

United States Nordic Ski Team

Top Contenders

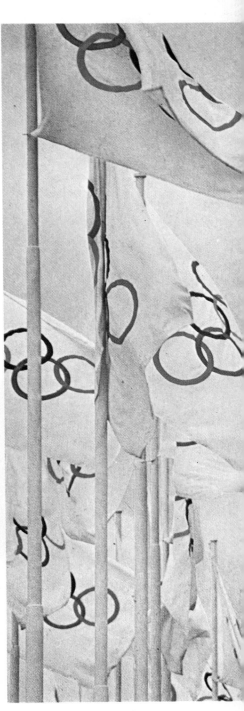

In Nordic cross-country skiing the Soviet women will continue to be strong. Raisa Smetanina, Nina Baldicheva and Galina Kulakova may be back to win medals for U.S.S.R. Also top contenders will be the women from Finland, Sweden, East Germany, Norway and the United States.

The Nordic men's events will be as exciting as ever. In the shorter cross-country events watch Bill Koch from the United States, Serpei Saveliev, Ivan Garanin, and Eugeny Beliaer from U.S.S.R. In the 50 kilometer cross-country event see if Ivar Formo of Norway can repeat his gold medal performance. The ski jump events may be dominated by Karl Schnabl, Toni Immauer, Reinhold Bachler and Hans Wallner from Austria; and Jochen Dannenberg, Henry Glass, and Hand-Georg Aschenbach from East Germany.

Jeff Denney

Pat Ahern

Walter Malmquist, U.S.A.

Jim Denney

Jon Denney

171

6

Biathlon

GOLD FOR AN UNKNOWN

Olympics can be a two-faced lady. She can destroy favorites, but she can also raise unknowns to unexpected heights. Magnar Solberg was one of the unknowns during the Olympic Winter Games at Grenoble in 1968. The thirty-one-year-old policeman from Trondheim was a total stranger, even to his fellow Norwegians, who are great fans of the biathlon. Although already advanced in years as an athlete, he had never participated in any important international competition, not to mention any Olympic Games.

His teammates, Ion Istad, world champion of 1966, as well as Ragnar Tveiten and Ola Waerhaug, ranked among the most experienced and successful biathlon specialists in the world. They were fast and strong on skis as well as accurate with their rifles. They justly deserved the confidence of their countrymen. But Magnar Solberg? Nobody knew why he was chosen as the fourth member of the Norwegian team. Solberg was terribly disappointing when he took part in a pre-Olympic competition in Switzerland, and the Norwegians would have liked to send him back to Norway. Yet the same Magnar Solberg won the biathlon gold medal at the Olympic Games. There were not too many spectators assembled that cold and wet morning of February 12 when sixty competitors representing fourteen nations started the 20-kilometer (about 12.4 miles) biathlon in one-minute intervals. The French did not particularly care for this event, which had been added to the Olympic program only eight years before at Squaw Valley. Many regarded it as a competition for soldiers, and anything military really is not compatible with the Olympic spirit.

This prejudice, however, is discredited by an examination of the history of skiing. The oldest known picture of a skier, the rock painting of Roedoey, Norway, which was discovered in 1929 and dates back to 3000 B.C., shows a man on something that looks very much like today's skis, carrying a weapon in his hands. This ancient skier could be called the first biathlon athlete on record. All the other pictorial documents, especially the old Russian stone sketches, also show hunters on skis. In the books of Bishop Olaus Magnus of Uppsala, Sweden, dating back to 1539, numerous winter hunting scenes can be found. Interesting are the descriptive texts of these pictures. One of them

Magnar Solberg

reads: "Those are the Laplanders, who with opened and long woods tied to their feet roam swiftly at will over mountains and valleys to hunt . . ." It is a curious fact that the youngest Winter Olympic sport is actually older than all the others!

The modern biathlon competitor can therefore be compared to a hunter rather than to a soldier. Every 4.5 kilometers (4923 yards) he has to fire five shots at a target 150 meters (492 feet) away. He has to shoot in a prone position at the first and third targets and standing up at the others. The target he has to hit is only 12.5 centimeters (5 inches) or 35 centimeters (14 inches) in diameter.

Magnar Solberg hit the targets as if they were twice their size. With his third starting position, the unknown Norwegian began his lonely race behind the strong Alexandr Tikhonov of the U.S.S.R. and Poland's Stanislaus Szczepaniak. The course was wet and strenuous, but Solberg, six feet tall and weighing only one hundred fifty pounds, did not seem to notice it. He felt a strange driving force within him. With almost automatic motions, he unslung his rifle from his back and took aim with such a steady hand it was as if he had not been skiing at all. The Soviet contender had skied a little faster, but did not shoot as well at the first two targets. This cost him two penalty minutes, which were added to his time of 1:12.40.0 hours. Solberg's time was 1:13.45.9 hours, and he did not miss a single shot.

The first starters were already close to the finish line when the rain began to fall. The Olympic gods were against the reigning world champion, Victor Mamatov of the U.S.S.R. His starting number was 58. The gods were also against the other favorites, Ion Istad and Ola Waerhaug. They all started in the last section and had no chance because of a progressively worsening course. Only the incredibly strong Vladimir Groundartsev of the U.S.S.R. could manage to overcome those handicaps to win the bronze medal.

Gold fell upon a man, however, whom nobody had known before. Magnar Solberg experienced his greatest moment. Only after he had crossed the finish line did the strain become noticeable. There he had to admit to the photographers who wanted to take pictures of a happy champion: "I am very happy, but too tired to smile."

174

Klas Lestander

The First Olympic Biathlon
Squaw Valley—1960

The biathlon became a part of the Winter Olympic Games because of the work of one man, General Gustav Dyrssen, a member of the International Olympic Committee for Sweden. The Winter Olympics already had a heavy program, and there were many objections to including this little-known competition. Despite the opposition, General Dyrssen went to California three years before the 1960 games were to be held at Squaw Valley and persuaded the organization committee to introduce the biathlon as a new discipline in the program.

Not all the IOC members knew what a winter biathlon consisted of. This is understandable, since the competition had seldom been heard of. Briefly, the biathlon is a 20-kilometer cross-country course including uphill and downhill sections across which the competitor must ski with a rifle slung across his body. At four points along the course the competitor must stop to fire five shots at a target. There is a 200-meter range after 6.5 kilometers, a 250-meter range after 9.5 kilometers, a 150-meter range after 12.5 kilometers and a 100-meter range after 15 kilometers. In 1960, at the first three ranges the competitor chose his own firing position, but at the last range he had to fire standing up with no support. Every failure to hit the target adds two minutes to the competitors' actual running time for the course. Thus very much depends on expert marksmanship.

To the surprise of even his own countrymen, the Swedish carpenter Klas Lestander won the event in 1960. On the track itself he was not very fast and in running time alone would have been placed only fifteenth out of the thirty competitors, all of whom finished. Lestander hit the target with every one of his 20 bullets, so that no penalty minutes were added to his running time. In the shooting section the Norwegian Ola Waerhaug came next with only one bullet missing the target. However, his total time of 1:38:35.8 hours, including two minutes of penalty for the one stray shot, put him in seventh place.

Prone Position Shooting

The Frenchman Victor Arbez was an excellent skier. His running time of 1:25:58.4 hours beat Lestander's by almost 7:5 minutes. He missed the target with 18 shots out of 20, which added 36 minutes penalty and put him at twenty-fifth place. Even the most expert skier could not overcome a disadvantage like that in the biathlon. The four participating Frenchmen had no luck at all at shooting. Out of their combined 80 shots they missed the targets 68 times, collecting a combined penalty of 136 minutes. Biathlon enthusiasts can easily excuse this. To command a steady hand for shooting after each strenuous section of the course is extremely difficult. Only Lestander proved himself really capable in the competition, although the runners-up Tyrvainen of Finland and Privalov of the U.S.S.R. also proved themselves to be good shots. The U.S. team was also hurt by poor shooting. The U.S. quartet comprised John Burritt, who finished fourteenth; Richard Mize, twenty-first; Gustav Hanson, twenty-third; and Larry Damon, twenty-fourth.

On to the Next Target

Results, Biathlon
1960 (Squaw Valley)

		Hits	Time	Penalty	Total
1.	Lestander, Sweden	20	1:33:21.6	0:00.0	1:33:21.6
2.	Tyrvainen, Finland	18	1:29:57.7	4:00.0	1:33:57.7
3.	Privalov, U.S.S.R.	17	1:28:54.2	6:00.0	1:34:54.2
4.	Melanjin, U.S.S.R.	16	1:27:42.4	8:00.0	1:35:42.4
5.	Pshenitsin, U.S.S.R.	17	1:30:45.8	6:00.0	1:36:45.8
6.	Sokolov, U.S.S.R.	15	1:28:16.7	10:00.0	1:38:16.7
7.	Waerhaug, Norway	19	1:36:35.8	2:00.0	1:38:35.8
8.	Meinila, Finland	15	1:29:17.0	10:00.0	1:39:17.0
9.	Werner, Germany	14	1:29:33.8	12:00.0	1:41:33.8
10.	Hermansen, Norway	16	1:34:20.1	8:00.0	1:42:20.1

Start of Relay Race

Coaches Study Shooting Results

Innsbruck—1964

In 1964 at Innsbruck, Finland's Veikko Hakulinen, rated the favorite, managed only a fifteenth place as the Soviet team swept the first two positions. Charlie Akers of Andover, Maine, was the first American across the line, finishing sixteenth. The other American finishers among the top forty-nine were Bill Spencer, thirtieth; Peter Lahdenpera, thirty-sixth; and Paul Renne, thirty-ninth—all of the U.S. Army.

Grenoble—1968

In 1968 the biathlon was still a comparatively new Olympic sport. The skills of the long-distance skier and the excellent marksman that it demanded made it a contest best suited for the military and for frontier police in mountainous countries. As expected, the race was a duel between the Scandinavians and the Soviet Union, with Norway's Magnar Solberg winning the gold medal and the U.S.S.R.'s Alexandr Tikhonov winning the silver. Tikhonov actually was the better skier, but he twice missed targets and this cost him the first place.

Results, Biathlon (Individual) 1968 (Grenoble)	Total Time (Hours)
1. Magnar Solberg, Norway	
2 in 1:13:45.9 hrs., no penalty	1:13:45.9
2. Alexandr Tikhonov, U.S.S.R.	
1 in 1:12:40.0 hrs., 2 min. penalty	1:14:40.0
3. Vladimir Groundartsev, U.S.S.R.	
5 in 1:16:27.4 hrs., 2 min. penalty	1:18:27.4
4. Stanislaus Szczepaniak, Poland	
10 in 1:17:56.8 hrs., 1 min. penalty	1:18:56.8
5. Arve Kinnari, Finland	
8 in 1:17:47.9 hrs., 2 min. penalty	1:19:47.9
6. Nikolai Pousanov, U.S.S.R.	
7 in 1:17:14.5 hrs., 3 min. penalty	1:20:14.5

177

Franz Vetter, Austria

On the Course

In the biathlon relay the situation was reversed, with the Soviets taking the gold, although the Swedish were the better shooters. One of the early surprises was the fine performance of the American team, but imprecise shooting later on dropped them to eighth place. The year 1968 was the first time the biathlon relay event was held in the Olympic Games. Fourteen teams from fourteen countries competed. Every competitor lapped a 2.5-kilometer course three times, and there were two shooting exercises of eight shots at five targets. The competitor had to go back 200 meters for each target they did not hit.

Results, Biathlon Relay
1968 (Grenoble)

		Targets Missed	Individual Times (Minutes)	Total Time (Hours)
1. U.S.S.R.	Tikhonov	1	33:28.9	
	Pousanov	1	34:07.2	
	Mamatov	0	32:53.2	
	Groundartsev	0	32:33.1	2:13:02.4
2. Norway	Waerhaug	1	35:12.1	
	Jordet	2	34:06.8	
	Solberg	0	32:26.4	
	Istad	2	33:04.9	2:14:50.2
3. Sweden	Arwidson	0	34:13.3	
	Eriksson	0	35:03.8	
	Petrusson	0	35:00.0	
	Olsson	0	33:09.2	2:17:26.3
4. Poland	Rozak	2	36:46.3	
	Fiedor	1	36:40.6	
	Lukaszczyk	1	34:01.9	
	Szczepaniak	0	32:50.8	2:20:19.6
5. Finland	Suutarinen	3	38:05.0	
	Floejt	1	35:57.3	
	Vaehaekylae	0	32:52.3	
	Kinnari	1	33:47.2	2:20:41.8
6. E. Germany	Kluge	1	36:48.1	
	Jahn	1	36:22.5	
	Koscha	0	35:22.7	
	Speer	2	33:21.2	2:21:54.5

178

Tagging in Biathlon Relay

Sapporo—1972

At Sapporo in 1972, thirty-two of the fifty-four participants were already on the course when a white curtain fell from the sky, enveloping the course to such an extent that the competitors could not even see the targets. The event had to be called off. When the race was repeated, the conditions were good and the champion from Grenoble, Norwegian Magnar Solberg, gave a repeat performance. Over the 20-kilometer course he was the fourth fastest and he collected only two penalty minutes for the shooting.

The improvement in the U.S. team was due to improved shooting. Peter Karns, a graduate of the University of Utah and the 1970 national champion, finished fourteenth. This equaled John Burritt's finish place in 1960, the first year of the biathlon competition. Following Karns' fourteenth place, the U.S. entries wound up twenty-fourth, forty-first and forty-fifth out of fifty-four entries.

Results, Biathlon (Individual)
1972 (Sapporo)

	Total Time (Hours)
1. Magnar Solberg, Norway, 2 min. penalty	1:15:55.50
2. Hansjorg Knauthe, E. Germany, 1 min. penalty	1:16:07.60
3. Lars-G., Arwidson, Sweden, 2 min. penalty	1:16:27.03
4. Alexandr Tikhonov, U.S.S.R., 4 min. penalty	1:16:48.65
5. Yrjo Salpakari, Finland, 2 min. penalty	1:16:51.43
6. Esko Saira, Finland, 5 min. penalty	1:17:34.80

The Japanese led after the first lap of the biathlon relay. In spite of that, the U.S.S.R. still won unchallenged. It was a great surprise that the second place was won by the Finns. The other Scandinavians placed only fourth and fifth. A most pleasant surprise for the United States was sixth place in the relay. The same group who participated in the individual event represented the United States in the relay: Peter Karns, Dennis Donahue, Dexter Morse and Jay Bowerman. This quartet earned an Olympic diploma for their place in this event, on the program for only the second time.

Magnar Solberg

Shooting Under Heavy Snow

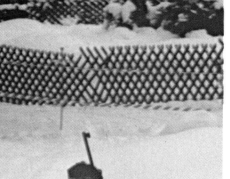

Lyle Nelson, U.S.A.

Results, Biathlon Relay
1972 (Sapporo)

(10 teams from 10 countries. Every competitor lapped a 2.5-km. course 3 times and there were 2 shooting exercises of 8 shots at 5 targets. The competitor had to ski a 20-meter course for every target missed.)

		Individual Times (Minutes)	Total Time (Hours)
1. U.S.S.R.	Tikhonov	28:54.48	
	Safin	26:48.51	
	Biokov	28:15.90	
	Mamatov	27:46.02	1:51:44.92
2. Finland	Saira	28:52.04	
	Suutarinen	28:52.04	
	Ikola	28:45.79	
	Roeppaenen	27:22.09	1:54:37.25
3. E. Germany	Knauthe	28:11.72	
	Meischner	28:35.86	
	Speer	28:50.72	
	Koschka	29:19.37	1:54:57.67
4. Norway	Svendsberget	28:23.86	
	Hovda	29:43.80	
	Nordkild	29:41.97	
	Solberg	28:34.78	1:56:24.41
5. Sweden	Arwidson	28:23.09	
	Petrusson	29:32.78	
	Wadman	27:52.03	
	Olsson	31:09.50	1:56:57.40
6. U.S.A.	Karns	28:50.37	
	Morse	28:43.56	
	Donahue	29:01.97	
	Bowerman	30:48.48	1:57:24.32

Innsbruck—1976

Marksmanship was again the key word in the biathlon event at Innsbruck in 1976. The failure of either of the former world champions, Finland's Heikki Ikola and top-ranked Alexandr Tikhonov of the U.S.S.R., to win the gold medal was a surprise. Ikola was runner-up. Nikolai Kruglov, a twenty-five-year-old army lieutenant, thought he had been eliminated after missing two early shots and being assessed the penalty, which was added directly to the actual time for completing the course. As it turned out, Kruglov and Ikola both missed two targets, but Kruglov skied the distance 17 seconds faster for the gold.

180

ki Ikola, Finland

In the first six places the U.S.S.R. had three, Finland two and Italy one.

The biathlon relay was decided almost strictly on marksmanship, the combined shooting of four expert cross-country skiers. In summary, the gold medal was again captured by the Soviet Union over Finland and East Germany simply because its biathletes didn't miss a single shot at the target. The order of finish on the Innsbruck course repeated Sapporo four years earlier. Each skier carried two five-bullet magazines, each with six extra cartridges. On the 7.5-kilometer lap there were two shooting "stations" set up. At the initial one, 2.5 kilometers into the course, there were five black targets 150 meters away to be hit from a prone position. At the 5-kilometer mark there was another station where five more shots were taken from a standing position.

When the target was hit, a red light flashed. If it was not hit within four shots, the biathlete started on a 150-meter penalty tour. Thus this was a distance penalty as opposed to a time penalty for the individual event.

The only real battle was for the bronze. West Germany's Klaus Gehrke was 1:45 ahead of East Germany's Manfred Geyer. Despite not missing a target, he was overtaken by his opponent and was nipped by only 10 meters in the final accounting. Kruglov and Tikhonov handled the final two laps for the winning Soviet foursome.

No. 9 Alkolai Kruglov, U.S.S.R.

With new leadership among the coaches and managers, all former Olympic biathletes, it was expected that the United States would continue the progress reflected in the results at Sapporo four years before. Such was not the case. Peter Karns had finished fourteenth at Sapporo, equaling the best U.S. individual finish. He was head coach of the 1976 Olympic team. Two of the four U.S. entries were jinxed. John Morton was down with influenza and never started. Lieutenant Peter Dascoulias was eliminated when the stock of his rifle was broken in a freak accident.

Heikki Ikola, Finland

Thus the top finisher was Captain Lyle Nelson, number one in the Olympic trials. He placed thirty-fifth and another newcomer, Martin Hagen, placed forty-seventh. There were fifty-one finishers.

At Sapporo the biathlon relay team of the United States had finished sixth out of ten teams. At Innsbruck they came in eleventh in a field of fifteen entries.

Results, Biathlon 1976 (Innsbruck)

Individual (20 km.)
1. Nikolai Kruglov, U.S.S.R.   1:14:12.26 (2)
2. Heikki Ikola, Finland   1:15:54.10 (2)
3. Alexandr Elizarov, U.S.S.R.   1:16:05.57 (3)
4. Willy Bertin, Italy   1:16:50.36 (3)
5. Alexandr Tikhonov, U.S.S.R.   1:17:18.33 (7)
6. Esko Saira, Finland   1:17:32.84 (2)

Figures in parentheses indicate missed targets in the shooting.

Relay (4 x 7.5 km.)
1. U.S.S.R. (Ivan Bjakov, Alexandr Elizarov, Nikolai Kruglov, Alexandr Tikhonov)   1:57:55.64
2. Finland   2:01:45.58
3. E. Germany   2:04:08.61
4. W. Germany   2:04:11.86
5. Norway   2:05:10.28
6. Italy   2:06:16.55

Martin Hagen, U.S.A.

Heikki Ikola, Finland

Vladimir Alikin, U.S.S.R.

Glen Jobe After Frosty

Don Nielsen, U.S.A., Tagging Glen Jobe

Martin Hagen, U.S.A.

Top Contenders

The people in these pictures are top contenders for Lake Placid, 1980. Racing in the World Cup at Anterselva, Italy were Martin Hagen, U.S.A., and Heikki Ikola from Finland. At the World Championship race in Ruhpolding, Germany were Vladimir Alikin and Nikolai Kruglov from Russia; Frank Ullrich from East Germany, and Lyle Nelson, Don Nielsen and Glen Jobe from the United States. The biathlon is a 20-kilometer cross-country ski course including uphill and downhill sections across which a competitor must ski with a rifle slung over his body. At certain points along the course he must stop and fire at a target.

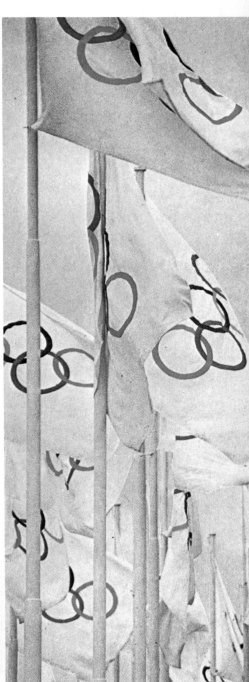

Nikolai Kruglov, U.S.S.R., Shooting;
Frank Ullrich, East Germany, Skiing

Lyle Nelson, U.S.A., on the Course

183

184

7

Luge-Tobogganing
A FRESH START FOR AN ANCIENT SPORT
INNSBRUCK—1964

In France the vehicle is a luge. In Germany they call it a rodel. Americans don't know what to call it because most have never heard of it, although a toboggan is a close relative. This difficulty posed problems for Master Sergeant Volley Cole, whose task it was to recruit candidates for the American luge team to enter in the 1964 Olympics at Innsbruck.

It took some doing, for no one had ever ridden a luge, which is less mechanized than a bobsled and requires manual controls. Few knew what he was talking about. Fewer still appeared interested in caroming down an ice-coated 1063.76-meter-long sluice at 60 miles per hour.

Sergeant Cole finally recruited a ten-member team from army personnel and two young women. They practiced in Germany because there were no American facilities for luge racing.

Austria's Josef Feistmantl and Manfred Stengl won the two-man event, and a second Austrian team took the silver medal in a race marred by a crash in which Californians Ronnie Walters and Jim Higgins missed death by a fraction of an inch. The second U.S. luge, with Ray Fales and Nick Mastromatteo aboard, finished last among thirteen competitors.

Injuries hampered whatever opportunities the Americans had in the event. Elizabeth Gould of Rydal, Pennsylvania, was injured in practice trials. This left Dorothy Ann Hirschland as the only American contender in the women's singles tobogganing. She had to withdraw, so the United States had no entry in the event.

Only Helene Thurner of Austria, who took third, could dent the Germans' hold on the men's and women's divisions. The men of West Germany took all the medals in the singles and their female counterparts took first and second ahead of Thurner. Francis Feltman, thirteenth, Robert Neely, seventeenth, John Hessel, twenty-second, and George Farmer, twenty-ninth, were the four American men to finish in the singles.

Flat Out

GRENOBLE—1968

In 1968 the rare breed of tobogganers were still having difficulties meeting the requirement of twelve participating nations as the minimum number for an Olympic event at Grenoble. They also experienced many troubles and disappointments during their second Olympic competition. Their sleds, weighing approximately forty pounds, caused them to suffer more than the participants in any other sport because of unfavorable weather conditions. Almost daily the men and women carried their sleds piggyback up to the starting point early in the morning only to be told that the course would never hold up to the trial runs of twenty-six women and fifty-seven men. The ice was approaching snow conditions and the sharp runners of the sleds zooming down at speeds close to 50 m.p.h. would surely have cut through to the concrete foundation of the chute. Only four days before the end of the games were the organizers able to hold three runs of the singles competition for men and women. Finally, on the very last day, the weather did cooperate and the course presented itself in perfect condition for the doubles.

The second mishap had little to do with the sport itself. It did, however, have a direct influence on the distribution of all three medals. There seemed to be no way to stop a sweep of East Germany in the women's competition. After two runs Ortrun Enderlein, the undisputed queen of tobogganists, was leading. Her two teammates, Anna-Maria Müller and Angela Knösel, were in second and fourth positions. Suddenly, before the third and deciding run, one jury member discovered that the runners of the women's sleds had been heated artificially. This had been strictly prohibited by a recent ruling. Other observers were summoned, and the jury had no choice but to disqualify the East German trio.

186

What's My Time?

The sport was beginning to gain popularity, and there was great admiration for the courageous athletes, especially the women, who looked more like members of a ballet troupe than competitors in a tobogganing contest. They appeared strangely out of place when they jumped fearlessly on their sleds in a running start to catapult themselves down the icy chutes. The most fragile-looking of them all, Erika Lechner of Italy, turned in the fastest times and won the gold medal. World champion Thomas Köhler of East Germany failed by a few hundredths of a second to overtake the Austrian Manfred Schmid. He and his teammate Bonsack did not miss their last chance and won the doubles competiton.

Prospects in 1968 for a high rank in the luge were not bright for the United States. For one thing, there were no Olympic-type facilities in the United States, and the squad could not get much training at a Canadian base before departing on a tour of Europe to gain much-needed experience. There was little time for training on the tour, and even in Grenoble unseasonably warm weather often prevented use of the Olympic run for precompetition testing.

The women representing the United States had less than two years of luging experience, placing fourteenth, sixteenth and seventeenth in a field of twenty-one entries for the singles. Against the vastly experienced European entries, the U.S. cause was a doomed one.

At one time the men's two-seater races were canceled and the U.S. sleds were packed up and shipped home. The races were suddenly rescheduled at the last moment, and only one U.S. pair got to the starting line. They could not qualify during the practice runs. In the men's singles the highest ranking for the United States was twenty-sixth.

Two Man Practise

The sport is popular in the Alpine countries. It had been included only in the previous Olympic Games at Innsbruck. No competitor from a non-European country had been in the top list of performers. The tobogganing took place in a stop about twenty-eight miles from Grenoble. The ice chute was 1094 yards long and had a vertical drop of 109 yards. The weather was far from favorable and the start had to be postponed several times.

In the men's singles the decision was between competitors from Austria and the two Germanys and Poland. The thawing ice made for slow times. Schmid of Austria won the gold medal, while the two East Germans won the silver and the bronze. Zbigniew Gawior was fourth.

Results, Men's Singles
1968 (Grenoble)

(50 toboggans from 14 nations. Only 3 out of 4 proposed runs took place. Feb. 15, 1968.)

	1st Run sec.	2nd Run sec.	3rd Run sec.	Total min.
1. Schmid, Austria	57.16	57.73	57.59	2:52.48
2. Köhler, E. Germany	57.68	57.47	57.51	2:52.66
3. Bonsack, E. Germany	57.90	57.63	57.80	2:53.33
4. Gawior, Poland	57.55	58.35	57.61	2:53.51
5. Feistmantl, Austria	57.78	58.06	57.73	2:53.57
6. Plenk, W. Germany	57.30	58.37	58.00	2:53.67

In the two-man event, which was held after everybody from countries outside Europe had already left, Klaus Bonsack and Thomas Köhler of East Germany won the gold medal. An Austrian pair won the silver and another East German pair took the bronze.

188

Round the Bend

Results, Men's Doubles
1968 (Grenoble)

(14 toboggans from 8 nations. Feb. 18, 1968.)

	1st Run sec.	2nd Run sec.	Total min.
1. Bonsack/Köhler, E. Germany	47.88	47.97	1:35.85
2. Schmid/Walch, Austria	48.16	48.18	1:36.34
3. Winkler/Nachmann, W. Germany	48.58	48.71	1:37.29
4. Plenk/Aschauer, W. Germany	48.70	48.91	1:37.61
5. Hörnlein/Bredow, E. Germany	48.80	49.01	1:37.81
6. Z. Gawior/R. Gawior, Poland	49.01	48.84	1:37.85

At last the women's event got under way. It was won by Ortrun Enderlein of East Germany. Places two and four also were taken by women from West Germany, while the bronze medal went to Erica Lechner of Italy. That was before the East Germans were all disqualified.

Results, Women's Singles
1968 (Grenoble)

(26 toboggans from 10 nations. Only 3 out of 4 proposed runs took place. Feb. 15, 1968.)

	1st Run sec.	2nd Run sec.	3rd Run sec.	Total min.
1. Erica Lechner, Italy	48.76	49.39	50.51	2:28.66
2. Christa Schmuck, W. Germany	49.15	49.84	50.38	2:29.37
3. Angelika Dünhaupt, W. Germany	49.34	49.88	50.34	2:29.56
4. Helena Macher, Poland	49.55	50.02	50.48	2:30.05
5. Jadwiga Damse, Poland	49.64	50.43	50.08	2:30.15
6. Dana Beldova, Czechoslovakia	49.22	50.36	50.77	2:30.35

Angela Knösel, Anna-Maria Müller and Ortrun Enderlein (all of East Germany) were disqualified.

Angelika Schafferer, Austria

Kathleen Homstad

Vera Zozulia, U.S.S.R.

SAPPORO—1972

Sapporo in 1972 saw the best-prepared group of men and women lugers the United States had entered in the Olympic competition since the ancient sport of European thrill seekers had been placed on the Olympic program eight years before.

The two Germanys and Italy continued to dominate the sport with experienced and daring lugers. There was not a more demanding or thrilling sport in the Olympic Games. For the first time, three U.S. entries in the men's singles and two entries in the doubles event all completed their prescribed number of runs. Only one of the three women completed all four runs.

At Grenoble, Kathy Homstad, then only sixteen, had finished fourteenth out of twenty-one lugers. At Sapporo, Kathy finished fifteenth out of twenty-three, nosing out the 1968 champion by a few hundredths of a second.

INNSBRUCK—1976

"May the best man win" was scarcely the appropriate battle cry for lugers at Innsbruck in 1976. It was equipment that counted and that made Olympic history. Streamlined sleds and customized helmets, some pointed and some egg-shaped, were the winning gear on display. Hans Rinn, East Germany's most talented luger, stuck to the 1972 fashions and was dethroned by team-

190

Ute Rührold, E. Germany

Margit Schumann, E. Germany

Elisabeth Demleitner, W. Germany

Ute Rührold, E. Germany

mate Detlief Günther, finishing third behind Josef Fendt of West Germany.

The women's competition had a familiar ring, with East Germany sweeping the medals. Margit Schumann, an army lieutenant, moved up from a third-place finish of four years earlier to win the gold medal by .225 second over Ute Rührold, also from East Germany, who had earned the silver at Sapporo.

There was a three-way battle for medals in the two-seaters event, which was part of the bobsled run for the first time. Hans Rinn gained a measure of revenge for himself, pairing with Norbert Hahn. After earning an advantage of .002 second on the first of two runs, he increased the lead over the West German pair to .28 second on the second run to win the gold. Third place was snared by the home forces of Austria. Of the nine medals available in luge, eight were shared by the Germans. Austria won its first medal in luge since the inaugural events at Innsbruck in 1964.

The only bobsled run in North America was at Lake Placid. It had been converted to a combination bobsled-luge run, making it available for American lugers. Even with an established training base and a newly recruited European coach, Piotr Rogowski, formerly of Poland, any improvement in the U.S. team was not noticeable at Innsbruck.

The luge run at Innsbruck was perhaps the safest on which international competitions were ever held. There were no serious injuries.

For the first time in four Olympic Games the entire U.S. luge squad finished all runs in the men's singles, men's two-seaters and women's singles competitions.

Kathleen Homstad, on her third Olympic team, again paced the women. She wound up twenty-first out of twenty-six entries. Rick Cavanagh, a seven-year luger, topped the U.S. men. He wound up twenty-fifth out of forty-three entries and with Bob Berkley, his 1972 partner, finished twenty-third out of twenty-five entries for the two-seater teams. Jim Murray had finished twenty-eighth in the last two Olympic Games. At Innsbruck he was twenty-sixth, one notch below Cavanagh, while Terry O'Brien, an Air Force enlisted man, was twenty-eighth as opposed to thirty-first at Sapporo.

Results, 1976 (Innsbruck)

Men's singles (four runs)
1. Detlef Günther, E. Germany
   (52.381, 52.101, 51.418, 50.882)   3:27.688
2. Josef Fendt, W. Germany   3:28.196
3. Hans Rinn, E. Germany   3:28.574
4. Hans-Heinrich Winkler, E. Germany   3:29.454
5. Manfred Schmid, Austria   3:29.511
6. Anton Winkler, W. Germany   3:29.520

Women's singles (four runs)
1. Margit Schumann, E. Germany
   (42.854, 42.830, 42.285, 42.652)   2:50.621
2. Ute Rührold, E. Germany   2:50.846
3. Elisabeth Demleitner, W. Germany   2:51.056
4. Eva-Maria Wernicke, E. Germany   2:51.262
5. Antonia Mayr, Austria   2:51.360
6. Margit Graf, Austria   2:51.459

Men's doubles (two runs only)
1. E. Germany (Hans Rinn/Norbert Hahn)
   (42.773, 42.831)   1:25.604
2. W. Germany (Brandner/Schwarm)   1:25.899
3. Austria (Schmid/Schachner)   1:25.919
4. W. Germany (Hölzwimmer/Grösswang) 1:26.238
5. Austria (Schmid/Sulzbacher)   1:26.424
6. Czechoslovakia (Zeman/Resl)   1:26.826

192

Right Turn

World Championships
Konigssee—1979

In the 1979 world championships at Königssee, West Germany, East Germany won the men's and women's titles and took the silver in the doubles. Its performance at Lake Placid was still surprising. The world champions, Detlef Günther and Melitta Sollman, repeated their performances. Ilona Brandt took the silver and Roswitha Stenzel took the bronze. Combined with Bernhard Glass's bronze-medal performance in the men's event, this gave the East Germans five of the six singles medals. Only Vladimer Shitov of the Soviet Union prevented a sweep. In all, it was six of nine medals going to East Germany and two more going to West Germany.

Of the North American performers, it was the women who looked the most promising. Danielle Nadeau of Montreal, Canada, finished in fifteenth place, while Donna Burke of Lake Placid took nineteenth. Nadeau and Burke had finished first and second in the North American championships two weeks previously.

Hans Rinn, E. Germany

Vladmir Shitou, U.S.S.R.

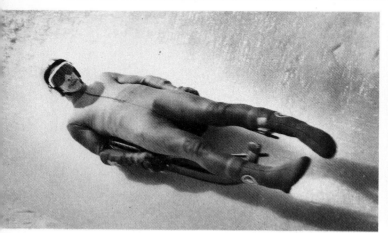

Detlef Guenther,
East Germany
1976 Gold Medalist

John Fee, U.S.A.

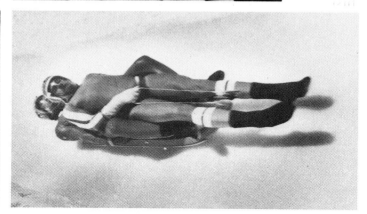

Ty Danco, U.S.A.

Richard Cavanaugh, U.S.A.

Jim Moriarity, U.S.A.

194

Top Contenders

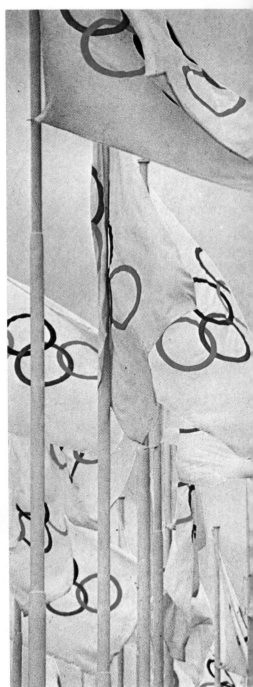

In the 1979 World Championships in Koenigssee, West Germany, the German Democratic Republic won the men's and women's titles and took the silver in the doubles. Its performance in Lake Placid was still surprising. The world champions, Gunther Dettlef and Melitta Sollman, repeated their performances. Ilona Brandt took the silver and Roswitha Stenzel took the bronze. This gave the German Democratic Republic five of the six singles medals. Only Vladimer Shitof of the Soviet Union prevented a sweep. Of the North American performances, it was the women who looked the most promising. Danielle Nadeau of Canada finished in fifteenth place while Donna Burke of Lake Placid took nineteenth place. Nadeau and Burke finished first and second in the 1979 North American Championships.

Among the outstanding American Luge experts that may be competing are: Ty Danco of Pepper Pike, Ohio; Gary Schmeusser of Wilmington, Delaware; Jim Moriarity of St. Paul, Minnesota; Debra Sanders of Monroe, New Hampshire; Debbie Genovese of Rockford, Illinois; Terry Morgan of Saranac Lake, New York; Steve Wilson and Erica Terwillegar of Lake Placid, New York.

Hans Rinn, E. Germany   Norbert Hahn, E. Germany

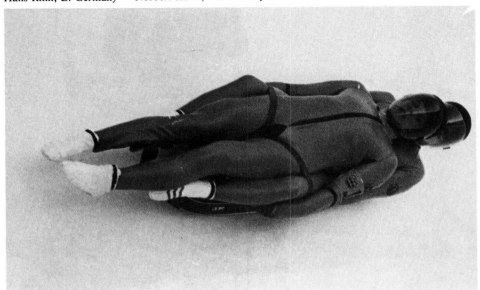

8

Bobsledding

MONTI'S DREAM

It was 1964 at Innsbruck, Austria. The Olympic bobsled competition was held at the Heiligenwasserwiese at the foot of the Patscherkofel mountain. Eugenio Monti of Italy was anxiously awaiting the last run of his most dangerous rival in the two-man competition. Suddenly there came a desperate cry for help over the loudspeaker. A bolt supporting the runners had broken on the sled of Tony Nash from England just as he was about to start his last run in an attempt to win the gold medal away from Monti.

The Italian did not hesitate long. He went over to his bob, took off a bolt, the counterpart of the broken one, and hurried up the hill to the starting place. He himself repaired the sled of his rival. Tony Nash and his brakeman Nixon finally started—and became Olympic champions. It was Nash who later proposed, when the International Sportswriters Association met to award the first Pierre de Coubertin Fair Play Trophy from UNESCO, that it be given to Monti. In May 1965 Monti became the first recipient of this valuable trophy.

Eugenio Monti was born January 23, 1928, at Dobaccio near Bolzano, Italy. He developed into an outstanding Alpine skier. In 1952 at Sestri Levante, Italy, he took a bad spill and required an operation on his left knee. One year later he fell again. This time the same cartilage operation had to be performed on his other knee. This settled matters for Monti. In 1954 he won the Italian collegiate championships once more in the long distance, the slalom and the Nordic combined, but the multitalented athlete had discovered his interest in bobsledding at Cortina d'Ampezzo.

Monti began to typify more and more the new breed of bobsledders. He weighed just 145 pounds, was five feet, nine inches tall and a strong believer in physical fitness. Nobody could handle the Podar bob better than he. The world championships of the following years turned into "Monti Festivals." Nobody faced the dangerous challenge of the icy shoots at St. Moritz, Cortina or Garmisch as seriously as he. He left nothing to chance. He himself carried the runners of his bob to the races and meticulously supervised their proper treatment. This included continuous polishing with woolen cloths until seconds before the actual run. Monti turned the examination of a course

Monti's 4-Man Team, 1956

into a sacred ceremony. He walked the course from start to finish and checked every small detail. Once he escaped disaster by jumping from the course just in time when another bob came rumbling down in a high-speed test run.

Monti, many times world champion, very much wanted to win his first Olympic championship at Innsbruck in 1964. However, he could not come to friendly terms with the course, just as he disliked the one at Alpe d'Huez (near Grenoble) four years later. He simply did not care for courses planned solely by calculations on the drawing boards. Monti was a driver by intuition. Nevertheless he never lost his nerves during a race and he never took unnecessary risks. Most of his victories were won during the last run and he broke course records only when he had no other choice. Innsbruck was Monti's major disappointment. There was talk of the end of the "Era Monti" and he himself talked about retiring. His brakeman Siorpaes, however, had developed new ideas about the construction of the Podar bob. Monti added another world championship in the two-man bob in 1966.

Monti had won nine world championships—but only two silver and two bronze medals in Olympic competiton—when he came to Alpe d'Huez in 1968. Now forty years old, Monti proved he had lost nothing of his fast reflexes and certainly nothing of his uncanny ability to be at his best when it really mattered. At Grenoble it really mattered. His victory in the two-man race could not have been any closer, and his team won the gold medal in the four-man bob by running the race only nine-hundredths of a second faster than the team of silver medalist Thaler of Austria.

Eugenio Monti's dream had finally come true: he had won his tenth and eleventh world championships and his first two gold medals. He smiled and announced to the press that he really was retiring.

A 1936 Garmish Team

The Beginnings of Bobsledding

The beginnings of bob sports go back to the year 1888, when in Switzerland Wilson Smith, an Englishman, made his first experiments to connect two sleighs by means of a board in order to go down the streets of St. Moritz. The first maker of bobsleds was C. Mathis, a blacksmith in St. Moritz. Another famous bobsled designer was the Italian Podar bobs. These men contributed to the great Italian successes in bobsledding.

Four-man bob races were included in the first Olympic Winter Games at Chamonix in 1924, and at Lake Placid in 1932 the two-man race was added.

Besides the vehicle, the pilot's sure eye, exact knowledge of the course and reaction ability all play important roles in bob races. The experienced cooperation of the entire crew, as well as a good start with as great a push as possible, is of great importance for the outcome of the race. In the past the weights of the members of the crew were often of decisive importance, but the decision in 1952 to limit the weights ended this advantage. Parallel to the improvement in the designs of the bobsled and in the preparation with the bob courses, the closeness of the results had increased. At Chamonix in 1924 the time difference between the second and the third bob in the four-man race was almost 14 seconds. At Cortina in 1956 the difference was only .29 second. The high speeds and the closeness of results soon led to the introduction of electrical timekeeping.

U.S.A. Silver Winners Oslo—1952

Results of Two-Man Bob Races through 1960

1960 (Squaw Valley)
No bob races

1956 (Cortina)
1. Italy I
(L. Dalla Costa, G. Conti)   5:30.14
2. Italy II
(E. Monti, R. Alverà)   5:31.45
3. Switzerland I
(M. Angst, H. Warburton)   5:37.46

1952 (Oslo)
1. Germany I
(A. Ostler, L. Niebert)   5:24.54
2. U.S.A. I
(S. Benham, P. Martin)   5:26.89
3. Switzerland I
(F. Feierabend, S. Waser)   5:27.71

1948 (St. Moritz)
1. Switzerland II
(F. Endrich, F. Waller)   5:29.2
2. Switzerland I
(F. Feierabend, P. Eberhard)   5:30.4
3. U.S.A. II
(F. Fortune, S. Carron)   5:35.3

1936 (Garmisch-Partenkirchen)
1. U.S.A. I
(I. Brown, A. Washbond)   5:29.29
2. Switzerland II
(F. Feierabend, J. Beerli)   5:30.64
3. U.S.A. II
(G. Colgate, R. Lawrence)   5:33.96

1932 (Lake Placid)
1. U.S.A. I
(J. H. Stevens, C. P. Stevens)   8:14.74
2. Switzerland II
(R. Capadrutt, O. Geier)   8:16.28
3. U.S.A. II
(J. R. Heaton, R. Minton)   8:29.15

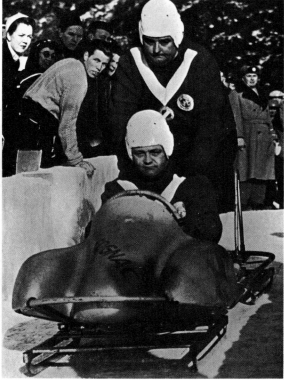

Winning 2-Man Teams—1952   Germany Winning Gold—1952   Germany Winning Gold—1952

Results of Four-Man Bob Races through 1960

1960 (Squaw Valley)
No bob races

1956 (Cortina)
1. Switzerland I
   (F. Kapus, G. Diener, R. Alt,
   H. Angst)   5:10.44
2. Italy II
   (E. Monti, U. Girardi,
   R. Alverà, R. Mocellini)   5:12.10
3. U.S.A.
   (A. Tyler, W. Dodge, C. Butler,
   J. Lamy)   5:12.39

1952 (Oslo)
1. Germany
   (A. Ostler, F. Kuhn, L. Nieberl,
   F. Kemser)   5:07.84
2. U.S.A. I
   (S. Benham, P. Martin,
   H. Crossett, J. Atkinson)   5:10.48
3. Switzerland I
   (F. Feierabend, A. Madörin,
   A. Filippini, S. Waser)   5:11.70

1948 (St. Moritz)
1. U.S.A. II
   (F. Tyler, P. Martin,
   E. Rimkus, W. D'Amico)   5:20.1
2. Belgium
   (M. Houben, F. Mansveld,
   G. Niels, J. Mouvet)   5:21.3
3. U.S.A. I
   (J. Bickford, T. Hicks,
   D. Dupree, W. Dupree)   5:21.5

Innsbruck—1964

There wasn't a bobsled run in all of Canada in 1964, but that didn't prevent Canada's four-man team at Innsbruck from scoring what U.S. coach Stan Benham called the "biggest upset in bobsledding history." Vic Emery drove his team down the chute at Igls four times for a total time of 4:14.46. Emery beat Italian Eugenio Monti, eight times a world champion, and the well-trained Austrian team. The only U.S. sled, driven by William Hickey, finished sixth, just three seconds behind in total elapsed time. Larry McKillip and Jim Larny, 1956 U.S. Olympic teammates, won fifth place in the two-man bobsled event.

Grenoble—1968

The bobsled competition at Grenoble took place in Alpe d'Huez, more than ninety minutes away by car. The organizers took great pains and did not spare costs to improve the track by artificial means. This could not, however, insure that the program would be a success. The races were scheduled to take place in the evening. What the organizers could not prepare for was the wind from the Mediterranean that kept shifting snow onto the track, making it unusable. The starts had to be delayed time and time again. On top of that, the days had been warm and the sun had softened the surface of the track.

1936 (Germisch-Partenkirchen)
1. Switzerland II
   (P. Mussy, A. Gartmann,
   C. Bouvier, J. Beerli)   5:19.85
2. Switzerland II
   (R. Capadrutt, H. Aichele,
   F. Feierabend, H. Bütikofer) 5:22.73
3. Great Britain
   (F. McEvoy, J. Cardno,
   G. Dugdale, C. Green)   5:23.41

1932 (Lake Placid)
1. U.S.A. I
   (W. Fiske, E. Eagan,
   C. Gray, J. O'Brien)   7:53.68
2. U.S.A. II
   (H. Homburger, P. Bryant,
   F. P. Stevens, E. Horton)   7:55.70
3. Germany I
   (H. Kilian, M. Ludwig,
   Dr. H. Mehlhorn, S. Huber)   8:00.04

200

Switzerland's 4-Man Team—1956

After some runs the track was not in good enough condition to take fifty more bobs. As a result the evening runs had to be abandoned and were raced later in the competition at the unusual hour of five in the morning. It was still pitch-dark at that time, and 160 searchlights along the 1641-yard track showed the bobsledders the way.

The story of the two-man event became the story of Italians Eugenio Monti and Luciano de Paolis, his brakeman. Monti had his share of nine different world championship titles, but had never won an Olympic gold medal. Another favorite was the German Horst Floth. He was supported by brakeman Pepi Bader. Monti was the first in the lead. Then Floth managed to go out a tenth of a second faster in his run than Monti. If Monti could better Floth's performance, he would establish a new record of 1:10.05. This was Monti's last run, however, and Floth still had one to go. It turned out that Floth's time was 1:10.15. When the times of all four runs were added, they totaled equal times for Monti and Floth. Someone remembered that there was a special ruling for such a situation. The book of rules was consulted. It stated that whichever team had the fastest time in the first heat would be the winner. Monti won his gold medal.

Results, Two-Man Bob Race
1968 (Grenoble)

(22 bobs from 11 nations. 4 runs for each bob. Feb. 11.)

	1st Run	2nd Run	3rd Run	4th Run	Total
1. Italy I (Monti, de Paolis)	1:10.13	1:10.72	1:10.64	1:10.05	4:41.54
2. Germany I (Floth, Bader)	1:10.76	1:10.43	1:10.20	1:10.15	4:41.54
3. Rumania I (Panturu, Neagoe)	1:10.20	1:11.62	1:11.31	1:11.33	4:44.46
4. Austria I (Thaler, Durnthaler)	1:11.27	1:11.26	1:10.72	1:11.88	4:45.13
5. Great Britain (Nash, Dixon)	1:10.57	1:11.60	1:11.77	1:11.22	4:45.16
6. U.S.A. (Lamey, Huscher)	1:11.30	1:11.54	1:11.04	1:12.15	4:46.03

The four-man bobsled race took place on an icy and very fast track, as the temperature had dropped considerably. There was danger of a sudden thaw, and the officials did not want to submit the track to a risk of collapse. Therefore contestants were limited to two runs. Monti and his crew won a second gold medal, and nobody begrudged the popular Italian his second win. There had never been a more likable sportsman.

Results, Four-Man Bob Race
1968 (Grenoble)

(19 bobs from 11 nations. Only 2 out of 4 proposed runs took place. Feb. 17.)

	1st Run	2nd Run	Total
1. Italy I (Monti, de Paolis, Zandonella, Armano)	1:09.84	1:07.55	2:17.39
2. Austria I (Thaler, Durnthaler, Gruber, Eder)	1:10.08	1:07.40	2:17.48
3. Switzerland I (Wicki, Candrian, Hofmann, Graf)	1:10.65	1:07.39	2:18.04
4. Rumania (Panturu, Neagoe, Hristovici, Maftei)	1:10.59	1:07.55	2:18.14
5. Germany I (Floth, Bader, Schafer, Lange)	1:10.49	1:07.84	2:18.33
6. Italy II (Gaspari, Cavallini, Rescigno, Clemente)	1:10.24	1:08.12	2:18.36

U.S.A. Team—Innsbruck 1976

U.S.A. Team—Sapporo 1972

Sapporo—1972

In the 1972 bobsled events three medals were taken by West Germany, two by the Swiss and one silver by Italy. It was a comedown for Monti's heirs.

In the two-man event the reigning European champions, Wolfgang Zimmerer and Peter Utzschneider of West Germany, did not allow any room for argument and placed themselves at the top of the list after their very first run. At half time Zimmerer and Utzschneider were leading Switzerland's Jean Wicki and Edy Hubacher and their fellow countrymen Horst Floth and Pepi Bader. In their third run Zimmerer and Utzschneider bettered their time with the record run of 1:13.51, which left their bid for Olympic victory unchallenged. Finally, Floth and Bader broke this record with 1:13.07, which enabled them to overtake the Swiss team of Wicki and Hubacher for the silver medal.

Results, Two-Man Bob Race
1972 (Sapporo)

(42 participants from 11 countries. Length of course: 1563 m. 14 curves. Gradient differential: 132 m. Feb. 4/5.)

	1st Run	2nd Run	3rd Run	4th Run	Total
1. W. Germany II (Zimmerer, Utzschneider)	1:14.81	1:14.56	1:13.51	1:14.19	4:57.07
2. W. Germany I (Floth, Bader)	1:16.04	1:15.38	1:14.35	1:13.07	4:58.84
3. Switzerland I (Wicki, Hubacher)	1:15.61	1:15.36	1:14.36	1:14.00	4:59.33
4. Italy I (Gaspari, Armano)	1:15.62	1:16.52	1:13.71	1:14.60	5:00.45
5. Rumania I (Panturu, Zangor)	1:16.50	1:15.31	1:14.04	1:14.68	5:00.53
6. Sweden I (Eriksson, Johansson)	1:16.68	1:16.81	1:14.08	1:13.83	5:01.40

The tension of bobsledding shows itself at the start of a race. The contenders in the four-man sled races are as nervous as racehorses milling around at the starting gate. This is understandable, since the top speed of the race is decided at its very beginning. The initial heave and the push-off, like a spring uncoiling, are the secrets of the bob. The search for a united takeoff shows more than the temperament of the teams. Experts and fans can tell with eyes shut who is taking off.

Medalists: Gold, Switzerland;

Silver, Italy;

In the 1972 four-man bobsled event the British under the command of John Hammond counted quietly to themselves until they got their "go" like Lord Nelson's call; England expects every man to do his duty. The Rumanians under Ion Panturu gave themselves moral support with an enormous shout like D'Artagnan and his three musketeers, and the spectators joined in involuntarily. For Jean Wicki, the pilot of the Switzerland I team, the start took on moral dimensions. He requested "a serious push" from his three teammates—Edy Hubacher, Hans Leutenegger and Werner Camichel. They pushed off as though to the beat of drums. Their runs were as serious as their pushes. They had a first and a second place during the first two runs, and they achieved third place in both the third and fourth runs. That gave them a gold medal and placed them in front of Italy I, steered by de Zordo, and West Germany I, steered by Zimmerer.

Results, Four-Man Bob Race
1972 (Sapporo)

(76 participants from 11 countries. Length of course: 1563 m. 14 curves. Gradient differential: 132 m. Feb. 11/12.)

	1st Run	2nd Run	3rd Run	4th Run	Total
1. Switzerland I (Wicki, Leutenegger, Camichel, Hubacher)	1:10.71	1:11.44	1:10.21	1:10.71	4:43.07
2. Italy I (de Zordo, Frassinelli, dal Fabbro, Bonichon)	1:11.39	1:11.33	1:10.19	1:10.92	4:43.83
3. W. Germany I (Zimmerer, Gaisreiter, Steinbauer, Utzschneider)	1:11.18	1:11.75	1:10.30	1:10.69	4:43.92

The U.S. Olympic bobsled team reported to Sapporo without a single day's training on a bobsled run during the current season. For the first time in the post-WWII period the United States failed to place a sled among the top ten finishers. In the two-man event Lamey and Howard Siler wound up sixteenth, and Boris Said, with Tom Becker as braker, finished nineteenth out of a field of twenty-one. Previously, the U.S. two-man sleds had never finished lower than eleventh.

204

Bronze, W. Germany

The results in the four-man competition were even more disappointing. Lamey's sled overturned and was eliminated from the final standings. The Boris Said sled could do no better than fourteenth among the nineteen sleds in the race. In the four-man races the United States had won gold, silver and bronze medals in 1948, 1952 and 1956 respectively.

Innsbruck—1976

Only four nations placed among the first six in the bobsledding events at Innsbruck in 1976. They were Austria, East Germany, Switzerland and West Germany, with only Austria finishing outside the medal winners' circle.

After three years of intensive buildup and a single year of international competition, East Germany made its Olympic bobsled debut by winning both gold medals. The new hero of bobsledders was Meinhard Nehmer, a humorless and stern thirty-five-year-old. He believed that among the reasons for his success in bobsledding was his special aptitude for technical things such as fast automobiles.

Nehmer was one of four East German gold medalists in bobsledding who had been recruited from other sports. Bernhard Germeshausen, a braker, was a former decathlete. The rider Jochen Babcok had been a member of the national hockey team, and rider Bernhard Lehmann was a former discus thrower. Nehmer proved his superiority in both the two- and four-man races. In five of the eight runs Nehmer's sled was the fastest. Twice he was second and once he was third.

Every time there is a new hero, of course the former hero is displaced. Wolfgang Zimmerer of West Germany, also thirty-five years old, was the hero from the first half of the seventies decade. With a new braker, Manfred Schumann, Zimmerer was runner-up in the two-man race, and his sled placed third in the classic four-man event.

Thus Nehmer, a staff sergeant in the army, became the third bobsled captain in Olympic history to be a double gold winner. He joined Italy's Eugenio Monti, 1968, and West Germany's Anderl Ostler, 1952.

**Results of Bobsled Races
1976 (Innsbruck)**

Four-Man (4 runs)
1. E. Germany I
   (Nehmer, Babcok, Germeshausen, Lehmann)
   54:43, 54.64, 55.51, 55.85   3:40.43
2. Switzerland II
   (Schärer, Bachli, Marti, Benz)   3:40.89
3. W. Germany I
   (Zimmerer, Utzschneider, Bittner, Schumann)   3:41.37

Two-Man (4 runs)
1. E. Germany I
   (Nehmer, Germeshausen)
   56.24, 56.05, 55.87, 56.27   3:44.42
2. W. Germany I
   (Zimmerer, Schumann)   3:44.99
3. Switzerland I
   (Schärer, Benz)   3:45.70

Top Contenders

The 1980 bobsled races at Lake Placid will be exciting. East Germany made its Olympic bobsled debut at Innsbruck in 1976 and won both gold medals. Can Meinhard Nehmer the pilot and Bernd Germershausen the braker help their country repeat this feat? In 1972 West Germany won three of the six medals awarded. Will Wolfgang Zimmerer and Peter Utzschneider win medals for West Germany? The teams to watch should be Italy, Austria, Switzerland, Romania, East Germany, and West Germany.

The vehicle, the pilot's sure eye, knowledge of the course, and reaction ability all play an important role in bobsled races. The experienced cooperation of the entire crew is important for a good start. A great a push as possible at the beginning sometimes determines the outcome of the race.

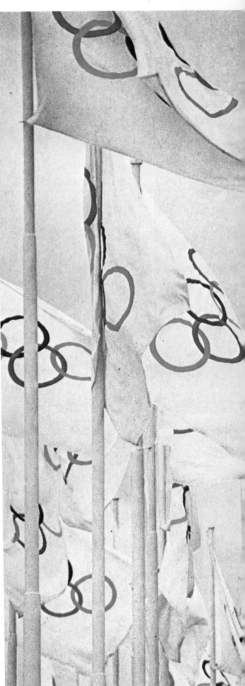

Lake Placid

1932—REVISITED

Behind the III Olympic Winter Games, which crowned Lake Placid as the winter sports capital of the 1930s, lies over a quarter century of successful experience in promoting and staging the sports of snow and ice. While winter sports had been the accepted thing in Europe for many years, it was not until shortly after the turn of the century that Americans in any number began to realize that snow was good for something besides snowballs. Lake Placid was a pioneer American resort in popularizing snow and in presenting its winter attractions to the public. Lake Placid suggests winter sports and winter sports suggest Lake Placid.

Although favored by nature with a climate and terrain ideally suited for winter diversion, it was several decades after Lake Placid had won world renown as a summer resort that anyone so much as thought of finding sport or recreation in its mountain fastnesses in winter. Outdoor sports were unheard of from Christmas to March.

Lake Placid is situated in Essex County, New York State, in the heart of the famous Adirondack forest preserve at an altitude of 2000 feet above the sea. The village itself lies along the shores of two beautiful lakes among Adirondack waters, Lakes Mirror and Placid. Surrounding the village and towering into the sky like great spires are the highest mountain peaks in the state, Tahawus (Mount Marcy), McIntyre, Haystack, Whiteface and Von Hoevenberg.

Lake Placid's winter season normally lasts from early December until late March. Zero temperatures are common. The air is clear and dry. Bright sunshine is plentiful. Snow and ice abound. Scenic effects surpass anything seen in summer. It is in this ideal natural setting that Lake Placid has built its international reputation as a winter rendezvous for young and old alike.

209

How It All Came About

The beginning was modest. In 1905, officials of the Lake Placid Club decided to keep one small clubhouse open all winter. A few hardy souls tried the Adirondack snow and found it good. They even found it enjoyable and hastened to tell their friends of their discovery. More came the next year, still more the year after. And so the annual winter trips to the snow-covered peaks and forest trails of the Adirondacks began. Today the community of Lake Placid plays host each winter to thousands.

Organized effort was necessary, however, in order to provide winter guests with things to do and things to watch. People had to be taught how to enjoy these outstanding facilities. With two lakes in the village, it was natural that ice sports should have found favor with Lake Placid residents in the early days.

Speed Skating

In tracing the history of speed skating at Lake Placid it is interesting to note that a majority of amateur speed-skating records were made on the Lake Placid tracks. Their enthusiasm fired by the deeds of Edmund Lamy, "Bobby" McLean and others, Lake Placid boys took to the ice in droves. Out of these groups were developed two North American champions in the 1920s, Charles Jewtraw and John Amos (Jack) Shaw. Jewtraw was the first winner of an Olympic Winter Games event. He defeated the greatest skaters of the world to take the 500-meter race in the I Olympic Winter Games at Chamonix, France, in 1924. Jewtraw's international fame as a speed skater did much to bring Lake Placid's winter reputation to the attention of the public.

Figure Skating

Figure skating had been enjoyed for many years by Lake Placid Club guests on flooded tennis courts in the rear of the main winter clubhouse. It was the building of the Olympic arena on the main street of the village in 1932, however, that stirred wider interest in this sport. Some of the greatest crowds of the Olympics thronged the arena to see such champions as Sonja Henie of Norway, Karl Schäfer of Austria and the Brunets of France in action.

Skiing

In the early years at Lake Placid snowshoes were the accepted means of travel in the woods in winter, a heritage from the Indians who for centuries roamed the surrounding mountains. Then winter guests found that it was good sport to get out on the forest trails on the webbed shoes. Skis became popular later, and now have almost entirely supplanted the snowshoe. The Lake Placid terrain is excellent for ski running.

Organized ski competitions in Lake Placid began February 21, 1921, when the Lake Placid Club held its first jumping meet on the original Intervales hill southeast of the village. Ski jumping, even in those days, appealed mightily to the winter-sports enthusiast. In 1921 the original Intervales hill of about 35 meters was completed. Intervales in 1927 was made into a 60-meter jump, generally recognized as one of the technically perfect hills of the world. Ski jumping is now accepted as a prime factor in Lake Placid's annual winter-sports schedule.

213

Hockey

Although for two decades the crack of stick against puck resounded over the frozen surface of Mirror Lake, it was only during the 1920s that this great winter game began to have the wide appeal that it enjoys today. Until the completion of the Olympic stadium during the winter of 1930-31, all hockey games were played on Mirror Lake. Now most of the winter schedule is played in the Olympic arena, where excellent ice is assured regardless of weather conditions and the spectators can watch the action in comfort. During the Lake Placid games in February 1932 for the first time in Winter Olympic history, hockey contests were played indoors, the new Olympic arena making the games on the program independent of variable weather.

214

Bobsledding

Bobsledding in 1932 was one of America's newest and most thrilling winter sports. The largest crowd of the III Olympic Winter Games, fourteen thousand, watched the four-man racing on one morning at the Mount Von Hoevenberg bob run. Bobsledding is another winter sport imported from Europe and started on its way to American fame by Lake Placid. When the idea of staging the III Olympic Winter Games in Lake Placid was first discussed, officers of the Lake Placid Club recognized that because of litigation the Olympic run could not be completed two years in advance of the games. They were impressed by the popularity of such foreign bob runs as those at St. Moritz, Davos and Schreiberhau, and saw the necessity of building a run at once. They pointed out that it was an American team piloted by William (Billy) Fiske, a resident of Europe for several years, that won first place for the United States at the II Olympic Winter Games in St. Moritz in 1928, even though at the time there was not a single bob run on the entire North American continent.

215

As a result, during the fall of 1929, on a steep hill near the Intervales ski jump, the club built the first technically engineered bob run in the Western Hemisphere. The winner of the Olympic two-man title and the second-place winner in the four-man bob, with their crews, received their initial training on the Intervales slide. Compared with the great Olympic slide on Mount Von Hoevenberg this first run today does not seem so thrilling, but when it was opened huge crowds were aghast at the speed with which the sleds shot round the dangerous curves.

From the time the first sled went down the Intervales slide, interest in the bob sport among Lake Placid residents and visitors began to develop. Crowds waited to ride, and crowds thronged the vantage points along the run to watch others ride. The judgment of those who built the run and prophesied its popularity was vindicated many times over. The next year, 1930, a Saranac Lake team on the Mount Von Hoevenberg slide set up a world's speed record for a recognized major bob run of 77 kilometers an hour. In the 1932 Lake Placid Winter Games, the United States took first- and third-place medals in the two-man bob event and the first-place gold and second-place silver medals in the four-man event.

III OLYMPIC WINTER GAMES—1932

How the Games Were Awarded to Lake Placid

Late in 1927, the year before the II Olympic Winter Games were staged at St. Moritz, Switzerland, members of the American Olympic Committee inquired unofficially as to whether Lake Placid would be in a position to hold the III Olympic Winter Games if they were awarded to the United States. Local sports leaders naturally were pleased at the implied compliment to Lake Placid's standing as a winter resort. They replied, however, that they would not even consider holding the games unless thoroughly convinced that they could meet the highest standards set abroad for Winter Olympic competitions.

Early in 1928 Dr. Godfrey Dewey of the Lake Placid Club, himself an ardent and capable winter sportsman, made a special trip abroad to study the conditions at prominent European winter resorts including Chamonix in France, Caux and Gstaad in the Vaud Alps, Grindelwald and Mürren in the Bernese Oberland, Engelberg and Arosa in central Switzerland, and Davos and St. Moritz in the Engadine. He was at St. Moritz at the time of the Olympics and made a careful study of the entire Olympic program at the Swiss resort.

Dr. Dewey's conclusions were that in those essential factors which money could not buy, such as winter climate, terrain and, especially, long and successful experience in the conduct of winter sports, Lake Placid could match the highest standards set abroad. Additional facilities and other things necessary for the conduct of the Olympics he felt certain could be provided by money and organization.

Returning to Lake Placid fired with enthusiasm as to the opportunity that would be Lake Placid's if this resort could secure the III Olympic Winter Games, Dr. Dewey immediately set about convincing the community that it could bid for the great international winter sports classic. He had already worked out a preliminary plan for staging the games in Lake Placid. At first many residents were aghast that there was even a possibility of this little mountain resort of fewer than four thousand people entertaining the winter sports world in 1932. The responsibility seemed too heavy, the task too great. But there were those who saw the vision at once, and they set about helping Dr. Dewey to convince others. To hear him tell of what St. Moritz had done and what Lake Placid could do was to be eager to start doing it.

Daily Program
Feb 4-15   Summaries   25c
**III Olympic
Winter Games**

Lake Placid, N Y
February 4-13, 1932

And Finally the Opening Day

At ten o'clock on the morning of February 4, 1932, the goal of four years of unremitting effort was reached as the athletes representing seventeen nations began the program of competition. The official Olympic winter sports consisted of skiing, speed skating, figure skating, hockey and bobsledding, as well as three demonstrations: sled-dog racing, curling and women's speed skating. Everything was in readiness, and even the weather, which had been anything but favorable immediately before the games, seemingly decided that it too should help; the morning of the opening day dawned bright and cold.

Lake Placid was in gala attire as befitted its position as host to the winter sports stars of the world and the thousands gathered to see them in action. Every Olympic facility was ready and waiting to do its part in the long program—the stadium, the indoor arena, the ski jump, the Mount Von Hoevenberg bob run and the forest ski trails. The athletes, most of whom had traveled thousands of miles for these tests of their skill against the best in the world, eagerly waited for the opening gun.

By tradition the opening ceremonies of the Olympic Winter Games are the most impressive on the entire program. The Organizing Committee was determined to make the opening of the Lake Placid games the most distinctive in the history of these international competitions. Promptly at ten o'clock members of the International Olympic Committee and the Organizing Committee were presented to Governor Franklin D. Roosevelt of New York. Then Governor Roosevelt, escorted by the Count de Baillet-Latour, president of the IOC, and Dr. Godfrey Dewey, president of the III Olympic Winter Games Committee, proceeded to his box in the reviewing stand.

219

As the strains of the American national anthem faded away into the encircling mountains, the parade of the athletes began. They came in by the main entrance at the east side of the stadium and marched around past the front of the grandstand, where sat Governor Roosevelt and the other officials. The teams marched by nations in alphabetical order: Austria, Belgium, Canada, Czechoslovakia, Finland, France, Germany, Great Britain, Hungary, Italy, Japan, Norway, Poland, Rumania, Sweden, Switzerland and the United States. Each nation's flag was carried in front of the delegation by a representative, marching alone. Preceding the standard bearer marched a Boy Scout with a placard held aloft indicating the name of the national delegation.

220

Parading with military precision, the different contingents swung past the
reviewing stand and around into the hockey box facing the tribunal of
honor. It was the most impressive sight of the games. The brilliant sun; the
multicolored uniforms, ranging from the somber blue of the Norwegians and
the Japanese to the white of the Americans; the hum of an airplane
overhead; the sparkling blue ice; and the cloudless sky above—all combined
to produce a picture of winter amateur athletics at its best.

Then to the strains of bugles and the cannon's salute, the great white
Olympic flag, with its five rings symbolizing the five continents joined

221

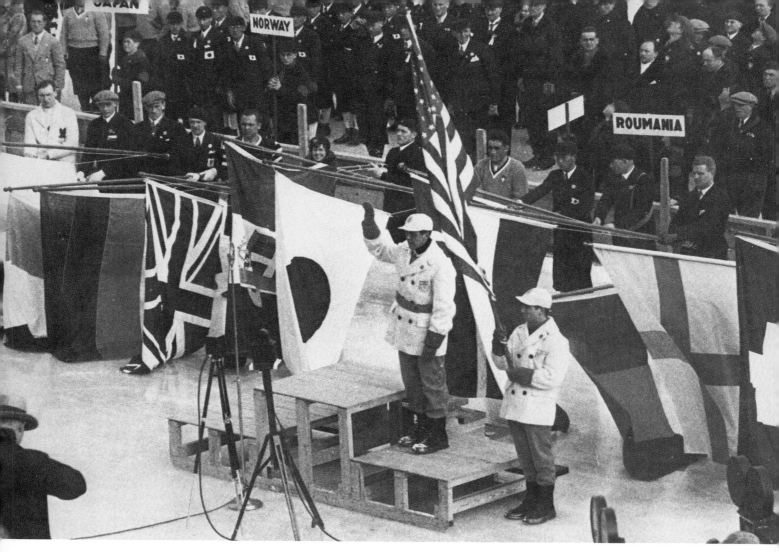

together in the amity of international sports competitions, was slowly hoisted to the top of the flagpole. Jack Shea, U.S. speed skater and a native of Lake Placid, had been selected to take the Olympic oath of amateurism. Stepping in front of the massed flags accompanied by the U.S. standard bearer, William Fiske Shea raised his right hand and repeated the oath as all other athletes also raised their right hands in token of assent: "We swear that we will take part in the Olympic Games in loyal competition, respecting the regulations which govern them and desirous of participating in them in the true spirit of sportsmanship for the honor of our country and for the glory of sport." The III Olympic Winter Games program was under way.

SECOND TIME AROUND

It has been forty-eight years, but this beautiful village in the rugged Adirondack Mountains is ready again. Some residents will say that the community of Lake Placid is the only complete winter resort in the United States because there is no other bobsled run in North America. Not content to use the old facilities, the Lake Placid Olympic Organizing Committee has done extensive new construction and renovation.

The entire length of the bob run has something new. It has been refrigerated. This new system will hold the ice longer and allow for a longer bob-run season. The racing times for this Winter Olympic Games on the bobsled may be the best ever.

The luge, the daredevil event in which each contestant lies on a sled, was not a part of the 1932 Lake Placid Olympics. A new luge slide has been constructed near the bob run. It too is refrigerated, in case the February 1980 weather in upstate New York proves unreliable.

Mount Van Hoevenberg will be the site of the Nordic skiing events and the biathlon. At the III Olympic Winter Games in 1932 the only skiing events were the Nordic cross-country races and ski jumping. The excellent cross-country trails are still here and ready, but there has been a major change in the ski-jumping facilities. Gone is the old 70-meter ski jump at Intervales.

223

Now there are two new hills — 70 meters and 90 meters — each with its new concrete tower. The landing hills have been carefully contoured and designed for the newer jumping techniques.

Also new on the program since 1932 are the Alpine skiing events. Lake Placid would have had a problem finding long, steep ski runs had it not been for New York State's development of Whiteface Mountain. In the late 1950s the state designed several new ski runs. Whiteface is just a few miles north of Lake Placid in Wilmington. Here the downhill, the slalom and the giant slalom events will take place. Whiteface has a drop of sufficient length and steepness to make it eligible for international competition. Not leaving anything to Mother Nature, snowmaking equipment has been installed the entire length of all Alpine runs at Whiteface.

A more personal aspect of the XIII Olympic Winter Games at Lake Placid is the interest of the Organizing Committee in doing the games as a family affair. Most of the persons involved are neighbors or live nearby. Many of the officials, the construction workers and the volunteers to snow-patrol the hills are dedicated townfolks. They are proud of their village and are looking forward to treating the many American and foreign visitors as new friends.

224

The Olympic Torch Relay Route

The Olympic flame, which will open the 1980 Olympic Winter Games in Lake Placid, will be carried to this small Adirondack community in a nine-day relay through some of America's most historic places.

The nearly thousand-mile torch relay route will commemorate the colonial heritage of the United States and also pass through the major population centers of the East Coast, beginning at Yorktown, Virginia, on January 31, 1980. The official route was planned by the Lake Placid Olympic Organizing Committee's chief of ceremonies and awards, George Christian Ortloff. He said, "The path of the Olympic torchbearers will itself become a historic route, and as such, it will take the flame past places which tell the story of American history, from the first English-speaking settlements in the New World to the towers of Manhattan."

The cities and towns along the route include Yorktown, Williamsburg, Hanover, Bowling Green, Fredericksburg, Mount Vernon, Alexandria and Arlington, Virginia; Washington, D.C.; Laurel, Baltimore and Rising Sun, Maryland; Newark and Wilmington, Delaware; Philadelphia, Pennsylvania; Princeton, South River and Perth Amboy, New Jersey; Staten Island, Brooklyn and Manhattan in New York City; Yonkers, Tarrytown, Peekskill, Poughkeepsie, Hyde Park, Hudson, Kinderhook and Rensselaer along the Hudson River in New York State; Saratoga Springs, Glens Falls and Ticonderoga along the historic Champlain Valley corridor in northeastern New York; and Amsterdam, Northville, Speculator, Indian Lake, Tupper Lake and Saranac Lake in the central Adirondack mountains.

The Olympic flame will be lighted in Greece, flown to Langley Air Force Base, near Yorktown, and transferred from Langley to Yorktown by sea. The single flame, carried by a relay of fifty-two runners (representing all parts of the United States) will go from Yorktown to Albany, New York. At Albany two teams of torchbearers, each with a flame, will travel different routes to Lake Placid, arriving at the same time on February 8, 1980.

225

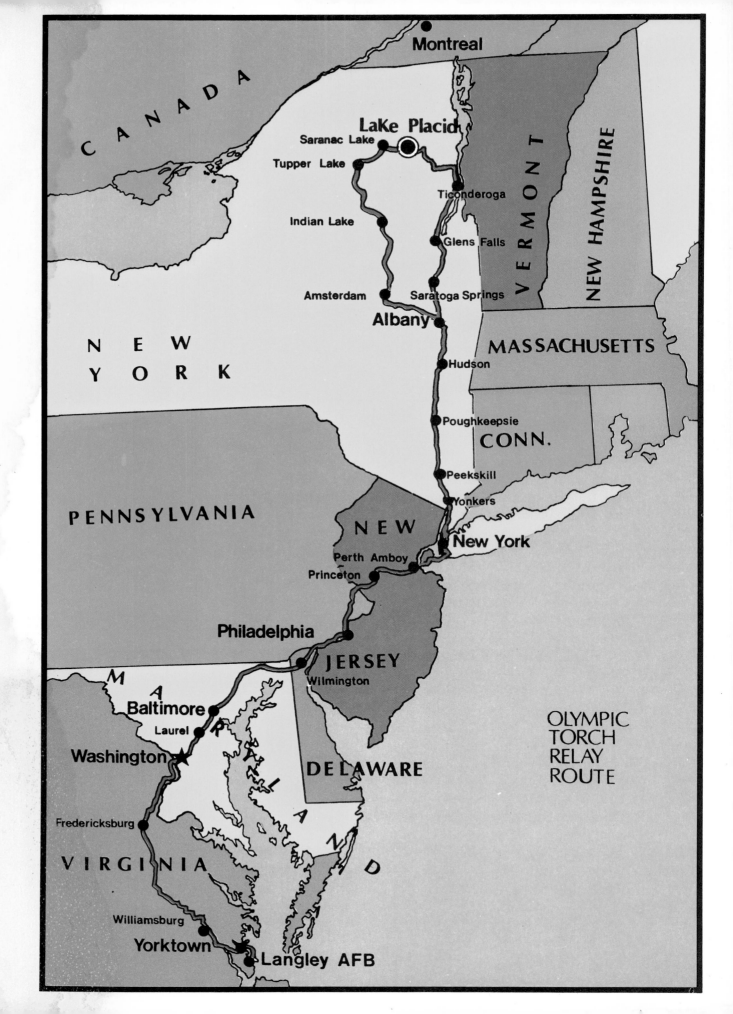

Montreal

CANADA

Lake Placid
Saranac Lake
Tupper Lake
Ticonderoga
Indian Lake
Glens Falls
Amsterdam
Saratoga Springs
VERMONT
Albany
NEW HAMPSHIRE
MASSACHUSETTS
Hudson
NEW YORK
Poughkeepsie
CONN.
Peekskill
PENNSYLVANIA
Yonkers
NEW
New York
Perth Amboy
Princeton
Philadelphia
JERSEY
Wilmington
MARYLAND
Baltimore
Laurel
Washington
DELAWARE
Fredericksburg
VIRGINIA
Williamsburg
Yorktown
Langley AFB

OLYMPIC
TORCH
RELAY
ROUTE

XIII OLYMPIC WINTER GAMES CEREMONIES

By George Christian Ortloff
Chief of Ceremonies & Awards
Lake Placid Organizing Committee

From the moment the Olympic Torch is lighted in ancient Olympia, Greece on January 30, 1980 until the last tongues of the dying flame disappear on February 24, 1980, in Lake Placid, the XIII Olympic Winter Games will be a ceremonial eyeful.

At the site of the first Olympic Games at Olympia, young Greek women, dressed as priestesses of old aim a parabolic mirror at the sun and the Olympic Flame is rekindled. An hour-long ceremony passes the flame to a torch and honors the founder of the modern Olympics, Pierre de Coubertin. Then the torch is relayed to Athens. A ceremony in the 50,000-seat stadium there officially transfers the torch to the Lake Placid Olympic Organizing Committee. The flame is flown to Langley Air Force Base, Virginia, and from there it is carried for nine days to Lake Placid. Festivals and pageants mark its passage through more than 100 cities and towns.

The Opening Ceremony is held in a 25,000 seat stadium, ringed by mountains, on a plateau above the AuSable River. An orchestra and chorus with a combined strength of six hundred performs, accompanied by three original compositions receiving their world premiere. The Olympic Hymn rings out as the five-ring flag is raised over the stadium.

George Christian Ortloff

One of the fifty two torchbearers, who has been selected only hours before, enters the stadium carrying the torch. The other fifty one, representing all the states, who have carried the flame almost 1600 km. to Lake Placid, form an honor guard as the final runner mounts the steps and lights the Olympic Flame which will burn through the end of the games.

Ceremonies continue daily, with award ceremonies conducted each evening on a magnificent crystal pavilion on frozen Mirror Lake. The gold, silver and bronze medals, created by Tiffany & Co., will be presented by Lord Killanin, president of the International Olympic Committee. As the last strains of each victor's national anthem echoes from the surrounding hills, a gold fireworks burst explodes high above, signaling to the countryside that a new Olympic champion has been crowned.

Finally, the athletes and officials assemble in the Olympic Field House on February 24 for the closing ceremony, where the flame is extinguished, the Olympic flag is taken down, and Lord Killanin invites the world to gather four years hence in Sarajevo, Czechoslovakia. The pageantry continues into the night, with firework displays, bands and celebrations in all parts of the village.

In all the ceremonies, the athlete has been the focus of attention. The "Olympics in Perspective" have honored the participants with simple, dignified and moving ceremonies, inspiring others to follow their footsteps, and reminding all of the awesome heritage of the three-thousand-year-old Olympic Games.

Index

SYRACUSE
BUFFALO

LAKE PLACID
VILLAGE

SKI
JUMP
COMPLEX

MT. VAN HOEVENBERG
BOBSLED RUN

NEW YORK CITY
300 miles

OSS
TRY
EX